An Introduction to Portuguese Employment & Labour Law

An Introduction to Portuguese Employment & Labour Law

A COMPREHENSIVE OVERVIEW OF THE PORTUGUESE LABOUR AND EMPLOYMENT LAWS

By Principal Professor
Guilherme Dray

in collaboration with
Catarina Granadeiro

ALMEDINA

AN INTRODUCTION TO
PORTUGUESE EMPLOYMENT & LABOUR LAW
A COMPREHENSIVE OVERVIEW OF THE PORTUGUESE LABOUR
AND EMPLOYMENT LAWS
AUTOR
Guilherme Dray
in collaboration with Catarina Granadeiro
EDITOR
EDIÇÕES ALMEDINA, S.A.
Rua Fernandes Tomás, n.os 76-80
3000-167 Coimbra
Tel.: 239 851 904 · Fax: 239 851 901
www.almedina.net · editora@almedina.net
DESIGN DE CAPA
Morais Leitão
PRÉ-IMPRESSÃO
EDIÇÕES ALMEDINA, S.A.
IMPRESSÃO E ACABAMENTO
DPS - Digital Printing Services
Outubro, 2019
DEPÓSITO LEGAL
462520/19

ALMEDINA | GRUPOALMEDINA

BIBLIOTECA NACIONAL DE PORTUGAL – CATALOGAÇÃO NA PUBLICAÇÃO
DRAY, Guilherme
AN INTRODUCTION TO PORTUGUESE EMPLOYMENT & LABOUR LAW
A Comprehensive Overview of the Portuguese
Labour and Employment Laws
ISBN 978-972-40-8108-3
CDU 349

This notebook was specially prepared as a support material to international students attending the courses on Employment and Labour law at the Faculty of Law of the University of Lisbon

TABLE OF CONTENTS

1.
General Overview on Portugal

1.1. Demography, Territory, and Identity

I. Portugal is a sovereign country founded in 1143. Portugal lies along the Atlantic coast of the Iberian Peninsula in South Western Europe. It shares a border with Spain in east and north, while the Atlantic dominates the coastline in west and south. Portugal occupies roughly 16 percent of the Iberian Peninsula.

Portugal is a Member State of the European Union since 1986, has a total area of 35,560 sq. mi. and about 10,500,000 inhabitants[1], including the islands of Azores and Madeira in the Atlantic Ocean. It is a democratic and representative Republic based on human dignity and the will of the people, committed to building a society which aspires to be free, fair and solidary.

Additionally, Portugal is also a full member of the United Nations, the Community of the Portuguese Language Speaking Countries (which is known by the abbreviation "CPLP") and NATO.

It is considered as a high-income economy by the World Bank[2].

[1] Source: *Instituto Nacional de Estatística, Censos 2011,* available at http://censos.ine.pt/xportal/xmain?xpgid=censos2011_apresentacao&xpid=CENSOS.

[2] Under the Gini index, a World Bank metrics which measures the extent to which the distribution of income (or, in some cases, consumption expenditure) among individuals or households within an economy deviates from a perfectly equal distribution, Portugal had an estimated 33.9 in 2015, meaning it was roughly the 33 richest country in the world as per these standards. (https://data.worldbank.org/indicator/SI.POV.GINI?locations=PT).

II. Portugal belongs to the Romano-Germanic Legal Family (best known as a civil law system). Broadly speaking, it is based on the Rule of Law and the primary source of law is the written law[3].

With regards to the hierarchy amongst legal acts, the Portuguese Constitution of 1976 is the most important source of law, enshrining fundamental rights as well as rules on the political organization of the country as a democracy, with general elections and separation of powers: the legislative power, the executive power and the judicial power, working in full independence.

It reflects the Constitutional history of the country – it is simultaneously a Constitution concerned with guarantees and a prospective Constitution. Bearing in mind the authoritarian regime defeated in 1974 and the possible detours occurred in 1975 it is a Constitution centered on the fundamental rights of citizens, workers and the separation of powers[4].

With regards to the system of private law, Portugal follows the model existing in the majority of the Romano-Germanic legal systems, with the following characteristics: The Portuguese Constitution prescribes the guarantees of a free market, freedom of initiative as well as the right to private property and several others, not less important, individual liberties.

In addition, the Portuguese system of private law received the influence of the Welfare State and the European Social Model which implies that beyond the liberal concept of individual liberties and the rule of law one must also consider the existence, at the same level, of social rights and the possibility of State assistance[5].

Generally speaking, social rights are those rights that the citizens can claim against the State on several social domains which range from health to education to employment to housing or social security[6].

Social rights are positive rights which translate the possibility of claiming action from the State in the areas within their scope. Positive rights differ from negative rights which are rights of protection of the citizens against

[3] See DÁRIO MOURA VICENTE, *Direito Comparado,* Volume I, 4ª edição, Revista e Atualizada, Almedina, Coimbra,2018, pp. 97 et seq.

[4] See JORGE MIRANDA, *Estrutura do Estado* in O Direito em Portugal – Madrid (2017), p.47-63.

[5] See GUILHERME DRAY, – *Equality, Welfare State and Democracy,* Almedina/The Luso-American Development Foundation, Coimbra, 2018.

[6] The Portuguese Constitution devotes title III to social rights, articles 58 to 79.

the State. Under these rights of protection citizens can react, for instance, in order to protect the right to property or privacy[7].

The rise of social rights laid the groundwork for the development of the Welfare State, under the principle of substantive fair equality. As a Member of the European Union, Portugal follows the Welfare State ideals based upon the principles of equality, common good and social justice.

1.2. Legal and Political Systems

I. As stated above with regards to its legal system, Portugal pertains to the family of *continental, civil* or *Romano-Germanic* legal systems, with a written Constitution and the prevalence of law rather than custom or judicial precedents[8].

Within the several sources of law, the written law is considered the primary and utmost important source of law. Among the types of existing written laws, the Constitution should be considered as the cornerstone of the legal system, but one should also not disregard the role of EU laws, international treaties, EU administrative regulations as well as the role of the laws enacted by the Parliament and the Government (Laws and Decree Laws) as well as the remaining secondary regulations of execution produced. Contrarily, customary law (custom) does not play a significant role. Legal doctrine or the works produced by academic scholars are also, altogether with customary law, ancillary or indirect sources of law.

II. Under the Portuguese Constitution, the bedrock values and founding principles enshrined in the Portuguese Constitution are the following[9]:

(i) Rule of Law;
(ii) Social Democracy;

[7] See Jorge Reis Novais, *Teoria jurídica dos direitos sociais enquanto direitos Fundamentais*, Coimbra Editora, 2010.

[8] Article 1.st of the Portuguese Civil Code, under the heading "Immediate Sources" refers as immediate sources of law the written law and corporate regulations. A definition of written law is then advanced in the next paragraph.

[9] See Jorge Miranda/Rui Medeiros, *Constituição Portuguesa Anotada*, Tomo I, Introdução Geral, Coimbra Editora, Coimbra, 2007.

(iii) Human Dignity;
(iv) Freedom;
(v) Equality;
(vi) Fundamental rights;
(vii) Separation and interdependence of powers (as the *res publica* framework is led by the three classical balanced branches: legislative, judicial and executive);
(viii) Political decentralization: granting certain political autonomy to the regions of Azores and Madeira;
(ix) Administrative decentralization: municipalities and parishes.

III. The Portuguese political system is grounded on three organisms.

The President of the Republic (*Presidente da República*), the head of state, is directly elected by the people and is a figure with relevant political powers but no legislative or executive powers.

The Parliament (*Assembleia da República* or *Parlamento*), currently with 230 members, is also directly elected by the people in general elections. Besides holding political power, the Constitution specifically vests the Parliament with the most important power – the authority to make laws.

The Executive ("*Governo*"), which is appointed by the President based on the result of general elections, takes on the Executive power and shares the legislative power with the Parliament. Some laws (Decree-Laws) may be issued freely by the Executive; in some areas, the Constitution allows the Executive to legislate on issues reserved to the Parliament (circumstances of "*reserva relativa*"); in others, the legislative power is reserved exclusively and absolutely to the Parliament (circumstances of "*reserva absoluta*"). The Government is composed by a Prime-Minister, who is the head of the Executive and by a number of ministers and secretaries of state. Both the Prime-Minister and the Ministers are appointed by the President of the Republic according to a proposal delivered by the leader of the party which accounted for most votes in the general elections who normally retains the role of Prime Minister.

The Portuguese system follows a semi-parliamentary model (or semi-presidential system) with a division of powers, as explained, between the President of the Republic, the Parliament and the Government with the corresponding political, legislative and executive powers. The last state power which must be referred in this account is the judicial power vested in the Courts which are sovereign bodies[10].

The Portuguese Constitution assigns to the Courts ("*Tribunais*") and to the judicial system as a whole the power to administer justice.

Due to the explained existing separation and interdependence of powers, the Courts exercise the judicial power independently from the political, legislative or executive powers.

The Courts are separate bodies of sovereignty within the Portuguese jurisdiction that pertain to administer justice by applying the law and neutrally assessing the cases submitted to them from a fair standpoint, through a careful examination of the presented evidence and with the background commitment to the discovery of truth by rendering a final and binding judgment.

Considering the existing system of sources of law in Portugal, Portuguese courts must obey to the law[11].

The Courts have the monopoly of the judicial power. In addition to the institutionalized system of courts and the application of the law to resolve disputes, alternative dispute resolution mechanisms have emerged such as conciliation, mediation and arbitration. Within the Labour legal framework, as we will see further on, these alternative dispute resolution mechanisms play a very important role regarding the collective bargaining and collective disputes.

[10] See Jorge Miranda, *Manual do Direito Constitucional*, Tomo I *Preliminares – O Estado e os Sistemas Constitucionais* – 8ª Edição, Coimbra Editora, Coimbra.

[11] Article 8 of the Portuguese Civil Code under the heading "Obligation to judge and obedience to the law" establishes the courts must not abstain from judging the cases submitted to them supporting their abstention in the lack or obscurity of the law or alleging unresolvable question regarding the litigation. Additionally, the second paragraph establishes a general duty of obedience to the law which cannot be misapplied under the pretext the law or the legal rule is unfair or immoral.

2.
Employment and Labour Law

2.1. General overview

I. Employment and labour law is the legal branch that governs the individual relationship between employer and employee, including corresponding rights and duties, as well as the collective relationship between trade unions and employers or associations of employers. In a nutshell, employment law governs the employment relationship and the employment contract, which is the contract that covers the work phenomena[12].

Employment and labour law belong to private law in the *summa divisio* between public and private law. More specifically, employment and labour law form a specific branch within civil law, with numerous specificities that confer systematic and dogmatic autonomy to this branch of law[13].

Historically, employment and labour law emerged in the 19.th Century as an instrument to protect the weaker party to the employment relationship – the employee – against an unlimited number of working hours, work

[12] Disclaimer: any reference to a legal rule or article should be construed to refer to a legal rule or article comprised in Law 7/2009, of February 12 also known as the Portuguese Labor Code or Labor Code of 2009 (also referred here by its acronym 'PLC' or 'LC').

[13] See Menezes Cordeiro, *Direito do Trabalho, I, Direito europeu, Dogmática geral, Direito Coletivo,* Almedina, Coimbra, pp. 37 et seq.; Pedro Romano Martinez, *Direito do Trabalho,* 7ª edição, Almedina Coimbra, 2015; pp 46 et seq.; Maria do Rosário Ramalho, *Da Autonomia Dogmática do Direito do Trabalho,* Almedina, Coimbra, 2001; Luís Menezes Leitão, *Direito do Trabalho, 3ª edição, Almedina, Coimbra, 2012,* pp 14 et seq.; Guilherme Dray, *O Princípio da Proteção do Trabalhador,* Almedina Coimbra, 2015, pp. 319 et seq.

accidents, low salaries, infant work and work devoided of human conditions. From those concerns steamed a group of rules and principles – a threshold of rights[14] – aimed at the protection of the employee in several areas: limitation of working hours, health and safety protection, prohibition of infant work, establishment of minimum wages, the right to rest and to leisure, protection in the event of maternity and a plethora of other rights and guarantees[15].

The underlying protection of the employee was the departure point of creation of Employment Law and what justifies its autonomy against Civil Law. Whilst Civil Law is based on equal relations between private parties at the same (horizontal) level, employment and labour law intends to govern vertical relations between employers, vested with economic and legal power over its employees, and other employees who are in a situation of economic dependency, and legal subordination[16].

For the above stated reasons, in contrast with the principle of private autonomy that governs civil law, Employment and Labour laws contain several compulsory dispositions which can't be waived by either party, in order to protect the employee.

While Civil Law is based on voluntary legal rules that can be freely replaced or waived by the parties, Employment and Labour law is characterized by the existence of several imperative and mandatory rules that cannot be waived or altered by the parties to an employment contract.

II. Employment and Labour law as a separate branch of law deals with two competing values: on one hand, employees that want the best independent job for the highest salary they can reach; on the other hand, employers pertain to maximize their production and profit making capacity by decreasing expenses, namely by paying lower salaries.

Bearing that in mind, the basic tenet of labour and employment law is to keep workers safe and to make sure they are treated fairly, whilst there are also rules which pertain to protect the interests of the employer.

[14] See Simon Deakin/Gillian Morris, *Labour Law*, 3rd edition, Butterworths, London, 2001, pp. 20 et seq.

[15] See Alvin L. Goldman and Roberto L. Corrada, *Labor Law in the USA, Third Revised Edition*, Wolters Kluwer, Law and Business, The Netherlands, 2011, pp. 21 et seq.

[16] See Guy Davidov, *A Purpositive Approach to Labour Law*, Oxford, 2018, pp. 30 et seq.

In this vein, while the underlying objective of employment and labour law is to protect employees against unscrupulous employers, modern Employment Law also tries to protect the employer's liberty of management and to promote flexible employment relations, within certain limits[17]. The idea is rather intuitive: without employers and wealthy Corporations there is no job market. For that reason, despite its underlying goal of protecting the employees, Employment and labour Laws must strike a fair balance between this protection, on one hand, and the employer's freedom of management, on the other[18].

2.2. Basic idea

I. As explained in the previous segment, the basic idea of Employment and Labour Law is the protection of the weaker party to the employment contract – the employee[19].

Despite this underlying idea, Employment and Labour law also pertains to guarantee the regular performance of the corporation.

The employer, who is the businessman or the owner of the corporation, the company or the undertaking, retains several powers to control the employees' activities, namely the management or directive power, which is the power to control and command the employee's performance; the regulatory power, which is the power to issue internal rules or to approve personal policy handbooks; as well as the disciplinary power, which means that in the event of employee's misconducts the employer may apply against him/her disciplinary sanctions or penalties, following an internal disciplinary procedure and without the previous intervention of a court.

Hence, while the employer is the owner of the corporation and retains the highlighted powers, being free to manage the company, the employee must comply with the instructions given by the employer.

Namely, the employee has to comply with the duty of obedience that is stated in the law. The employer can define the method and the type of

[17] See GUILHERME DRAY, *O Princípio da Proteção do Trabalhador*, cit., pp. 399 et seq.

[18] See GUILHERME DRAY, *O Princípio da Proteção do Trabalhador*, cit., pp. 319 et seq.

[19] See MANFRED WEISS, "Re-Inventing Labour Law?", *The Idea of Labour Law*, Edited by Guy Davidov & Brian Langille, Oxford University Press, United Kingdom, 2013, pp. 43-57.

work the employee is to do, as well as the working place or the working time schedule, while the employee has the duty to work under those orientations and the employer's directives.

In other words, the employee is subordinated to the instructions of the employer and is also economically dependent on his/her job, since the wages he/she receives are necessary to run his/her and his family's life[20].

That is the reason why up till today the employee is seen as the weaker party of the employment contract[21, 22].

II. The employment relationship tends, as a consequence, to be naturally unbalanced and unequal. On one side we have the owner of the corporation vested with several powers; on the other, we have the employee, who has to work under the employer's direction and depends on his/her job to earn a living.

Therefore, given this unbalanced and unequal relationship, Labour laws exist to sustain the protection of the employee and his/her dignity as such.

That is the cornerstone and the main purpose of Employment and Labour Laws[23].

2.3. Scope

I. Employment and Labour Laws aim to cover all aspects related to the employment situation.

On a first level, with regards to the individual employment relationship, employment laws deal with the employment contract. They regulate the formation process, the execution as well as the termination of the contract.

With regards to the *formation* of the contract, this branch of law deals with the duty of information, the *bona fide* principle which must preside to

[20] See Maria do Rosário Ramalho, *Tratado de Direito do Trabalho – Parte II*, 6ª edição, Almedina, Coimbra, 2016, pp. 32 et seq.

[21] See Menezes Cordeiro, *Direito do Trabalho, I*, cit., pp. 336 et seq. and 453 et seq.; Pedro Romano Martinez, *Direito do Trabalho*, cit., pp. 295 et seq.; Guilherme Dray, *O Princípio da Proteção do Trabalhador*, cit., pp. 165 et seq

[22] See João Leal Amado, *Contrato de Trabalho*, Coimbra Editora, 2009, pp. 12 et seq.

[23] See Harry Arthurs, "Labour Law after Labour", *The Idea of Labour Law*, cit., pp.190-208.

the conclusion of the contract, the rights of personality in *contrahendo* as well as the equality in the access to work and the legal requirements for the conclusion of an employment contract – capacity, possibility and proper form. With regards to the *execution* of the contract, the law expresses the rights and duties of the employer and the employee: rules which govern the workplace, working time, holidays and job functions, as well as salaries, the content of the contract and some specific categories of employees, such as pregnant employees and minors. The law also governs the distinction between permanent contracts (open-ended employment contracts) and non-permanent contracts (i.e. fixed-term, unfixed-term-contracts and temporary contracts) proposing its substantive and formal requirements.

Finally, regarding the termination of the contract, the law defines categories of termination, such as the expiration, revocation, dismissal by the employer and the resolution or the termination of the contract without just cause by the employee. As we will see further on, the Portuguese legal system does not apply the usually called "employment at will doctrine", under which both the employer and the employee can quit at any time and for any reason – for a good reason, for a bad reason or for no reason at all.

The Portuguese Constitution and the Labour Code state that the employer cannot dismiss the employee without just cause.

All these issues belong to what we usually call Employment Law[24].

II. On the other hand, Labour Law also deals with the relation between employers and employees representatives. It deals with the relations established between trade unions or working councils, on one hand, and the employer or employers′ associations, on the other. In this case, Labour Law rules the collective bargaining, the collective agreements and other sources that result from the negotiations between those collective undertakings. Labour Law also governs collective conflicts, such as strikes, and the ways to solve them, namely through conciliation, mediation and arbitration. In Portugal, the right to strike is a constitutionally protected right (article 57.th of the Portuguese Constitution). Ordinary law, enshrined in the Labour Code, develops the constitutional right to strike, establishing its legitimacy, principles and requirements. That is the collective labour area of law[25].

[24] See Luís Menezes Leitão, *Direito do Trabalho*, cit., pp. 197 et seq.

[25] See Pedro Romano Martinez, *Direito do Trabalho*, cit., pp. 1092 et seq.

So, in a nutshell, because of the existence of an unbalanced relationship between the employer and the employee, we have Employment and Labour laws aiming simultaneously at the protection of the employee and the preservation of the freedom of management of the employer. These laws cover both the individual relationship between the employer and the employee and the collective relations between the employers' associations and trade unions, the collective bargaining and the right to strike.

Basically, this is the scope of problems employment and labor laws deals with.

3.
Sources of law

3.1. General overview

I. As with all legal branches, we have general and specific sources of law applicable to the employment contract which governs the employment relationship between the employer and the employee as well as the previously referred collective relations between employers and trade unions.

Basically speaking, we have two types of sources of law: international and national, on one hand, and general and specific, on the other hand[26].

II. Article 1.st of the Portuguese Labour Code (PLC) contains and expresses the specific sources of law which are applicable to the employment relationship, stating that the employment contract is subject, in particular, to the instruments of collective labour regulations, as well as to labour uses which are not contrary to the principle of good faith.

That implies that we have specific sources of law applicable to the employment relationship, like those that result from collective bargaining.

Nevertheless, the sources that are identified in article 1.st are not the single exclusive sources which govern the employment relationship. These are only the specific sources applicable to this branch of law. Beyond these sources we can also find general or common sources of law, i.e., sources that apply to other branches of law even if they are not expressly foreseen

[26] See MENEZES CORDEIRO, *Direito do Trabalho, I*, cit., pp. 262 et seq. and 453 et seq.; PEDRO ROMANO MARTINEZ, *Direito do Trabalho*, cit., pp. 161 et seq.

in the referred article 1.st of the PLC. For instance, let's consider the Portuguese Constitution: although it is not expressly enshrined in article 1.st of the Portuguese Labour Code, it is an important and general source of employment law, as we will see further on.

II. Additionally, we also have international sources that are very important to employment law, playing a core role for this branch of law, in connection with the internationalization of Employment Law fostered during the second half of the XX Century, after the II World War. During this time period, several covenants and treaties were enacted by the International Labour Organization (ILO), a special agency of the United Nations, and multiple Directives on employment Regulations were approved at the European Union level.

Portuguese Employment Law contains several principles which steam from international law, namely from the ILO's Constitution (1919) and its Declaration of Philadelphia (1944). For example, under the Declaration of Philadelphia, the ILO declared its main principles which have greatly inspired Portuguese Law. They state as follows:

- Labour is not a commodity;
- Freedom of expression and of association are essential to sustained progress;
- Poverty anywhere constitutes a danger to prosperity everywhere[27].

Under this Declaration, the ILO announced the main goal of Labour Law, which is to seek justice in the workplace and to provide protection to the employee, by minimizing his/her vulnerabilities without jeopardizing the employer's freedom of management.

Those principles still govern Modern Labour Law.

The basic idea of Employment Law is still the protection of the employee despite the evolution that occurred in the last three decades.

[27] We are here referring to the Declaration of Philadelphia adopted in May 10, 1944, concerning the aims and purposes of the International Labor Organization, which may be found at: https://www.ilo.org/wcmsp5/groups/public/---dgreports/---dcomm/documents/normativeinstrument/wcms_698995.pdf

3.2. Specific sources of law

I. As referred above, Employment and Labour Law comprises several sources of law, of general and specific nature. Due to the fact that Employment Law embraces freedom of association, unionism and collective bargaining, there are several sources of law which regulate the employment contract beyond the law itself, such as those which refer to instruments of collective labour regulations.

Hence, the sources of law which apply to Portuguese Employment Law are the following:

- 1948 Declaration of Human Rights of the United Nations (articles 23.rd – 25.th);
- Portuguese Constitution of 1976 (articles 53.rd – 57.th);
- International Employment Law (*e.g.* EU Directives/ILO Covenants);
- National Law (Labour Code of 2009 and its amendments);
- Collective agreements;
- Customs;
- Employment practices;
- Employment Contract;
- Court decisions and legal doctrine, as ancillary sources.

We will now take a closer look at these sources of law.

II. The Declaration of Human Rights of the United Nations (1948) includes several provisions related to employment[28].

Firstly, article 23.rd states that (1) everyone has freedom of choice of employment, the right to work, the right to just and favorable conditions of work and to protection against unemployment. (2) everyone, without undue discrimination, has the right to equal pay for equal work. (3) everyone who is employed has the right to just and favorable remuneration ensuring for himself/herself and his/her family an existence worthy of human dignity, and to be supplemented, if necessary, by other means of social protection. (4) everyone has the right to form and to join trade unions in order to protect his/her interests.

[28] See at https://www.un.org/en/universal-declaration-human-rights/index.html

Secondly, article 24.th declares that everyone has the right to rest and leisure, including a reasonable limitation of working hours and periodic paid holidays.

Finally, article 25.th states that (1) everyone has the right to a standard of living adequate for the health and well-being of himself/herself and of his/her family, including food, clothing, housing, medical care and needed social services, as well as the right to security in the event of unemployment, sickness, disability, widowhood, old age or other lack of livelihood in circumstances beyond his/her control, (2) motherhood and childhood are entitled to special care and assistance. All children, whether born in or out of wedlock, shall enjoy the same social protection.

III. The Portuguese Constitution contains several provisions on employment, the majority aiming at protecting the employee[29].

This legal instrument contains a specific Section entitled "*Workers' rights, freedoms and guarantees* "e from article 53.rd to article 57.th. Due to this inclusion, some Portuguese authors state our Constitution contains an "Employment Constitution" which frames the employment relationship.

Firstly, article 53.rd (Job security) states that workers are guaranteed job security, and dismissal without just cause or for political or ideological reasons is prohibited.

Secondly, article 54.th (Workers' committees) states that workers have the right to form workers' committees to promote and defend their interests and democratically intervene in the life of their enterprise.

Thirdly, article 55.th (Freedoms concerning trade unions) states that workers are free to form, belong and operate trade unions as a condition and guarantee of the building of their unity in defense of their rights and interests.

Fourthly, article 56.th (Trade union rights and collective agreements) stipulates that trade unions have the competence to protect and promote the defense of the rights and interests of the workers they represent.

Finally, article 57.th (Right to go on strike and prohibition of lock-out) states the right to strike and forbids lock out.

[29] See JORGE MIRANDA/RUI MEDEIROS, *Constituição Portuguesa Anotada*, cit., comments on articles 53.rd et seq.; GUILHERME DRAY, *O Princípio da Proteção do Trabalhador*, cit., pp. 454 et seq.

IV. Additionally, the Portuguese Constitution contains several provisions specifically targeted at employment in its Title III, about the economic, social and cultural rights and duties.

Article 58. th (Right to work) states that everyone has the right to work.

Article 59.th (workers' rights) declares that regardless of age, sex, race, citizenship, place of origin, religion and political and ideological convictions, every worker has the right: a) To remuneration for his/her work in accordance with its responsibility, nature and quality, in respect for the principle of equal pay for equal work and in such a way so as to guarantee a proper living; b) To organized work under conditions of social dignity and in such a way so as to provide personal fulfilment and to make it possible to reconcile work with family life; c) To work in safe and healthy conditions; d)To rest and leisure time, a maximum limit on the working day, a weekly rest period and periodic paid holidays; e) To material assistance when the worker involuntarily finds himself/herself in a situation of unemployment; f) To assistance and fair reparation when the worker is victim of a work-related accident or occupational illness[30].

V. The Portuguese Labour Code comprises a provision on the specific sources of Employment and Labour Law, stating (in its article 1.st) that the employment contract is submitted to instruments of collective labour regulation as well as to employment practices, submitted to the principle of good faith[31].

The instruments of collective labour regulation (ICLR) are identified in article 2.nd of the PLC

The instruments of collective labour regulation may be negotiated or non-negotiated (n.er 1), depending on the way they are formed. If they result from a negotiation between employers and employee's representatives, they are negotiated; if they result from an administrative act issued by the Government, they are not-negotiated.

[30] See Jorge Miranda/Rui Medeiros, *Constituição Portuguesa Anotada*, cit., comments on articles 58th and 59th.

[31] See Luís Gonçalves da Silva, *Código do Trabalho Anotado*, 11ª edição, Pedro Romano Martinez/Luís Miguel Monteiro/Joana Vasconcelos, /Pedro Madeira de Brito, Guilherme Dray /Luís Gonçalves da Silva, Almedina, Coimbra, 2017, comments on articles 1rst and 2nd of the Portuguese Labor Code.

VI. The negotiated ICLR refers to the collective convention, the membership agreement and an arbitration decision issued in a voluntary arbitration process (article 2.nd, n.er 2).

The collective conventions are agreements concluded by trade unions and employers or employers' associations. Depending on the undertakings or the employer's association which conclude these conventions, they can have different subtypes, as follows (n.er 3):

a) A collective contract is the collective employment convention concluded between a trade union and an employer's association;
b) A collective agreement is the collective employment convention concluded between a trade union and several employers for several undertakings or companies;
c) A single-undertaking agreement is the collective employment convention concluded between a trade union and an employer for a specific company or undertaking.

VII. The membership agreement, also referred to as adhesion agreement, is the agreement under which an employer or a trade union adhere to preexisting collective conventions in force. With the adhesion to the collective agreement, this agreement becomes binding to the new members that adhere to it. The adhesion agreement is thus an agreement concluded between the new member that wants to be part of the collective convention in force and its counterpart. The adhesion agreement is foreseen in article 504.th of PLC, which specifies that adhesion may not result in an amendment to the content of the Convention.

VIII. The arbitration decision issued in a voluntary arbitration process occurs when the parties that are bargaining a collective agreement and that do not reach an agreement assent on submitting the conflict around its negotiation to voluntary arbitration. The arbitration award has the same effect as a collective agreement. The voluntary arbitration regime is enshrined in article 506.th of the PLC, under which parties may always agree to submit to arbitration the issues resulting from, inter alia, the interpretation, integration, conclusion or review of a collective agreement.

The arbitration award is the final subtype of negotiated ICLR's.

IX. The non-negotiated instruments of collective bargaining are the administrative extension act, the administrative employment conditions act and the arbitral decision issued in a mandatory or necessary arbitration (article 2.nd, n.er 4)[32].

X. The administrative extension act extends the collective agreement or the arbitral award in force, in whole or in part, to employers and workers comprised within the scope of the business and professional sector defined in that instrument. The administrative extension act is issued by the Ministry of Employment and will imply weighting social circumstances and economic reasons which justify it, in particular the identity or analogy of economic and social situations considered in the extension (article 514.th).

XI. The administrative employment conditions act is an administrative act issued by the Ministry of Employment that creates a new ICLR. This emission is possible where social and economic circumstances justify it and if there is no union of employers 'association nor can the administrative extension act be issued. The administrative employment conditions act is subsidiary: it may only be issued in the absence of any other ICLR in force (article 517.th).

XII. Finally, the mandatory or needed arbitration award is a decision issued when arbitration becomes imperative, which is very rare. Mandatory arbitration is foreseen in article 508.th of the PLC; the necessary arbitration is governed under article 510.th[33].

XIII. Giving the fact that we have several sources of employment law, one may find competing sources of law covering the same subject with different solutions. In other words, we may have conflicts between distinctive sources of law. For example: we may have conflicts between what is stipulated in the law and in instruments of labour regulation; conflicts between the law and individual employment contracts; and conflicts between the instruments of labour regulation and individual employment contracts.

[32] See Luís Gonçalves da Silva, *Código do Trabalho Anotado*, cit., comments on articles 1rst and 2nd of the Portuguese Labor Code.
[33] See Luís Gonçalves da Silva, *Código do Trabalho Anotado*, cit., comments on articles 508.th to 514th of the Portuguese Labor Code.

When this happens, legal rules must solve these conflicts so as to define which source will be applicable in an employment situation and thus rule the contract. More on this can be found in the next section.

3.2.1. Conflict of sources of law

I. The Portuguese Labour Code tries to solve all the conflicts of sources of law that may emerge, by establishing two rules of conflicts, respectively comprised in articles 3.rd and article 476.th [34].

II. Article 3.rd is the most important provision in this regard, solving conflicts between the law and ICLR, as well as conflicts between the law and employment contracts[35].

The first conflict we are faced with is the conflict between the law and instruments of collective labour regulations. That is to say, a conflict between a legal rule and a rule resulting from a collective convention, for example, as a result of a collective negotiation.

Regarding this conflict, article 3.rd, n.er 1, states that legal rules that govern the employment contract can be removed by instruments of collective labour regulation unless those rules are imperative, i.e., if the legal rules are not imperative, the collective agreement (for instance) will prevail. Contrarily, legal rules that govern the employment contract cannot be removed by any administrative employment conditions act (n.er 2). We may conclude, as a consequence, that the lawmaker favored the collective agreements over the law, unless the law is imperative. The reason is easy to strike: if the collective agreement is a result of a private bargaining between the employer and the trade unions and if both of them agree on creating different employment conditions than those legally created, then the legislator accepts the result of that negotiation and the removal of the law, regardless of ascertaining if the agreement is more favorable for the employee than the law.

[34] See João Leal Amado, *Contrato de Trabalho,* cit., pp. 38 et seq

[35] See Menezes Cordeiro, *Direito do Trabalho,* cit., pp. 390 et seq.; Guilherme Dray, *O Princípio da Proteção do Trabalhador,*cit., pp. 487 et seq.; Luís Gonçalves da Silva, *Código do Trabalho Anotado,* cit., comments on articles 3.rd of the Portuguese Labor Code.

Nevertheless, in specific cases, foreseen in article 3.rd, n.er 3, the legal rules that govern the employment contract may only be removed by instruments of collective labour regulations when the law is not imperative and if these instruments are more favorable to the employees. This is the requirement whenever we face one of the following subjects:

a) Rights of personality, equality, and non-discrimination;
b) Protection in parenthood;
c) Child work;
d) Employees with reduced working capacity, disability or chronic illness;
e) Worker-student status;
f) Employer's duty of information;
g) Limits on the daily and weekly working time periods;
h) Minimum duration of rest periods, including the minimum period of annual holiday;
i) Maximum duration of night worker's work;
j) Fulfilment and guarantees of salary;
k) Chapter on prevention and repair of occupational accidents and diseases and legislation that regulates them;
l) Transmission of undertaking or businesses;
m) Rights of the employee's elected representatives.

This means that in the above referred cases the law prevails over the ICLR if the instruments of collective labour regulations are less favorable to the employees.

So, in a nutshell, we may conclude as follows: as a general rule, the collective agreements may prevail over the law, unless the law is imperative (article 3.rd, n.er 1); if we deal with the subject matters expressed in article 3.rd, n.er 3, related to matters which can compromise the employee's dignity, then the ICLR can only replace the law if it contains more favorable rules to the employees.

III. If the conflict is between the law and the individual employment contract, we shall apply article 3.rd, n.er 4. In this case, the legal rules that govern the employment contract tend to prevail. They can only be removed by an employment contract if the latter establishes improved conditions to the employee and if the legal rules are not imperative (n.^{er} 4). That is to say: as the employment contract is negotiated between the employer and the employee individually (i.e. without the participation of trade unions) the lawmaker is likely more protective. The employment contract will only prevail over the law if it is more favorable for the employee. If not, the employer could impose less favorable and less protective conditions to the employee as those comprised in the law.

The law also clarifies that whenever a legal rule that governs the employment contract states that it can be removed by an instrument of collective bargaining, it is understood that it cannot be replaced by an employment contract (n.^{er} 5)[36].

IV. Finally, with regards to the conflicts between instruments of labour regulation and employment contracts, article 476.th (Principle of the most favorable treatment) of the Portuguese Labour Code provides that the provisions of an instrument of collective labour regulation may only be excluded by an employment contract whenever such individual contract establishes better conditions to the employee[37].

V. Let´s gather an example to best understand article 3.rd, on a conflict surrounding working time.

Consider the legal rule comprised in article 203. rd of the Portuguese Labour Code which states the employee's working day goes up to 8h a day and 40h a week. Imagine the event where the collective agreement says the normal working period corresponds to 7h a day and 35h a week. And, finally, gather the event where the employment contract comprises a clause stating that the working time is 10h a day and 50h a week. In this case, we have a conflict between different sources of law. We have a hierarchical conflict of sources. Therefore, if we have a conflict, we must solve it, for the following reason: at the end of the day, we have to know whether the employee should

[36] See MENEZES CORDEIRO, *Direito do Trabalho,* cit., pp. 390 et seq.; GUILHERME DRAY, *O Princípio da Proteção do Trabalhador,* cit., pp. 487 et seq.; LUÍS GONÇALVES DA SILVA, *Código do Trabalho Anotado,* cit., comments on articles 3.rd of the Portuguese Labor Code.

[37] See LUÍS GONÇALVES DA SILVA, *Código do Trabalho Anotado,* cit., comments on article 476.th of the Portuguese Labor Code.

work 40h a week (as stipulated by law), 35h a week (as agreed on the ICLR) or 50h a week (as stipulated in the employment contract).

In order to solve this conflict, we must apply the referred article 3.rd of the Portuguese Labour Code to solve the conflicts between the legal rules and the collective agreements, on one hand, and between the legal rules and the employment contract, on the other hand; finally we must also apply article 476.th to solve the conflicts between the collective agreement and the employment contract.

In this particular case, we have to apply the specific rule foreseen in article 3.rd, n.^{er} 3, since the collective agreement governs the limits on the duration of normal daily and weekly work periods (article 3.rd, n.^{er} 3, subparagraph *g)*). In fact, the law can be replaced by the collective agreement but only if this agreement is more favorable to the employee. In the above exemple, the collective agreement can replace the law since it establishes a maximum threshold (35h) below the limits created by the law (40h) which is more favorable to the employee. The law establishes a limit of 8h a day and 40h a week of working time but admits the creation of other limits below those thresholds. In other words, since the law is not absolutely imperative, the collective agreement can replace the law. Moreover, in this particular case, the solution created by the collective agreement is more favorable to the employees than the provision of the law. Therefore by applying article 3.rd, n.^{er} 3 of the Portuguese Labour Code, the collective agreement prevails.

On the second conflict which occurs between the collective agreement and the employment contract, we must apply article 476.th. Under this rule, the contract can replace the collective agreement only if it contains a more favorable regime to the employee. That is not the case in this particular situation, and so the contract cannot prevail.

We can also analyze the conflict between the law and the contract, with the same results. Under article 3.rd, n.^{er} 4, the law prevails over the contract, unless the contract contains a more favorable regime to the employee. That is not the case as well. In this case, since the employment contract contains a clause that states that the working period is 10h a day and 50h a week, we are forced to conclude that this regime is not more favorable to the employee than the legal regime and violates the maximum limits stated in the law.

In the end, when applying both articles 3.rd and 476.th we conclude that the collective agreement prevails against the law and against the contract. Summing up, in this particular case the employee should work only 7h a day and 35h a week according to the terms negotiated in the collective agreement.

Having said that, a final question remains: what is the validity of the employment's contract clause that infringes the law? Under article 121.st of the Portuguese Labour Code that clause is void, null and ineffective, since it violates a provision of imperative law. That doesn't mean the employment contract is globally ineffective. The contract is valid, only the null clause will be declared null and extracted from the contract, because it is an out-of-limits clause[38].

3.2.2. The scope of collective agreements

I. Collective agreements are the most important negotiated ICLR, since they are concluded between the employer or the employers organizations and the trade unions, as the employees representatives.

Whenever a collective agreement is concluded, we have to grasp its scope: who are those that are bound by this agreement; what is the material scope of the agreement; to which circumstances will the agreements apply; and what is their duration. Basically, we must gather the personal, material, and the geographic scope, as well as the duration of these agreements.

The answer for these questions depends partly on the content of the collective agreement.

In terms of *personal scope* of application, there is a rule in the Portuguese Labour Code under which the collective agreement bounds both the contractors (the employer or the association of employers, on one hand; and the trade union, on the other) as well as the union employees that are affiliated with that same union. That means that the collective agreement is not binding nor covers non-union employees or those that are affiliated with another trade union that hasn't signed the collective agreement. That is what we usually call the *principle of affiliation,* expressed in article 496.th of the Portuguese Labour Code. The collective agreement is applicable to those who signed it and those who are represented by the latter. Furthermore,

[38] See Pedro Madeira de Brito, *Código do Trabalho Anotado*, cit., comments on articles 121.st of the Portuguese Labor Code.

non-union employees can also choose individually to be bound by a specific collective agreement that is in force. In that case and for that purpose they have to express their will to be under the scope of application of that agreement (article 497.th). That is what we usually call as an "individual adhesion"[39].

II. Secondly, we must determine the *material scope* of application, which will define the situations that are under the scope of these agreements. The collective agreement is *vertical* when its aim is to cover a specific sector of activity. It is *horizontal* when it is based on a professional scope. This may be important, whenever there is a concurrence between a *vertical* collective agreement and a *horizontal* collective agreement. Under article 481.st of the Portuguese Labour Code, if we have a concurrence between a *vertical* and a *horizontal* collective agreement the one which prevails is the *vertical* collective agreement. The *material* scope of application shall be defined by the parties to the agreement. This information is mandatory, under article 492.nd, n.er 1, subparagraph *c)*, that states that the collective agreement must inform its material and geographic scope of application[40].

III. Thirdly, we have the *geographic* scope of application, which tells us about the geography where the collective agreement is applied. For instance, the collective agreement may be applied only in a specific city, in a region or at a national level. The geographic scope of application is important to determine where the instrument will be applicable.

IV. Finally, the *duration* or the length of these agreements depend on the will of the contractors. For example, we may have an agreement with a foreseeable duration of 1, 2, or 5 years depending on the deal between the employer and the union. The Portuguese Labour Code states in its article 499.th that the collective agreement is in force and shall be renewed in accordance with the terms laid down therein. It is also considered that if the Convention does not provide for a term of validity, we may consider by

[39] See Luís Gonçalves da Silva, *Código do Trabalho Anotado*, cit., comments on articles 496.th and 497th of the Portuguese Labor Code.
[40] See Luís Gonçalves da Silva, *Código do Trabalho Anotado*, cit., comments on article 492.nd of the Portuguese Labor Code.

default that the collective agreement is in force for a period of one year and is successively renewed for an equal period[41].

3.2.3. Hierarchical conflict of sources

I. Because of the existence of multiple sources of law, we may have a significant number of conflicts. Let's consider, for instance, a conflict with regards to the probation period, which is the period that starts after the beginning of the execution of the contract and during which both the employer and the employee can terminate the contract at any given time without previous notice, without just cause, and without the need for any compensation.

Bearing in mind that the law states that the probation period for the generality of the employees corresponds to 90 days (article 112.th), consider, now, that the collective agreement states a probation period of 60 days and that the employment agreement expresses a probation period of up to 120 days[42].

In this case, we have a conflict of different sources of law providing different solutions for the same situation regarding the probation period. Legally speaking we have a hierarchical conflict of sources. Therefore, since we face a conflict, we must solve it for the following reason: we must know what is the working period that must be attained by the employee.

In order to determine it, we should apply article 3.rd of the Portuguese Labour Code (PLC), aimed at solving the conflicts between the law and the collective agreement, on one hand, and the conflict between the law and the employment contract, on the other. Moreover, we also have to apply article 476.th PLC to solve the conflict between the collective agreement and the employment contract.

II. In this particular case, we have firstly to apply the general rule expressed in article 3.rd, n.er 1. That means, as we already know, that the law

[41] See Luís Gonçalves da Silva, *Código do Trabalho Anotado*, cit., notes on article 499.th of the Portuguese Labor Code.

[42] About the probation period, see Luís Miguel Monteiro, *Código do Trabalho Anotado*, cit., comments on articles 111.st et seq. of the Portuguese Labor Code.

can be replaced by the collective agreement no matter if the latter contains either a more or a less favorable regime for the employee. The only legal requirement is that the law itself is not imperative. In this particular case, by establishing a smaller probation period (60 days, instead of 90 days), the collective agreement expresses a regime that is more favorable for the employee, since it establishes a maximum threshold below the limits legally created. Actually, that would mean that 60 days after the performance of the contract the employer could no longer dismiss the employee without just cause. So, since the collective agreement creates a regime more favorable to the employee and bearing in mind that the law is not imperative, allowing a reduction of the probation period, the collective agreement could replace it. Moreover, in this particular case, the law is clear: article 112.th, n.^{er} 5, expresses that "*The duration of the probation period may be reduced by means of an instrument of collective labour regulation or by a written agreement between employer and employee*".

Therefore, by application of article 3.rd, n.^{er} 1 of the Portuguese Labour Code, the collective agreement prevails.

III. The second conflict occurs between the collective agreement and the employment contract. To solve it, we must apply article 476.th. Under this rule, the contract can replace the collective agreement whenever it contains a more favorable regime to the employee than the provisions of the law. That is not what happens in this particular case. In our example, while the collective agreement states a probation period of 60 days the employment contract contains a probation period of 120 days; this leads us to conclude that the employment contract is less favorable than the collective agreement. Hence, the contract cannot prevail.

IV. We can also analyze the conflict between the law and the contract, but we will reach the same solution. Under article 3.rd, n.^{er} 4, the law prevails over the contract unless the latter contains more favorable terms to the employee. It is not the case here. Since the employment contract contains a clause that states a probation period of 120 days, we must conclude that this regime is not more favorable to the employee than the legal regime, which states a probation period of 90 days. Besides, as we said before, the law clarifies this solution through a specific rule, as article 112.th, n.^{er} 5, expresses that "*The duration of the probation period may be reduced (...) by written agreement between employer and employee"*. I.e.: the employment contract can reduce the duration of the probation period but cannot enlarge it.

In conclusion, by applying both articles 3.rd and 476.th the collective agreement prevails over the law and also prevails over the contract.

V. Finaly, the probation period applicable in this case would be 60 days, under the rules convened in the collective agreement. Connecting this regime with the one regarding the personal scope of the collective agreements, this solution would be applicable only if the employee was affiliated with the trade union that signed such agreement, as previously referred (article 496.th PLC). On the other hand, since the employment contract contradicts the law regarding the probation period, that specific clause of the contract should be considered null and void (article 121.st of the PLC) and must be suppressed.

4.
Employment contract

4.1. Concept

I. Under Portuguese Law, the employment contract is a contract in which a natural person undertakes, through retribution, to provide his or her activity to another person(s), within an organization and under their authority. This is the definition stated in article 11.th of the Portuguese Labour Code, which lies very close to the definition comprised in article 1152.nd of the Portuguese Civil Code, which defines the employment contract as the one in which a person undertakes, by way of remuneration, to provide his intellectual or manual skills to another person, under the authority and direction of this person[43].

The overarching characteristics of the employment contract are the legal and economic subordination of the employee[44]. Under an employment contract, the provider of an activity promises to work under the control and the direction of the employer, being paid a salary as compensation. He/she doesn't control the business and must work under the surveillance and direction of the employer[45].

[43] See MENEZES CORDEIRO, *Direito do Trabalho, I*, cit., pp. 59 et seq.; PEDRO ROMANO MARTINEZ, *Direito do Trabalho*, pp 291 et seq.; LUÍS MENEZES LEITÃO, *Direito do Trabalho*, cit., pp. 95 et seq.

[44] See JOÃO LEAL AMADO, *Contrato de Trabalho*, cit., pp. 12 et seq. and pp. 53 et seq.

[45] See MARIA DO ROSÁRIO RAMALHO, *Tratado de Direito do Trabalho – Parte II*, cit., pp. 32 et seq.

II. In its bare essence, the employment contract is a bilateral agreement by which both parties assume obligations: the employee assumes the duty of working under the direction and control of the employer, while the employer assumes the duty of paying a salary to the employee, usually on a monthly basis. This contract is nominated and typical, as it is referred and expressed in the law. Besides, the law contains a specific regime that governs the relationship between the employer and the employee. This contract is also onerous, since it involves the payment of a salary, which is a statutory obligation[46]. So as to protect the employee and guarantee its dignity, Portuguese law defines a minimum monthly salary to all workers, which is defined by the Government after consulting the Social Concertation Permanent Commission, a permanent organization that includes representatives from the Government, the employers and the employees.

III. The main characteristic of the employment contract is the existence of legal subordination, which means that the employee works under the control and direction of the employer. The employer has the right to control the time, place and type of work as well as the method and manner the manner in which the worker performs the activity. The employer has, therefore, the right to define where the employee has to work, the tools and equipment he/she must use, the working schedule he/she must accomplish, where he/she should present himself/herself to work, and so on. In case of non-accomplishment of the employee's duties or an obligation to which he/she is bound to, the employer may exercise a disciplinary power to sanction him what requires a preliminary disciplinary procedure, with the corresponding possibility of applying penalties without a previous court decision. That's something unique within the scope of private law: as a consequence of any misconduct incurred by the employee, the law confers upon the employer the power to apply penalties against the latter without a previous court ruling[47].

The employee depends on the wages he/she receives to carry out his/her and his/her family's life, and he/she does not control the production process, which is the responsibility of the employer. It is the employer that controls the relation of the corporation with all its stakeholders and the community

[46] See ALVIN L. GOLDMAN and ROBERTO L. CORRADA, *Labor Law in the USA,* cit., p. 91.

[47] See PEDRO ROMANO MARTINEZ, *Direito do Trabalho,* pp 295 et seq.

as a whole, including the regulatory agencies. Moreover, the employer controls price definition, as well as the aims and direction of the productive process. The overall management of the corporation is a competence of the employer; therefore, the employee depends on someone else´s direction to receive his/her salary at the end of the month. That´s the reason why legal doctrine usually emphasizes that the employee is economically dependent on the employer.

In a nutshell: the employee undertakes, through retribution, to provide his or her activity and skills to another person(s), within an organization and under their authority. The employer is legally authorized to exercise the power of direction, and is conferred the power to manage and control the employee´s performance; the employee has the corresponding duty to obey his/her direction.

The employer is envisaged as the owner of the corporation and the employee depends on his/her wages to carry out his/hers family's life. The employer is empowered with disciplinary power, in the event of misconduct, while the employee cannot exert the same power against the employer. Thus, the relationship between the employer and the employee is unbalanced and unequal by two different points of view: legal and economic[48].

IV. This is the reason why employment law is aimed at the protection of the employee, providing a wide range of rights to protect him/her against unscrupulous employers and the potential abusive exercise of the employer´s powers. Under employment law, the employee is entitled to a several range of rights. For example: he or she is entitled to a minimum wage; to periods of rest and an annual period of paid holidays; to a Christmas bonus; to an insurance against work accidents; to maternity or paternity leave in case of childbirth; to a limitation of working hours; and to protection against unmotivated dismissal. Labour law is generally aimed at the protection of the employee, through imperative rules. This is its basic idea. That is also why parties often times seek to evade the employment contract, establishing alternative arrangements to achieve the same results, namely through the conclusion of contracts for the provision of services.

[48] See Guilherme Dray, *O Princípio da Proteçao do Trabalhador*, Almedina Coimbra, 2015, pp. 19 et seq.

This scape led to a certain 'grey area' within this subject: the distinction between an employee and an independent contractor. The first is the person who concludes an employment contract, performing the activity under the control and direction of the employer; the second is the person who concludes a provision of services contract, working autonomously.

V. The provision of services contract is a contract foreseen in the Portuguese Civil Code (article 1154.th) under which a provider performs a service to a beneficiary, doing it autonomously. Since the provider is independent, the law doesn't grant him/her any specific protection. In fact, while under the employment law the employer has to guarantee the employee a monthly salary, annual subsidies, paid holidays, overtime pay, and public holidays and has also to provide safe and healthy conditions of work, such obligations do not exist in a provision of services relationship. The reason is easy to grasp: while the employee depends legally and economically on the employer, the provider of services, as an independent contractor, works autonomously and without any exclusivity, being economically and legally independent.

So, due to the existing gap between those two contracts and the rights reserved by law to the employee, the employer has incentives to evade an employment contract and to favor a provision of services contract instead.

As we will see further on, if the provision of services contract follows all the characteristics of an employment contract, legal authorities namely employment courts may decide that regardless of the label not being that of an employment contract it is a fraudulent definition and in reality it is a true employment contract.

For the stated reason, the distinction between an employment contract and a provision of services contract as well as the distinction between an employee and an independent contractor is very relevant and must be emphasized[49].

[49] See Pedro Romano Martinez, *Direito do Trabalho*, pp 307 et seq.

4.2. Distinction between an employment contract and a provision of services contract

I. The distinction between an employee and an independent contractor is a core issue given the consequences of such classification. It is likely the most relevant issue of modern employment law and a topic that feeds many legal disputes[50].

While a broad legal framework and a set of rights offered by national laws and collective agreements protects the employee, the same protection is not extended to an independent contractor. While the protection of workers is at the heart of employment law and expressed both in international and national sources, the same is not applicable to independent contractors.

The reason for this distinction is easy to grasp: while the employee works under the employer's control, depending on him/her on a legal and economic basis, the independent contractor, in theory, may work for several beneficiaries and does not depend exclusively on a specific beneficiary. That is the meaning of autonomous and independent work, which defines the independent contractor[51].

It is sometimes difficult to determine whether an employment relationship exists especially when the rights and obligations of the parties are not clearly defined, and an employment relationship stands in disguise.

In order to prevent disguised employment relationships operating under the radar, laws will define perimeters surrounding the concepts of employees and independent contractors.

For that purpose, the lawmaker usually allows a broad range of ways to determine the existence of an employment relationship and the true nature of the contract. Those instruments are centered around legal indicators aimed at proving the existence of legal subordination, on one hand, and on legal presumptions, on the other, through which we may conclude that an employment relationship is presumed to exist if one or more relevant indicators are present. In both cases, by using a legal test, such as evidentiary mechanisms or subordination indexes, or by the use of legal presumptions, the interpreter or the judge should be able to assess the true nature of the contract. In other words, they must determine the existence of subordination

[50] See João Leal Amado, *Contrato de Trabalho*, cit., pp. 64 et seq.

[51] See Pedro Romano Martinez, *Direito do Trabalho*, pp 310 et seq.

or dependence, even if someone signed a disguised contract for the provision of services.

The purpose of the legal test or the legal presumption is to decide what business is at stake and whether we have an employment contract or not.

In the event we apply a legal presumption that points towards the existence of an employment contract, then the law reverts the burden of proof[52].

If there is a reversion of the burden of proof, the employer must prove that that specific contract is truly a provision of services contract rather than an employment contract. The employer will then have to prove that he/she had no intention to disguise an employment contract and that the written contract is truly a provision of services contract.

Ultimately, the qualification of a contract as an employment contract or a provision of services contract is decided by the courts. To issue such decision, courts usually apply the above referred legal test to find what kind of relation comes to surface[53].

[52] See Pedro Romano Martinez, *Código do Trabalho Anotado*, cit., notes on articles 11.st and 12.th of the Portuguese Labor Code.

[53] See, for example, the decision of the UK Court of Appeals (Civil Division), 19/12/2018, process UBER B.V., UBER London Limited, Uber Britannia Limited, vs. Yaseen Aslam, James Farrar, Robert Dawson & others. The Court decided that the Claimants were employed by UBER as employees, despite the label of the contract concluded by the parties. Regardless the written contract that qualified UBER drivers as independent contractors, the Court, following the previous decisions from the Employment Tribunal and the Employment Appeal Tribunal, concluded that the UBER drivers should be treated as employees for the purpose of applying the Employment Rights Act 1996, the National Minimum Wage Act 1998, and the Working Time Regulations 1998. To ground its decision, the Court applied the leading case *Autoclenz Ltd v Belcher [2011]*, UKSC 41, stating that the tribunals are not bound by the label used by the parties, since they are obliged to discover the true nature of the contract. The court qualified the UBER drivers as employees based on the following indicators: the drivers were integrated into the UBER business of providing transportation services; they were excluded from establishing a business relationship with passengers; UBER interviewed and recruited the drivers; UBER controlled the key information and excluded the driver from it; the drivers worked on the understanding that UBER would indemnify them for bad debts; UBER required drivers to accept trips and/or not cancel trips, and enforced the requirement by logging off drivers who breached those requirements; the UBER fixed the fare and the driver could not agree a higher sum with the passenger; UBER used to subject drivers through the rating system to what amounts to a performance management disciplinary procedure; UBER handled complaints by passengers, including complaints about the driver; and the drivers were subject to various controls by UBER. The Court found out that UBER drivers did not operate businesses

II. The ILO, in its Recommendation n.[er] 198, approved in 2006[54], concerning the employment relationship, recommends all its members to formulate and apply a clear national policy in order to guarantee effective protection for workers who perform work in the context of an employment relationship, including measures to:

(a) Provide guidance for the parties concerned, employers and workers, on effectively establishing the existence of an employment relationship and to distinguish between employed and self-employed workers;
(b) Prevent disguised employment relationships in the context of, for example, other relationships that may include the use of other forms of contractual arrangements which hide the true legal status, noting that a disguised employment relationship occurs when the employer treats an individual other than an employee and in a manner which hides his or her true legal status as an employee. Those situations can arise where contractual arrangements have the effect of depriving workers of the protection they are due;
(c) Ensure standards which are applicable to all forms of contractual arrangements, including those involving multiple parties, so that employed workers have the protection they are owed;
(d) Ensure that standards applicable to all forms of contractual arrangements establish who is liable for the protection contained therein;
(e) Provide effective access to those concerned, in particular employers and workers, to appropriate, speedy, inexpensive, fair and efficient procedures and mechanisms for settling disputes regardless of the existence and terms of an employment relationship;
(f) Ensure compliance with, and effective application of, laws and regulations concerning the employment relationship; and

on their own account and therefore rejected the label of agency and the characterization of the relationship in the written documentation. To come up with this decision, the Court applied the usually called "legal test", used to find whether a provider of services should be qualified as an employee or an independent contractor. Under this legal test, the courts should examine all the circumstances and evidences of the case of which the written agreement is only a part.

[54] Seeathttps://www.ilo.org/legacy/english/inwork/cb-policy-guide/employmentrelationshi precommendationno198.pdf

(g) Provide for appropriate and adequate training in relevant international labour standards, comparative law and case law to the judiciary, arbitrators, mediators, labour inspectors and other individuals responsible for dealing with the resolution of labour disputes and enforcement of national employment laws and standards.

With regards to the determination of the existence of such an employment relationship, the ILO recommends that it should be guided primarily by the facts relating to the performance of work and the remuneration of the worker, notwithstanding how the relationship is characterized, contractually or otherwise and regardless of how it has been agreed between the parties. For that purpose, Members should promote clear methods for guiding workers and employers with regards to the determination of the existence of an employment relationship, considering the following:

(a) Allowing a broad range of means for determining the existence of an employment relationship;
(b) Providing for a legal presumption that an employment relationship exists where one or more relevant indicators are present; and
(c) Determining, following prior consultations with the most representative organizations of employers and workers, that employees with certain characteristics, in general or in a particular sector, must be deemed to be either employed or self-employed.

The Recommendation also states that Members may consider to define clearly the conditions the conditions applied for determining the existence of an employment relationship, for example, by defining in their laws and regulations concepts of subordination or dependence, or by other means put forward specific indicators of the existence of an employment relationship. Those indicators might include:

(a) The fact that the work is carried out according to the instructions and under the control of another party; involves the integration of the worker in an organization or an enterprise; is performed solely or mainly for the benefit of another person; must be carried out personally by the worker; is carried out within specific working hours or at a workplace specified or agreed by the party requesting the work; is of a particular duration and has a certain continuity; requires the worker's availability; or involves the provision of tools, materials and machinery by the party requesting the work[55];

(b) Periodic payment of remuneration to the worker; the fact that such remuneration constitutes the employee's sole or principal source of income; provision of payment in kind, such as food, lodging or transport; recognition of entitlements such as weekly rest and annual holidays; payment by the party requesting the work for travel undertaken by the worker in order to carry out the work; absence of financial risk for the worker.

The ILO Recommendation also establishes that the settlement of disputes concerning the existence and terms of an employment relationship should be a matter for industrial or other tribunals or arbitration authorities to which workers and employers have effective access in accordance with national laws and practice. The competent authorities should adopt measures with a view to ensure respect for the implementation of laws and regulations concerning the employment relationship regarding the various aspects considered in the Recommendation; for example, through labour inspection services and collaboration with social security administration and tax authorities. With regards to the employment relationship, national labour administration and associated services should regularly monitor the enforcement of its programs and processes.

III. It is not easy to classify a specific relationship as an employment contract or a provision of services contract, since we may trace common features in both contracts.

When deciding if there is an employment relationship, the overarching aspect we should look for is whether the employer has the right to control and to penalize the employee and the degree to which he/she exercises such rights. If we conclude that he/she has the right and effectively

[55] Based on this idea, the Paris Court of Appeals, in a decision issued on January 10 of 2019, qualified the contract concluded between a UBER driver and UBER as an employment contract, namely based on the fact that Uber managed all the business and controlled the driver's performance, namely by sending them messages asking "*Etes-vous encore là*? (are you still there?)" whenever the driver didn't answer calls from UBER.

exercised control over the time and work performed by the employee or exercises his disciplinary power in the event of misconduct then we are tilted to conclude that such relationship is based on the tenets of legal and economic dependency and, as a consequence, that we face an employment relationship.

Even when you find a written contract classifying the employee as an independent contractor, the administrative agencies or courts may say that´s not the case and that the employment contractual arrangements were not assumed to deprive the worker of the protection granted by employment laws. In this case, the employer may incur in major liability.

The comprehensive method or the legal test commonly used in Portugal by legal doctrine, academics and opinion makers as well as employed by the courts, to distinguish whether you have an employment relationship or an independent contract, is the evidentiary mechanism or the index of subordination method ("indicia method" or "*método indiciário*", in Portuguese), that uses several indicators in order to determine if you have a relationship with legal subordination or not.

Those indicators, which characterize an employment relationship, are mainly the following:

a) The work is carried at a workplace specified or agreed by the party requesting the work;
b) The provision of tools, materials and machinery (such as a laptop, a van or a uniform) by the party requesting the work;
c) The work is carried out in specific working hours determined by the party requesting the work;
d) The employee works out according to the instructions and under the control of the party requesting the work;
e) The employee is integrated in the organization of the enterprise;
f) The employee receives periodic payments as remuneration and such remuneration constitutes the employee's sole or principal source of income;
g) The party requesting the work acknowledges certain certain employee entitlements such as weekly rest, annual holidays, and paid vacations;
h) Absence of financial risk for the employee, given he/she is paid every month despite the financial results of the employer; the salary is

usually fixed, and whether the employee does a good or a bad job he/she still gets his/her salary;

i) The employee is usually required to attend company meetings;
j) Employees get usually group benefits, such as health insurance or medical assistance;
k) The employee cannot subcontract other employees to perform his/her own duties;
l) If the provider is entitled to manage other employees, that usually means that he is an employee rather than an independent contractor.

IV. Based on these indicators, the Portuguese legislator created a presumption regarding the existence of an employment contract comprised in article 12.th of the Portuguese Labour Code[56].

Under that article the existence of an employment contract is presumed to exist if, within the scope of the relationship between the person providing an activity and that who benefits from it, some of the following characteristics are found:

a) The activity is carried out in a place belonging to or determined by the beneficiary;
b) The equipment, tools and instruments of work used belong to the beneficiary of the activity;
c) The activity provider controls the start and end times of the service, keeping a work schedule, determined by the beneficiary of the service;
d) A certain amount is regularly paid – fixed remuneration – to the activity provider, in return for the service he/she provides;
e) The activity provider performs a managing or leadership role in the organization structure of the company.

If, under these indicators, the courts conclude that the employer disguised an employment contract by entering into an apparent provision of services contract with the end goal of depriving the employee of the protection he/she is owed under the Portuguese Labour Code, the employer incurs in extensive liability.

[56] See Pedro Romano Martinez, *Código do Trabalho Anotado*, cit., notes on article 12.th of the Portuguese Labor Code; Luís Menezes Leitão, *Direito do Trabalho*, cit., pp. 118 et seq.

Moreover, the Portuguese legislator enacted in 2013 Law n.er 63/2013, of 27.th August, that contains a procedure to be adopted in case of improper use of the services contract.

Under this law, if the labour inspector of the Authority of Working Conditions identifies, during an inspection routine, the existence of a situation of provision of activity apparently independent under conditions analogous to the employment contract based on the terms described in article 12.th of the Portuguese Labour Code, he/she should notify the employer to, within 10 days, rectify the situation or state what he/she finds convenient.

If this period expires without the rectification of the situation by the employer, the labour inspector shall submit the process within five days to the prosecution services of the Public Attorney, together with all the evidence gathered, for the purpose to initiate a lawsuit to affirm the existence of an employment contract.

The intention of the parties is important to determine whether we have an employment contract or not, but is not the determining factor. The final decision on the nature of the contract pertains to the courts and they are not bound to the label employed by the parties.

5. Personality rights

5.1. General overview

I. Personality rights are the rights of an individual related to his or her own personality, namely the right to life, physical and moral integrity, the right to privacy and the right to control the commercial use of name, image, likeness or other aspects of one´s identity[57].

To have legal personality means to be capable of holding legal rights and obligations within a certain legal system, such as entering into contracts, the ability to sue and being sued. Legal personality is a prerequisite to legal capacity and the ability of any legal person to amend rights and obligations[58].

Legal persons are of two kinds: natural persons and judicial persons, i.e., entities like corporations, which are treated by law as having legal relevance. For natural persons, the holding of personality rights is automatic from the moment they are born. That is the rule affirmed in the Portuguese Civil Code. Since birth, a person holds personality and natural rights, like the right to life or to physical and moral integrity (Portuguese Civil Code, article 66.th).

Generally speaking, personality rights have the following characteristics: they are personal, hence they are linked to personality goods instead of economic goods; they are non-transferable, since they cannot be transferred to anybody; they are absolute, since they are *erga omnes* rights which must

[57] See Menezes Cordeiro, *Direito do Trabalho*, cit., pp. 534 et seq.

[58] See Guilherme Dray, *O Princípio da Proteção do Trabalhador*, cit., pp. 361 et seq.

be respected by everybody regardless of the inexistence of a specific legal relationship; and they contain an ethical structure and approach as they deal with personality aspects of our life, such as physical and moral integrity, name, image, likeness, privacy and confidentiality.

Personality rights play on a Civil Law level the same role that fundamental rights play at a Constitutional Law level. There are however some differences. While fundamental rights are negative rights affirmed in Constitutional texts, i.e., rights of protection of the citizen against the State in order to protect his/her own privacy, property, and freedom to self-development against the State's interference, personality rights are rights that must be used within the context of horizontal relations, i.e., between two or more private persons at a private level. Fundamental rights are rights stated in the Fundamental Law to protect the citizen against the State; personality rights are rights expressed in the Civil Code to protect an individual against other individuals in his/her private sphere.

In Portugal, while fundamental rights are affirmed in the Portuguese Constitution of 1976, from article 24.th (right to life) throughout article 47.th (Freedom to choose a job and access to public service), including the right to personal integrity (article 25.th), to freedom and security (article 27.th), to the *habeas corpus* (article 31.st), the right to safeguards in criminal procedure (article 32.nd), deportation, extradition and right of asylum (article 33.rd), the rights to inviolability of home and correspondence (article 34.th), to freedom of expression and information (article 37.th), to freedom of the press and media (article 38.th), to freedom of conscience, of religion and of any form of worship (article 41.st), the right to meet and to demonstrate in public (article 45.th) and the freedom of association (article 46.th). Personality rights are affirmed in the Portuguese Civil Code of 1966[59].

The Portuguese Civil Code contains in its article 70.th a general protection of personality which comprises and protects different aspects of an individual's personality against other individuals. Basically, article 70.th states that the law protects individuals against any unlawful interference or threat of harm to their physical or moral personality. Moreover, it states that regardless of the liability that may arise, a threatened or offended person may require appropriate action to the circumstances, in order to prevent

[59] See the notes of articles 24th et seq. of the Portuguese Constitution by Jorge Miranda/Rui Medeiros, *Constituição Portuguesa Anotada*, cit.

the consummation of the threat or mitigate the effects of the offense committed[60].

After this general clause containing a general protection of personality rights, the Portuguese Civil Code expresses several specific personality rights, such as the right to a name (article 72.nd), the right to the confidentiality of letters and missives (article 75.th); the right to confidentiality of family and other confidential written memories (article 77.th); the right to one's image (article 79.th); the right to privacy (article 80.th) as well as the regime of voluntary limitation of personal rights, stating that any voluntary limitation on the exercise of personal rights is void if it is contrary to the principles of public order and that the voluntary limitation, when lawful, is always revocable notwithstanding the obligation to compensate the damage caused to the legitimate expectations of the other party (article 81.st).

As results from all the above we have a set of fundamental rights affirmed in the Portuguese Constitution (articles 24.th and following), namely some specific employee's fundamental rights (articles 53.rd and following.), and personality rights affirmed in the Portuguese Civil Code (articles 70.th and following); moreover the Portuguese lawmaker, decided when drafting the Portuguese Labour Code, in 2003, that this law should also contain specific rights of personality to be applied within the employment relationship.

The underlying reasons for this option can be summarized in four points: firstly, it was not logical to have personality rights expressed in the Civil Code to regulate horizontal relations and not to have them at private vertical relations, such as the employment relation, where the employee is under the control of the employer; secondly, because there are specific problems to the employment relationship that justify tailored regulation; thirdly, because in an employment relationship the employee affects his or her own person to provide an activity and therefore the risk of having his/her personality rights violated is bigger than in a horizontal relation; finally, because the growth of technology of information and communication and its use by the employers to control the employee's performance makes the employee's personality rights more vulnerable. The use of remote surveillance equipment to

[60] See Menezes Cordeiro, *Tratado de Direito Civil Português, I, Introdução, Fontes do Direito, Interpretação da Lei, Aplicação das Leis no Tempo, Doutrina Geral, 4ª edição, Reformulada e Atualizada,* Almedina, Coimbra, 2012, pp. 931 et seq.; Guilherme Dray, *Direitos de Personalidade. Anotações ao Código Civil e ao Código do Trabalho,* Almedina, Coimbra, 2006.

control the employee's performance; the use of databases which processes data about the employee; the use of equipment able to monitor and control the contents of email correspondence; the use of medical tests to control the existence or the probability of some diseases or drug consumption; all these new tools can threaten the personality rights of the employee. For all these reasons, the Portuguese legislator decided in 2003 to create a specific Section of the Portuguese Labour Code on personality rights within the scope of employment. This Section is still comprised in the Portuguese Labour Code of 2009.

This reveals how ambitious was the Portuguese legislator when dealing with an issue as important as this one. The Portuguese Civil Code of 1867 (seldom referred to as "*Código de Seabra*") was the first European Code to regulate in a systematic way the so-called "natural rights" of the citizens; the Portuguese Labour Code of 2003 was also the first European Labour Law Code that created a specific Section on the employment personality rights.

The existence of that specific Section (articles 14.th to 22.nd) does not refrain the application of the fundamental rights affirmed in the Constitution nor the personality rights affirmed in the Civil Code. We have a complementary relationship between these three pieces of legislation. When applying the Portuguese Labour Code, we can still apply the Portuguese Civil Code (for instance, article 81.st on the voluntary limitation of personality rights) and the Portuguese Constitution (for instance, article 18.th, under which any restriction of a fundamental right shall obey to the principles of necessity and proportionality). Additionally, the Portuguese Labour Code presents us answers to several problems that we may find in an employment relationship[61].

Personality rights linked to employment are very important to the affirmation of an idea of *full citizenship*. The existence of jobs, dignity at work and the accomplishment of minimum labour standards are part of this citizenship idea and of the free development of one's personality. Therefore, the idea of *citizenship at work* is part of the civil values of freedom, self-determination and free development of one's personality. Consequently it is an essential ingredient for freedom, democracy and citizenship. Citizenship at work depends both on the affirmation of *equality and fair opportunities in*

[61] See the notes of GUILHERME DRAY regarding articles 14.th – 22.nd of the Portuguese Labor Code, at *Código do Trabalho Anotado*, cit., pp138 et seq.

the access to employment and within the context of an employment contract on the enforcement of *rights of personality*. The idea is intuitive: despite signing an employment contract, the employee remains a citizen able to express his or her thoughts and opinions at the workplace. That is also the basic idea that arises from the ILO' Declaration of Philadelphia, which affirms that all human beings, irrespective of race, creed or sex, have the right to pursue both their material wellbeing and their spiritual development in conditions of freedom and dignity, of economic security and equal opportunity[62].

5.2. Specific personality rights

I. The Portuguese Labour Code contains several personality rights: the freedom of expression and opinion (14.th); the right to physical and moral integrity (15.th); the right to privacy (16.th); the protection of personal data (17.th); the regulation of biometric data (18.th); the regime of medical tests and examinations (19.th); the protection against surveillance remote tools (20.th and 21.st); and the confidentiality of messages and information (22.th). Personality rights are bilateral, as they protect both the employee and the employer and its representatives. However, they are generally more important for the protection of the employee, which is the weakest party of the employment relationship.

II. The freedom of expression stated in article 14.th means that within the scope of a company the employee's freedom of expression, thought and opinion is accepted.

Generally speaking, the freedom of expression at the workplace and within a company is a precondition for the protection of the worker and his/her citizenship rights at work. The fact that the worker is bound to provide an activity under the command, rules and the direction of others under legal subordination does not mean that he annihilates his/her possibility to exhibit and disseminate freely in the workplace his/her thoughts and opinions about multiple aspects of public social life, as a normal citizen would. Article 14.th of the Portuguese Labour Code allows a worker to

[62] See Guilherme Dray, *O Princípio da Proteção do Trabalhador,* cit., pp. 361 et seq.

express freely his ideas and political opinions at the workplace and assert freely his convictions, both religious and political, as well as his/her trade unions. affiliations. The freedom of expression and opinion at the workplace is not however unlimited – the second part of the provision establishes that this specific right of personality ceases if its exercise violates someone else's rights of personality (including those of the employer or of the other workers) in a disproportionate way or if it jeopardizes or prejudices the regular performance or the normal functioning of the company. For instance, it is not allowed for an employee on the grounds of his/her freedom of expression to: denigrate, defame or insult a coworker, the employer or his representatives; to participate in demonstrations that put in risk the normal function of the company; to use a sticker saying "Jail for Rich People" in the front desk of a Five Star Hotel; to wear a T-Shirt of a sports team while selling tickets at the front desk of the rival team; or to write a political speech as a speech-writer using an ideological discourse contrary to the ideology expressed by the political leader for whom he/she is working. In determining the employee's rights of free speech within the corporation we must seek a fair balance between the interest of the employee, as a regular citizen, in commenting upon matters of public concern, and the interest of the employer, in promoting the efficiency and image of the corporation through his employees. The employee is entitled to freely express his or her opinions on matters of public concern, but he or she cannot be disruptive to the course of business, undermine the employer's authority, threaten the employer's authority to run the company, create insurrections, destroy the close working relationships within the corporation or jeopardize the corporation's image before its clients or the community[63].

III. Article 15. th establishes the right to physical and moral integrity[64].

Under this article, the employer, including the natural persons who represent him/her, and the worker, shall enjoy the right to their physical and moral integrity, in a peaceful work environment. This article must be connected to article 29.th, that prohibits moral and sexual harassment at

[63] See the notes of Guilherme Dray on article 14.th of the Portuguese Labor Code, at *Código do Trabalho Anotado*, cit., pp. 138 et seq.

[64] See the notes of Guilherme Dray on article 15.th of the Portuguese Labor Code, at *Código do Trabalho Anotado*, cit., pp. 149 et seq.

the workplace. Therefore, within a power relationship, as the employment relationship, those that are in a more powerful position (namely those in senior positions) cannot use their status to harass those that are in a less powerful function or position (namely junior staff). Both moral and sexual harassment (article 29. th) and physical and moral integrity violations (article 15. th) violate personality rights. This includes violence and harassment in the workplace, including public and private area if they are considered as work areas ; in places where the worker is paid, takes a rest break or a meal, or uses sanitary, washing and changing facilities; during work-related trips, travel, training, events or social activities; through work-related communications, including those enabled by information and communication technologies; in employer-provided accommodation; and when commuting to and from work[65].

IV. Article 16.th contains the right to privacy[66].

Under this article, the employer and the worker must respect the personality rights of the counterparty. Particularly, they should reserve the other's right to privacy. The right to guarantee the privacy of private life or the right to be let alone shall include access to and disclosure of aspects relating to the intimate and personal sphere of the parties, in particular in relation to family, affective and sexual life, health, political and religious beliefs. That also means that both parties have the right to privacy regarding communications, correspondence, image and voice, as further developed under provisions 20.th to 22.nd of the PLC.

V. Related to the right of privacy, article 17.th states that the employer cannot require a job applicant or a worker to provide information on (a) their private life, unless this information is strictly necessary and relevant to assess their suitability for the performance of employment and the written

[65] About harassment at the workplace, see the ILO Convention n.er 190 and Recommendation n.er 206, both adopted in June 21st, 2019.

[66] See the notes of Guilherme Dray on article 16.th of the Portuguese Labor Code, at *Código do Trabalho Anotado*, cit., pp. 151 et seq. See also Guilherme Dray, "O direito à reserva da intimidade da vida privada. O artigo 80.º do Código Civil de 1966", *Revista de Direito Civil, Centro de Investigação de Direito Privado,* Faculdade de Direito da Universidade de Lisboa, Ano II (2017), Número 3, António Menezes Cordeiro (Dir.), pp. 673-699.

statement with the reasoning thereof; and inquire on (b) their health or condition of pregnancy, unless justified by the particular requirements inherent to the nature of the professional activity at hand and the reasoning given in writing. Additionally, that same article 17.th expresses that the information provided about health or condition of pregnancy must be delivered to a physician, who can only communicate to the employer if the employee is or is not able to carry out the activity. Besides, the candidate to employment or the worker who has provided information of a personal nature shall have the right to control his/her personal data, being able to take note of its content and the purposes for which it is intended, as well as to require its correction and update. In a nutshell: article 17.th deals with personal data, following the principles and rules regarding the protection of personal data expressed in the European Union Charter for Fundamental Rights (article 8.th) and in the Regulation (EU) 2016/679 (General Data Protection Regulation – GDPR), under which everyone has the right to the protection of personal data concerning him or her and such data must be processed fairly for specified purposes and on the basis of consent of the person concerned or through other legitimate legal basis. Everyone has the right of access to data which has been collected concerning him or her, and the right to have it rectified. Moreover, the processing of personal data revealing racial or ethnic origin, political opinions, religious or philosophical beliefs, or trade union membership, and the processing of genetic and biometric data for the purpose of uniquely identifying a natural person, data concerning health or data concerning a natural person's sex life or sexual orientation shall be prohibited (article 9.th GDPR). These rules can easily be misapplied in the work environment and that is why they are expressly foreseen in article 17.th of the PLC[67].

VI. Article 18.th[68] provides that the processing of biometric data is only permitted if the data to be used are necessary, appropriate and proportionate to the objectives to be attained. Using the concept expressed at the GDPR (article 4.th), biometric data' means personal data resulting from specific

[67] See the notes of Guilherme Dray on article 17.th of the Portuguese Labor Code, at *Código do Trabalho Anotado*, cit., pp. 154 et seq.

[68] See the notes of Guilherme Dray on article 18.th of the Portuguese Labor Code, at *Código do Trabalho Anotado*, cit., pp. 159 et seq.

technical processing relating to the physical, physiological or behavioral characteristics of a natural person, which allow or confirm the unique identification of that natural person, such as facial images or fingerprint identification. Under the above referred article 18.th, biometric data shall be kept for the period necessary to achieve the treatment purposes for which they are retrieved and shall be destroyed at the time of transfer of the worker to another place of work or termination of the employment contract. Before, the legal doctrine used to sustain that the processing of biometric data at the workplace was only lawful if used to provide access to the employer's premises or to control the employee's attendance and compliance with the working schedule. Previous to the approval of the European Union GDPR and under the PLC, the use of biometric data depended on prior authorization by the National Data Protection Commission (article 18.th, n.^{er} 1). That prior authorization is no longer necessary, since under the GDPR these national administrative agencies no longer have the competence to enact previous administrative authorizations, but rather to monitor and guarantee the enforcement of the GDPR and national laws regarding data protection.

VII. Article 19.th foresees the possibility of undertaking medical tests and exams[69].

It is stated that in addition to the situations provided for in specific legislation on occupational safety and health, the employer may not, for the purposes of admission or maintenance of employment, require a job applicant or a worker to perform or be submitted to medical tests, except where they are intended to protect the worker or third parties, or where particular requirements inherent to the activity so warrant it. In any case, the employer must provide, in writing, to the applicant the grounds or motives for taking said medical tests. Besides, the employer may not, under any circumstances, require the job applicant or the worker to perform or be submitted to pregnancy tests. Moreover, the doctor or the physician responsible for the medical tests can only communicate to the employer if the worker is or is not fit to carry out the activity. The violation of these provisions by the employer is considered a very serious offense.

[69] See the notes of Guilherme Dray on article 19.th of the Portuguese Labor Code, at *Código do Trabalho Anotado,* cit., pp. 151 et seq.

VIII. Articles 20.th and 21.st refer to remote surveillance[70].

Basically, they establish that the employer may not use remote surveillance in the workplace by making use of technological equipment, for the purposes of controlling the worker's professional performance. The use of equipment is only lawful whenever it is used for the purposes of protection and security of people and goods or when particular requirements inherent to the nature of the activity so justify it. In these cases, the employer shall inform the worker of the existence and purpose of the means of surveillance he/she intends to use and shall indicate at the workplace that he/she is using remote surveillance, by publishing a sign where it reads, as appropriate: "*This place is under surveillance of a circuit closed television*" or "*This place is under surveillance of a closed circuit television, proceeding to the recording of image and sound*", followed by an identifying symbol. Again, the use of means of remote surveillance in the workplace used to depend on the authorization of the National Data Protection Commission, which is the national authority that stands for the privacy of citizens. After the publication of the European GDPR this authorization is, however, no longer needed but this administrative agency continues to have the competence to control the lawfulness of these mechanisms. Particularly, the agency may supervise if the use of these means is necessary, appropriate and proportionate to the objectives to be attained. Under the law, the personal data collected by means of distance surveillance shall be kept for the period necessary to achieve the purposes of its intended use and shall be destroyed at the time of transfer of the worker to another place of work or termination of the employment contract.

A violation of these provisions by the employer is considered a very serious offense.

IX. Finally, article 22.nd provides on confidentiality of messages and access to information[71].

[70] See the notes of Guilherme Dray on article 20.th and 21.rst of the Portuguese Labor Code, at *Código do Trabalho Anotado*, cit., pp. 161 et seq.

[71] See the notes of Guilherme Dray on article 19.th of the Portuguese Labor Code, at *Código do Trabalho Anotado*, cit., pp. 151 et seq. See also Guilherme Dray, "Comunicações Eletrónicas e privacidade no contexto laboral", *Prontuário de Direito do Trabalho*, II, 2016, Centro de Estudos Judiciários, Almedina, Coimbra, 2016, pp. 103-131.

Under this provision, the employee has the right of reserve and to confidentiality regarding the content of his/her messages of personal nature as well as access to non-professional information that he or she sends or receives namely through email. Anyhow, the Law states that this general rule shall not affect the employer's power to establish rules for the use of the corporation's communication channels, namely the use of email.

The prevailing idea is one of fair balance.

By applying employment personality rights, our task is to seek a fair balance between the employee's interest, as a citizen, and the employers' interest in promoting the regular performance of the company through his/her employees.

The idea of fair balance is discussed in several court rulings by Portuguese courts.

For instance, in September 8th 2014, the Oporto Court of Appeals ("*Tribunal da Relação do Porto*") considered that the publication of insults against the employer on a Facebook page can, in certain circumstances, be unlawful and therefore justify the dismissal of the employee with just cause, in particular where there is no expectation that such comments will remain confidential and comprised within the employee's right to privacy. The basis of this decision is that although article 14.th provides the employee's freedom of expression he or she cannot use it to defame or diminish the employer on social media, where there is no expectation of privacy. Here, the freedom of expression must be balanced with other people's rights of personality, like the right to honor and the right not to be defamed.

In a similar decision ruled by the Lisbon Court of Appeals ("*Tribunal da Relação de Lisboa*") in September 24th 2014, the court considered that the employee who offended and defamed the President of the Board of Directors of the company for which he worked on Facebook, exceeded the bounds of the freedom of expression, considering that it "*cannot cover the violation of the rights of the employer and its representatives. (...). In other words: it is not necessary to resort to gross and personal offense, as well as to defamation to assert and claim a right*". In this particular case, the employee posted on his Facebook page a message where he stated the employer was a "*great liar, Pinocchio (...)*" and that he and his management team were grossly incompetent, emphasizing that "*If they do not know how to manage a hotel than get out and go manage a Tasca (In Portuguese this refers to a very humble establishment which can roughly be translated to "Tavern"), you bunch of incompetents*". The employee ended the message by using the option to "*share with friends*" thus inviting his friends to spread the message with other employees as well as the whole Facebook community. The court considered that although it is a settled understanding of the jurisprudence that the legal and constitutional protection of the confidentiality of personal messages restrains the employer from gathering evidence to instruct a disciplinary process through access to personal messages, in this particular case the employee could not have a reasonable expectation of secrecy in the disclosure of the content since he knew that his message would be public to several persons. Therefore, the Court concluded that he used such message to defame and humiliate the employer, violating his own personality right of moral integrity expressed in article 15.th of the Portuguese Labour Code. The Court concluded that the freedom of expression stated in the article 14.th cannot be used to defame or denigrate somebody else's personality rights.

On the contrary, in another case, regarding the confidentiality of email, the Portuguese Supreme Court decided on July 5th 2007 that the email message sent by an employee to her workmate, in which she criticized her superior and the Vice-President of the corporation, was protected under the right to confidentiality of messages stated in article 22.nd of the Portuguese Labour Code, as the message was private and the employee had a legitimate expectation of privacy. The message was sent directly and exclusively to one colleague and was read by accident by the employer. In this case, the court considered that the content of the message was private and therefore the employee had the right to privacy and to confidentiality regarding the content of said message. The employer could not use this message as evidence to dismiss the employee. Moreover, there were no rules at corporate level prohibiting the use of email for private purposes. As a consequence, the dismissal was null and void. The Court condemned the employer to reinstate the employee, to payback and to pay her a severance compensation for the damages she suffered.

6.
Equality and non-discrimination at the workplace

6.1. General overview

I. Equality and non-discrimination, as well as meritocracy, are tenets which are crucial for social mobility, for the development of citizenship and for the self-development of personality.

It is currently agreed that the principle of equality and non-discrimination is part of the democratic ideals. Internationally, it forms part of several legally binding documents, such as the 1948 *Universal Declaration of Human Rights*[72], the 1965 *Convention on the Elimination of all Forms of Racial Discrimination*[73], the 1966 *International Covenant on Civil and Political Rights*[74],

[72] Article 1.st of the *Universal Declaration of Human Rights*, approved by the United Nations General Assembly on 10 December 1948, determines that *"all human beings are born free and equal in dignity and rights"*, and article 2.nd of the same legislative act states that *"Everyone is entitled to all the rights and freedoms set forth in this Declaration, without distinction of any kind, such as race, color, sex, language, religion, political or other opinion, national or social origin, property, birth or other status"*.
[73] Article 5.th of the *Convention on the Elimination of all Forms of Racial Discrimination*, approved by the United Nations General Assembly on 21 December 1965, provides that *"States Parties undertake to prohibit and to eliminate racial discrimination in all its forms and to guarantee the right of everyone, without distinction as to race, color, or national or ethnic origin, to equality before the law"*, namely in the exercise of *"rights to work (and) to free choice of employment"*.
[74] Article 2.nd of the *International Covenant on Civil and Political Rights*, approved by the United Nations General Assembly on 16 December 1966, provides that *"each State Party to the present Covenant undertakes to respect and to ensure to all individuals within its territory and subject to its jurisdiction the rights recognized (...), without distinction of any kind, such as race, color, sex, language,*

the *International Covenant on Economic, Social and Cultural Rights*, also from 1966[75], the 1979 *United Nations Convention on the Elimination of all forms of Discrimination against Women*[76], as well as several International Labour Organizations' conventions[77], treaties and declarations of rights of certain regional organizations, namely the *Treaty on European Union*[78], the *Charter of Fundamental Rights of the European Union*[79] and the *African Charter on Human and Peoples' Rights*[80].

religion, political or other opinion, national or social origin, property, birth or other status". Moreover, article 26.th prohibits discrimination and establishes equal and effective protection against discrimination on any ground, *"such as race, color, sex, language, religion, political or other opinion, national or social origin, property, birth or other status"*.

[75] Article 2.nd, paragraph 2, of the *International Covenant on Economic, Social and Cultural Rights*, approved by the United Nations General Assembly on 16 December 1966, provides that *"The States Parties to the present Covenant undertake to guarantee that the rights enunciated in the present Covenant will be exercised without discrimination of any kind as to race, color, sex, language, religion, political or other opinion, national or social origin, property, birth or other status"*.

[76] Article 2.nd of the *The United Nations Convention on the Elimination of all forms of Discrimination against Women*, approved by the United Nations General Assembly on 17 December 1979, determines that *"State Parties condemn discrimination against women in all its forms"* and *"agree to pursue by all appropriate means and without delay a policy of eliminating discrimination against women"*.

[77] Regarding the specific field of access to employment, the ILO's Convention No. 111 on Discrimination in Respect of Employment and Occupation (1958), and the ILO's Convention No.156 on Equal Opportunities and Treatment for Male and Female Workers (1981), stands out. The subject of equality and non-discrimination forms part of the axis created by this Organization and is commonly called by the latter as *"Decent Work"*. Its main goal is to *"ensure that people can find work, which is essential to moving out of poverty; and that the work they find is "decent" – in terms of providing a living for the worker and for his or her family, to being carried out under reasonable conditions and above all to ensure that the worker's fundamental rights are respected"* – see, in this regard Lee Swepston, "ILO Standards and Globalization", *Bulletin of Comparative Labour Relations*, Wolters Kluwer Law & Business, Netherlands, No. 55, 2005, p.11 et seq.

[78] Article 2.nd of the *Treaty on European Union*, as last amended by Article 1-A. of the Lisbon Treaty, determines that *"The Union is founded on the values of respect for human dignity, freedom, democracy, equality, the rule of law and respect for human rights, including the rights of persons belonging to minorities. These values are common to the Member States in a society in which pluralism, non-discrimination, tolerance, justice, solidarity and equality between women and men prevail"*.

[79] Article 21.st of the *Charter of Fundamental Rights of the European Union*, adopted on 7 December 2000 by the European Parliament, the European Council and the European Commission, as amended on 12 December 2007, in Strasbourg, provides that *"Any discrimination based on any ground such as sex, race, color, ethnic or social origin, genetic features, language, religion or belief, political or any other opinion, membership of a national minority, property, birth, disability, age or sexual orientation shall be prohibited"*.

II. The same occurs in Portugal. Both our Fundamental Law and the Portuguese Labour Code contain several provisions on equality, namely regarding the access to employment and equality at the workplace.

6.2. The Portuguese Constitution

I. The Portuguese Constitution of 1976 received the idea of equality before the law as a material unitary principle, covering both the *prohibition of privileges and discriminations*, and the *obligation of differentiating*, as a compensation for social inequalities[81].

The principle of equality is provided for in article 13.th of the Portuguese Constitution, as a general principle according to which all citizens shall have the same social dignity and be equally treated before the law, providing additionally that no one shall be privileged, favored, suffer prejudice, be deprived of any right, or exempted from any duty because of his/her ancestry, sex, race, language, territory of origin, religion, political or ideological convictions, education, economic or social status as well as sexual orientation.

II. Besides containing a general prohibition on discrimination, the principle of equality set forth in the Portuguese Constitution, particularly in articles 9.th and 81.st, also undertakes a social function, which implies the obligation to eliminate or mitigate the social, economic and cultural inequality intended to pursue a legal and material equality, or rather a real equality[82]. Thus, article 9.th reaffirms that the State shall *"promote the well-*

[80] Article 2.nd of the *African Charter on Human and Peoples' Rights*, approved by the African Union Heads of State and Government's Conference on 26 July 1981, determines that *"Every individual shall be entitled to the enjoyment of the rights and freedoms recognized and guaranteed in the present Charter without distinction of any kind such as race, ethnic group, color, sex, language, religion, political or any other opinion, national and social origin, fortune, birth or any status"*. On the other hand, article 15.th recognizes the right to work under equitable and satisfactory conditions, and the right to receive equal pay for equal work.

[81] See Jorge Miranda/Rui Medeiros, *Constituição Portuguesa Anotada*, notes on article 13.rd.

[82] In this regard, see João Filipe Moreira Sabino, *"Os Direitos Fundamentais nas Relações de Trabalho"*, *Human Rights and Labor Law*, Flávia Piovesan/Luciana Paula Vaz de Carvalho (coord.), Editora Atlas, São Paulo, 2010, pp. 64 et seq.

being and quality of life of the people and the real equality of all Portuguese (...)" (article 9.th, subparagraph *d*)), whereas article 81.st determines that the State has a primary obligation *"to promote social justice, ensure equal opportunities and make the necessary corrections on the unequal distribution of wealth and income, in particular through tax policy"*[83]. Therefore, the Portuguese Constitution reaffirms the Welfare State in its system of values and, in this context, enshrines several social rights, as true *"positive discriminations"*[84].

III. Finally, this framework also explains the rules set forth in the Constitution, applied to certain types or categories of people more vulnerable, such as children, pregnant women, young people, disabled people and workers, the latter as a unitary and cross-sectional category. It was, therefore, based on this understanding and in line with said political and constitutional aim to achieve real equality[85] that the constitutional revision of 1982 contained an autonomous chapter (Chapter III of Title II – articles 53.rd to 57.th) specifically devoted to workers' rights, freedoms and guarantees – the commonly called *"Labor Constitution"*. Simultaneously, together with those perceptive rights, the Constitution ensured the "credit claims" set out in Chapter I of Title III, with regards to the economic, social and cultural rights (articles 58.th and 59.th)[86].

Therefore, the purpose of said legislation is to promote a real equality between citizens, by granting special rights of protection, namely those of workers, seen as a category of citizens who tend to be in a situation of inferiority which might compromise their freedom to bargain in equal terms.

[83] In this regard, see GUILHERME DRAY, *"Igualdade e não discriminação"*, Insert on Labor Law, *Revision of 2009*, Coimbra Editora, Coimbra, 2009, pp.123-138; *"O Sentido Jurídico do Princípio da Igualdade: Perspectiva Luso-Brasileira"*, Brazilian Journal on Constitutional Law, No. 2, Jul./Dez. 2003: pp.113-137; and *"O Princípio da Igualdade no Direito do Trabalho – sua aplicabilidade no domínio específico da formação de contratos individuais de trabalho"*, Almedina, Coimbra, 1999.

[84] See JORGE MIRANDA, *Manual de Direito Constitucional*, Part IV, *Fundamental Rights*, pp. 237 et seq., exemplifying some phenomena of *"positive discrimination"* provided for in the Constitution.

[85] In this regard, see JOÃO FILIPE MOREIRA SABINO, *"Os Direitos Fundamentais nas Relações de Trabalho"*, Human Rights and Labour Law, cit., pp. 64 et seq.

[86] On the distinction between *"rights, freedoms and guarantees"* and *"economic, social and cultural rights"*, see JORGE MIRANDA, *"O regime dos direitos, liberdades e garantias"*, *Studies on the Constitution*, III, pp. 41 et seq.

This is the reason why, as mentioned above, article 13.th, paragraph 1, allows for – or rather imposes – citizens' discrimination and differentiation by the legislator, in order to promote substantial and real equality amongst them.

Thus, the principle of equality enshrined in the Constitution has, as stated above, two approaches to it: a *negative approach*, consisting on the prohibition of privileges and distinctions as well as the prohibition of arbitrariness and discrimination; and a *positive approach*, resulting in the obligation to treat differently the different situations, as a way to compensate unequal opportunities[87], on behalf of social justice.

IV. In brief, the Portuguese Constitution of 1976 provides for both an *equality before the law*, as a liberal principle, and the *real equality of the Portuguese*, as a social principle. We may highlight two different perspectives regarding the principle of equality: a negative perspective, as a way to prevent privileges and discriminations, and to prohibit arbitrariness; and a positive perspective, based on the pursuit of the aforementioned real equality, by imposing positive discriminations, particularly regarding employment, in the name of the principle of social justice and emphasizing the role of the Welfare State.

6.3. The Labour Code

I. Besides the general provision of the principle of equality laid down in article 13.th of the Portuguese Constitution, the principle of equal access to employment and at work is also reaffirmed in the Portuguese Labour Code. The Labour Code treats equal access to employment and at work in a unified way, broadening the constitutional range of factors likely to justify a discriminatory practice – in light of said Code, factors such as *genetic heritage, reduced work capacity, chronic illness* and *trade-union membership* are also distinctive elements that shall be considered as non-valid causes

[87] See GUILHERME DRAY, "*O Princípio da Igualdade no Direito do Trabalho*", cit., p. 107, and "*O Sentido Jurídico do Princípio da Igualdade: Perspectiva Luso-Brasileira*", *Brazilian Magazine of Constitutional Law*, cit., p.117.

for discrimination, even though they are not included in article 13.th of the Constitution.

Following the U.S. legacy and tradition, that influenced all the European countries in this regard after the approval of the U.S. *Civil Rights Act of 1964*, cases of *disparate treatment* and *disparate impact* are addressed in the Portuguese Code under the concepts of *direct discrimination* and *indirect discrimination* (articles 23.rd and 25.th). These provisions: guarantee the right to equal access to employment and at work (article 24.th), establish the reversal of the burden of proof where a discriminatory practice is invoked (article 25.th), prohibit the existence of collective agreements or rules of procedure that are contrary to the principle of equality and non-discrimination (article 26.th), accept the adoption of positive or affirmative measures that benefit a traditionally disadvantaged group (article 27.th), provide for compensation on patrimonial and non-patrimonial damages in case of a discriminatory practice (article 28.th), prohibit harassment, namely sexual harassment (article 29.th), and contain a number of provisions relating to equality and non-discrimination on grounds of gender (articles 30.th to 32.nd)[88].

II. Under article 23.rd, paragraph 1, subparagraph *a*) of the Labour Code, a *direct discrimination* occurs whenever, due to a discrimination factor, a person is treated less favorably than someone else placed in a similar situation. However, this provision should be read together with article 24.th, paragraph 1 of the same Code, according to which the employee or job applicant has the right to have equal opportunities and treatment regarding access to employment, professional training and promotion, professional career, and working conditions, and cannot be privileged, benefited or harmed because of, *inter alia*, his/her ascending line, age, sex, sexual orientation, marital status, family status, economic status, education, origin or social status, genetic heritage, reduced working capacity, disability, chronic disease, nationality, ethnic or racial origin, place of origin, language, religion, political or ideological beliefs and trade-union membership.

Similarly, article 25.th, paragraph 1, states that the employer cannot discriminate a worker, whether *directly* or *indirectly*, namely on the basis of

[88] On the Portuguese Labor Code and the legal provisions related to equality and non discrimination, see the notes of Guilherme Dray, *Código do Trabalho Anotado*, cit., pp. 166 et seq.

the factors listed in article 24.th, whereas paragraph 5 of that same article, on the burden of proof, determines that the employee who claims to be discriminated shall only indicate the worker in relation to whom he/she is being discriminated against; by doing so, it will be up to the employer the burden of proving that the difference in treatment is not based on any element of discrimination.

Thus, a *direct discrimination* will occur whenever distinctive practices will result in a weaker or disadvantageous treatment by the employer with regards to differentiating certain groups on the basis of specific characteristic elements or by targeting specific categories of workers. Therefore, a distinctive practice based merely on the confirmation of a common feature amongst a group of individuals, such as racial origin, gender, sexual orientation, religion, affiliation or age[89], among other distinctive features listed in the Constitution or the Labour Code, will be considered as illegal.

III. What is at stake, therefore, is a reproaching judgment on certain "categorical" motivations for a differentiated treatment, contrary to the values and principles protected by the labour system. As sustained amongst Portuguese doctrine, namely by MONTEIRO FERNANDES, it is not the differentiation itself that is at stake but the reasonableness of the motivation and the unlikeliness of adopting distinctive practices based on certain characteristics common to particular groups of people[90].

IV. As a rule, factors such as race origin, sex, religion, political affiliation and beliefs and ideological convictions, or being membership to a particular religious' community are not, given the axiological values of the system, lawful reasons for distinctive practices. Therefore, any differential treatment

[89] Regarding age-based discrimination, see TERESA COELHO MOREIRA, *"A discriminação em razão da idade no contexto de uma população envelhecida na UE"*, Equality and Non Discrimination, *Studies on Labor Law*, Almedina, Coimbra, 2013, pp. 9-78. For this Author, the latest actions within the European Union regarding age-based discrimination are not directly related to a bigger concern with personal rights or even the dignity of older workers, but, and above all, with *"economic reasons and the difficulties of financing social security systems. Thus, if until recently the voluntary early retirement was encouraged, currently the opposite is true, as the crisis in social security has resulted in workers' penalization in case he/she retires earlier. Thus, the age of retirement is more and more postponed"* (pp. 12-13).

[90] See MONTEIRO FERNANDES, *"Observações sobre o princípio da igualdade de tratamento no Direito do Trabalho"*, I, *Studies in Homage to Dr. António de Arruda Ferrer Correia*, pp. 1014 et seq.

on the basis of one of these factors should be regarded as discriminatory and illegal[91].

Not only the defense of human dignity is proclaimed, but also the irrelevance of certain socially identifiable factors (such as racial origin or sex) as capable of justifying different treatments. As stated by MONTOYA MELGAR, discrimination based on *"typical reasons, historically entrenched and contrary to human dignity"* shall be unacceptable[92].

V. Similarly to the doctrine of *disparate impact* provided for in Title VII of the U.S. 1964 *Civil Rights Act*, the Portuguese Labour Code establishes, in article 23.rd, paragraph 1, subparagraph *b*), the concept of *indirect discrimination* – in light of this article, an *indirect discrimination* occurs whenever a provision, criterion or apparently neutral practice is likely to cause a discrimination, placing the person in a disadvantaged situation when compared to others, unless that provision, criterion or practice is objectively justified by a legitimate purpose and the means to achieve it is both appropriate and necessary.

In other words, even if there is no direct intention to discriminate, there might still occur a situation of *indirect discrimination* if the employer's actions, although apparently neutral, concretely (and indirectly) injure someone belonging to a certain group of people.

The concept of indirect discrimination appears in the Portuguese Labour Code following the transposition of EU Directives n.er. 2000/43/EC of 29 June 2000, implementing the principle of equal treatment between persons irrespective of their racial or ethnic origin[93], and n.er. 2000/78/EC of 27 November 2000, establishing a general framework on equal treatment in employment and occupation[94].

[91] See LUÍS MENEZES LEITÃO, *Direito do Trabalho*, cit., pp. 204-205.

[92] See MONTOYA MELGAR, *Derecho del Trabajo*, 30 th ed. Tecnos, Madrid, 2009, p. 313.

[93] Under article 2.nd, paragraph 2, subparagraph *b)* of the Council Directive No. 2000/43/EC, *"indirect discrimination shall be taken to occur where an apparently neutral provision, criterion or practice would put persons of a racial or ethnic origin at a particular disadvantage compared to other persons, unless that provision, criterion or practice is objectively justified by a legitimate aim and the means of achieving that aim are appropriate and necessary"*.

[94] Article 2.nd, paragraph 2, subparagraph *b)* of the Council Directive No. 2000/78/EC, determines that *"indirect discrimination shall be taken to occur where an apparently neutral provision, criterion or practice would put persons having a particular religion or belief, a particular disability, a*

The implementation of the concept of *indirect discrimination* has been carried out by doctrine and case law, particularly by the Court of Justice of the European Union, although with several years of delay when compared with the case law of the U.S. Supreme Court. Portuguese doctrine, namely Maria do Rosário Ramalho, reaffirms that the setting of a uniform academic hiring requirement by the employer, which, although apparently neutral, has proportionally different effects on workers of a particular ethnic group, generally less educated, is considered as an *"indirect discrimination"*, whenever such academic requirement is not objectively justified for the activity to be carried out. The author also notes that this concept can be associated with the definition of *systemic discrimination*, which occurs in cases involving a certain sector of activity or professional category, where the percentage of workers belonging to a particular *group* or *sex* is much higher than that of other workers. In this case, the imbalance is a result of a discriminating factor in the hiring process, by employing criteria objectively unjustified in view of the performed activity[95].

VI. Regarding case law, the matter has been addressed mainly in the European Union by the Court of Justice of the European Union (CJEU).

In the case *Lourdes Cachaldora Fernández vs. Instituto Nacional de la Seguridad Social (INSS), Tesorería General de la Seguridad Social (TGSS)*, before the CJEU, the Advocate-General Yves-Bot considered that a Spanish law which reduces a pension for permanent invalidity given to some part-time workers, introduces an indirect sex-based discrimination – although apparently neutral, this provision would affect mainly women. In fact, amongst part-time workers in Spain, female workers are much more numerous than male workers (80% in 2010 and 73% in 2013)[96].

*particular age, or a particular sexual orientation at a particular disadvantage compared with other persons unless: (i) that provision, criterion or practice is objectively justified by a legitimate aim and the means of achieving that aim are appropriate and necessary, or (ii) as regards persons with a particular disability, the employer or any person or organization to whom this Directive applies, is obliged, under national legislation, to take appropriate measures in line with the principles contained in article 5.*th *in order to eliminate disadvantages entailed by such provision, criterion or practice".*

[95] See Maria do Rosário Ramalho, *Tratado de Direito do Trabalho, Part II – Personal employment situations*, 4th edition, Almedina, Coimbra, 2012, p. 154.

[96] See case no. C-527/13 *Lourdes Cachaldora Fernández vs. Instituto Nacional de la Seguridad Social (INSS), Tesorería General de la Seguridad Social (TGSS)*, available at http://curia.europa.eu/

In the case *Maurice Leone, Blandine Leone vs. Garde des Sceaux, Ministre de la Justice*, and *Caisse nationale de retraite des agents des collectivités locales*, also before the CJEU, the Court held that, in relation to additional seniority, French legislation introduced an indirect discrimination. In practical terms, French law benefited public employees of both sexes provided they had interrupted their career for a minimum period of two consecutive months devoted to a child, what led to a much higher percentage of women benefiting from said law. In fact, given the mandatory basis and the minimum of two months of a maternity leave in France, female public employees were in a position in which they could benefit from that subsidy. Differently, the other cases of leave that would lead to the payment of a bonus, of which male public employees would benefit from, were merely optional and in some cases consisted in the absence of both the payment and the acquisition of pension rights. Therefore, the French legislation created a disadvantage affecting a large number of male workers and introducing an indirect sex-based discrimination[97].

In another case, the same Court held that, in connection with the disappearance of public employees' job posts due to a national economic downturn, workers who had benefited from a longer period of parental leave were penalized after being chosen as preferred targets for said firing, would represent an indirect discrimination, as it would negatively and significantly affect women, who traditionally benefit from larger periods of maternity leave[98].

jcms/upload/docs/application/pdf/2014-10/cp140135pt.pdf, access on July 2015.

[97] Check case C-173/13, *Maurice Leone* and *Blandine Leone/Garde des Sceaux, Ministre de la Justice*, and *Caisse nationale de retraite des agents des collectivités locales*, available at http://curia.europa.eu/jcms/upload/docs/application/pdf/2014-07/cp140102pt.pdf, access on July 2015. It should be noted, however, that in the final judgment the CJEU, despite the opinion of the Advocate-General, the court decided that the measure was justified under article 141.st, paragraph 4, EC, which should be interpreted as meaning that said provision does not cover national measures such as those at issue in the main proceedings, which merely allow the workers concerned to take early retirement with immediate payment of pension and to grant them a service credit upon their retirement, without providing a remedy for the problems which they may encounter in the course of their professional career – available athttp://www.cite.gov.pt/asstscite/downloads/Proc_C173_13.pdf, access on July 2015.

[98] See case C-7/12, Judgment of the Court of Justice (Fourth Chamber) of 20 June 2013 (request for a preliminary ruling Augstākās tiesas Senāts – Letonia) – Nadežda Riežniece vs.

In essence, such as in the *disparate impact* theory, there will be an indirect discrimination whenever an apparently neutral practice puts a person in a disadvantaged situation compared to others, due to a discrimination factor, unless such conduct is objectively justified by a legitimate purpose and the means to achieve it are both appropriate and necessary[99].

VII. Portuguese doctrine also accepts, just like the U.S. *Bona Fide Occupational Qualification*, that in the private domain the protection of both private autonomy and the freedom of negotiation requires that its restriction should only occur in extreme situations, when higher values so demand. In other words, restricting private autonomy should only be accepted when the system's axiological values are at risk, i.e., in cases involving the protection of the employee or the job applicant's dignity, as the most vulnerable contracting parties exposed to abusive, arbitrary or discriminatory practices committed by the employer.

As such, situations justified according to their own reasoning should not fall within the concept of *direct* or *indirect discrimination*[100].

Both article 25.th, paragraphs 2 and 3, and article 27.th of the Portuguese Labour Code address this topic.

Article 25.th, paragraph 2, states that although based on a discriminative factor, a behavior shall not be seen as a discrimination if it represents a *"justifiable and determining requirement"* for the professional capacity, due to

Latvijas Republikas Zemkopības Ministrija, Lauku atbalsta dienests, available at http://www.cite.gov.pt/asstscite/downloads/Proc_C7_12.pdf, access in July 2015.

[99] See also, on *indirect discrimination*, case *Elodie Giersch and others vs. État du Grand-Duché de Luxembourg*, in which the CJEU decided that Luxembourg law which makes the grant of financial aid for higher education studies conditional upon residence by the student in that Member State gives rise to a difference in treatment, amounting to indirect discrimination, between persons who reside in the Member State concerned and those who, not being residents of that Member State, are the children of cross-border workers carrying out an activity in that Member State – seecase C-20/12, available at:
http://www.gep.msess.gov.pt/acordaos_tribunaljustica/acordao_c-20-12.pdf..

[100] In fact, as affirmed by Simon Deakins and Gillian Morris, *"Discrimination in hiring is prohibited by statute only in relation to a number of specific criteria. In particular, decisions may not be based on sex, race or disability of the applicant. (...). Outside these areas of statutory intervention, the common law principle of freedom applies: an employer is free to refuse to hire a person for any reason, no matter how capricious, or for no reason at all"*- see Simon Deakins/Gillian Morris, *Labor Law*, 3rd edition, Butterworths, Londres, 2001, pp. 140-141.

the nature or context of the activity performed, given that *"the purpose is legitimate and the requirement proportionate"*. Paragraph 3 of that same article prescribes that age-based differences in treatment are allowed, as long as they are necessary and appropriate for achieving a legitimate purpose, namely regarding employment policy, labour market or vocational training[101].

In light of these principles, Portuguese doctrine[102] has been accepting the lawfulness of differentiating practices, (i) whenever the distinction is based on the nature of the future employment relationship and the type of functions required; and (ii) if that relationship demands a special ideological blend between the employer and the workers. In such cases, or whenever a distinction that offends a worker or job applicant's dignity is not at jeopardy, the employer's freedom of contract prevails.

VIII. In the first case, it is currently accepted that distinguishing workers based on the nature of the employment relationship to be developed or the type of labour activity, regardless of any social stereotype, should not be seen as discriminatory[103, 104].

In addition to the jobs legally prohibited or limited to specific categories of workers (namely women or children), due to the special hardship of the working conditions, the physical effort involved, the inherent danger or the risks involved for genetic function[105], including work performed

[101] In this regard, see our explanation on article 25.th of the Labor Code, *Código do Trabalho Anotado,* cit., pp. 177 et seq..

[102] See GUILHERME DRAY, *O Princípio da Igualdade no Direito do Trabalho,* cit., pp. 270-285.

[103] See LUÍS MENEZES LEITÃO, *Direito do Trabalho,* cit., pp. 154-155.

[104] See MONTOYA MELGAR, *Derecho del Trabajo,* 30th edition, cit., p. 312.

[105] The provisions relating to pregnancy protection cannot, however, serve as a basis of, or have as a result, a less favorable treatment with regards to access by pregnant women to employment. The CJEU has held this opinion, affirming that *"Article 2.nd subparagraphs 1 and 3 of Council Directive 76/207/EEC of 9 February 1976 on the implementation of the principle of equal treatment for men and women (...) preclude a refusal to appoint a pregnant woman to a post for an indefinite period on the grounds that a statutory prohibition on employment attaching to the condition of pregnancy prevents her from being employed in that post from the outset and for the duration of the pregnancy"* (see Judgment of the CJEU of 3 February 2000, case No. C-207/98, *Silke-Karin Mahlburg*). In the main, the CJEU considered that the provisions of the German Law on the Protection of Working Mothers (*Mutterschutzgesetz*), of 24 January 1952, stating that *"Pregnant women must not be assigned to heavy physical work or to work exposing them to the harmful effects of substances or rays, dust, gases or steam, heat, cold or humidity, vibrations or noise that pose a risk to*

in storerooms, boilers, mines, coal, iron and steel mining, police forces specialized in fighting against terrorism, and other jobs that require the use and regular and frequent handling of toxic substances, the limitation of certain activities to the applicants' physical characteristics, given the nature of the task to perform, is perfectly acceptable[106].

Thus, regarding sex-based discrimination, under article 25.th, paragraph 2, of the Labour Code, hiring women rather than men to perform a fashion show intended to promote women's clothing shall not be considered as a discrimination. Likewise, hiring a man over a woman to participate in a male federation tournament shall also not be seen as discriminatory. In another example, Portuguese doctrine, namely PEDRO ROMANO MARTINEZ, accepts the differentiation in jobs that require the existence of different health infrastructures, for employees of different sex: in light of this situation, it will be lawful for a ship-owner in a long-term fishing vessel to hire a male employee over a female employee when his entire crew consists of men, or vice-versa. In such case, hiring a different sex employee would involve an investment in new infrastructures that the employer may not be able to afford. Thus, in this case there is no arbitrary or unreasonable discrimination, nor discrimination intended to harm the exercise of rights by a certain category of employees.

In the abovementioned cases, it is clear that the nature of the tasks performed allows employers to distinguish and differentiate on the basis of gender. The same should be said regarding other differentiating elements, such as language or ethnicity of the employees, when such qualities are equally important for the task to be performed.

Thus, for an interpretation job, it will be lawful to exclude an employee who does not speak perfectly the required language; to represent a historical white person, it will be lawful to exclude a black person, and vice-versa; and

health" (§ 4 da *Mutterschutzgesetz*), do not justify a refusal to appoint a pregnant woman to a post for an indefinite period on the grounds that a statutory prohibition on employment attached to the pregnancy condition prevents her from being employed on that post from the outset and for the duration of the pregnancy. Similarly, the CJEU had already decided, in other preliminary ruling, that a refusal to employ a woman due to her pregnancy cannot be justified by the financial loss which an employer who appointed a pregnant woman would suffer for the duration of her maternity leave (see Judgment issued by the CJEU in 8 November 1990, Case C 177/88, *Dekker*).

[106] See GUILHERME DRAY, *O Princípio da Igualdade no Direito do Trabalho*, cit., pp. 279-282.

for a professional driver, it will be lawful to exclude a disabled person if he/she is not capable to drive that specific vehicle.

All these cases are essentially concerned with the employee's adaptability to the task to be performed. The cause for excluding an applicant is not discriminatory nor exists a discriminatory intent. In any case, the purpose should be lawful and the requirement should be proportional. In other words, the underlying purpose of the distinction should relate to the need to adjust the employee or job applicant to the job and the nature of the professional activity, and it should also meet the principles of proportionality and adequacy.

IX. Likewise, the distinctions made on the basis of political or religious convictions, in the case of jobs requiring a particular ideological closeness between employers and their workforce, particularly in terms of political parties, trade unions, religious congregations or newspaper offices sharing a certain well-defined party line[107], should not be considered discriminatory – in these cases, the work does not have neutral character, being subject to religious or political purposes[108]. In these situations, linking the employee to the aims of the organization to which he/she belongs becomes much more evident.

Thus, it will be perfectly legitimate, for example, for a political party to refuse to hire an employee who does not share the same ideology, *maxime* when it is affiliated with another political party[109]. And it will also be legitimate for a religious congregation to only hire priests who share the

[107] These are the cases of labor relationships developed within the so-called "ideological companies" ("*tendenzbetriebe*", under German doctrine, "*Le organizzazioni di tendenza*", under Italian doctrine, and "*enterprises ideologiques*", under French doctrine). The specificities of such relationships, particularly on the termination of employment contracts, justify an autonomous study, which falls outside the limited scope of the present work. On this subject see, for all, F. SANTONI, *Le organizzazioni di tendenza e il rapporti di lavoro,* Giuffrè, Milano, 1993.

[108] These are the so-called *"tendency companies"*, which derive from the Germanic concept of *Tendenzbetriebe* – in this regard, see LÖWISCH, CASPERS and KLUMPP, *Arbeitsrecht,* 9th edition, Vahlen, München, p. 419.

[109] Moreover, it should be recalled that article 38.th of the Law on Political Parties – Organic Law 2/2003, of 22 August, amended and re-published by Organic Law 2/2008, of 14 May, accepts as a *"justified dismissal the fact that an employee is disaffiliated or makes propaganda against the party that employs him or in favor of a competitor's application"*.

same religion. Finally, it will also be legitimate for a political party's official newspaper to exclude those who are affiliated to other political parties that follow different or distant ideologies than the one embraced by the employer[110].

In the same line of thought, a wider restriction on the freedom of expression is accepted in these type of companies – by way of example, the doorman of a political party cannot bear a badge referring to another political party or the cleaning employee of a mosque cannot work showing a crucifix[111].

In the case of companies whose activity is inseparable from a certain ideological presumption (religious institutions, political parties, trade unions, among others) as well as of employees whose work is linked to "*the development of ideological values sustained by that company, it makes sense that they should share the same values and principles*", to the exact extent that their performance requires such ideological communion[112].

X. The Portuguese Labour Code was inspired by articles 9.th, 13.th and 81.st of the Portuguese Constitution and has its origin both in article 157.th, paragraph 4, of the *Treaty on the Functioning of the European Union,* and in EU Directive 76/207/EEC of 9 February, as amended by Directive 2002/73/EC of 23 September. As with the case of U.S. *affirmative actions,* the Portuguese Labour Code also accepts the so-called *positive measures.* Thus, article 27.th [113] of the Labour Code states that a temporary legal measure benefiting a group that is considered as having been disadvantaged due to a discrimination factor shall not be taken as discriminatory, as it aims to guarantee the exercise on an equal basis of the rights provided by law, or to correct situations of inequality persisting in social life[114].

The connection with the principle of *material equality* or *equal opportunities* is clear: more than putting forth formal equality, based on the classic

[110] In this regard, see *O Princípio da Igualdade no Direito do Trabalho,* cit., pp. 282-284.

[111] Example given by Luís Menezes Leitão, in *Direito do Trabalho,* 3rd edition, cit., p. 190.

[112] See Montoya Melgar, *Derecho del Trabajo,* 30th edition, cit., p. 316.

[113] See the notes of Guilherme Dray on article 27.th of the Portuguese Labor Code, at *Código do Trabalho Anotado,* cit., pp. 184 et seq.

[114] See Guilherme Dray, *Equality, Welfare State and Democracy,* Almedina/The Luso-American Development Foundation Coimbra, 2018, pp. 29 et seq.

declaration that all citizens are equal before the law, it reaffirms (and even encourages) the need to adopt temporary measures that impose a different treatment as a way to offset the inequalities in opportunities and treatment persisting in social life. Therefore, the Portuguese Code accepts the currently called *positive measures,* which embody the idea of *positive discrimination* and are understood in the context of an ideal of social justice, which sees equality not as the starting point but rather as the point of arrival. This allows for the implementation of measures which temporarily benefit groups of people traditionally ostracized, particularly based on gender, disability, and national or ethnic origin. Moreover, the Code also establishes some specific provisions that reinforce this idea, respectively in article 30.th et seq. (*gender equality*), article 84.th, paragraph 3 (*worker with reduced working capacity*) and article 86.th (*worker with disability or chronic illness*).

Based on this rule, several measures to increase the employability in a particular sector may be accepted, in particular a reduction in the payment of social security by the employer or the adoption of quotas for the admission of under-represented categories of workers, such as women or disabled individuals[115].

[115] In this regard, the case law of the Court of Justice of the European Union should be mentioned, including both the famous *Kalanke* decision (Judgment of the CJ of 17/10/1995 – Case C-450/93), ruling against the adoption of *a system of strict quotas,* and the *Marschall* decision (Judgment of the CJ of 11/11/1997 – Case C-409/95), who again said that, under certain conditions, such positive measures can be accepted, through the adoption of *a system of quotas dependent on candidates' abilities.* In case *Kalanke,* the Court of Justice of the European Union considered any system of strict quotas as unlawful, concluding that "*Article 2.nd* subparagraphs *1 and 4 of the Council Directive No. 76/207/CEE, of 9 February 1976, precludes national rules which, where candidates of different sexes shortlisted for promotion are equally qualified, automatically give priority to women in sectors where they are under-represented, under-representation being deemed to exist when women do not make up at least half of the staff in the individual pay brackets in the relevant personnel group or in the function levels provided for in the organization chart*". The absolute and unconditional priority for appointment or promotion of certain categories of people is unacceptable. However, a system of quotas dependent on candidates' abilities is both lawful and justified, as it promotes equal opportunities between men and women. These systems attribute benefits to certain people within disadvantaged groups in order to put them on an equal footing as other workers or job applicants, without assigning them a preferential right automatically triggered. Flexible systems are peacefully accepted by the EU Community case law (v.g. CJEU decisions of 11 October 1997 – case C-409/95, *Marshall* – and of 28 March 2000 – case C-158/97, *George Badeck*).

XI. The concepts of *disparate treatment*, *disparate impact*, *bona fide occupational qualification* and *affirmative action*, all expressed in the Portuguese Labour Code at the above referred article 23.rd and following, arose in the United States system long before the approval of our Labour Code, especially through the intervention of the U.S. Supreme Court, based on the Civil Rights Act of 1964[116].

Bearing its importance in mind, we will further analyze this topic below.

6.4. The Influence of the United States on the principle of equality

I. In this regard, it is important to highlight the often forgotten role played by the United States of America in the universal reaffirmation of the principle of equality[117]. The struggle for equal rights is part of the United States' history and, given its pioneering spirit it is also a landmark in the legal reaffirmation of the principle of equality. From the 1776 *Declaration of Independence*[118] to the 1964 *Civil Rights Act*, the path taken was always progressive and evolutionary, so much so that it can be said that equality and non-discrimination, on one hand, and social mobility, on the other hand, are part of the *American Way of Life* and the *American Dream*[119].

It is true that the 1787 U.S. Constitution[120], the first and most stable written constitution in the modern sense, did not include a Bill of Rights,

[116] See GUILHERME DRAY, *The Influence of the United States of America on Reaffirming the Principle of Equality in Employment in Portuguese Speaking Language Countries*, Almedina/The Luso-American Development Foundation, 2017, pp. 45 et seq.

[117] See GUILHERME DRAY, *The Influence of the United States of America on Reaffirming the Principle of Equality in Employment in Portuguese Speaking Language Countries*, cit.

[118] On the Declaration of Independence, see DAVID ARMITAGE, *"The Declaration of Independence: a Global History"*, Harvard University Press, 2007.

[119] See ALVIN L. GOLDMAN and ROBERTO L. CORRADA, *Labor Law in the USA, Third Revised Edition*, Wolters Kluwer, Law and Business, The Netherlands, 2011, p. 184.

[120] On the 1787 U.S. Constitution, see LAURENCE H. TRIBE, *The Invisible Constitution*, Oxford University Press, Oxford, 2008, and *American Constitutional Law, Volume I*, Foundations, 3rd edition, University Textbook Series, 2000; BRUCE ACKERMANN, *We The People – transformations*, II, Harvard University Press, 2000; LAURENCE H. TRIBE/MICHAEL C. DORF, *On Reading the Constitution*, by The President and Fellows of Harvard College, United States of America, 1991; HERMAN C. PRITCHETT, *The American Constitution*, McGraw-Hill Series in Political Science, Edited by Joseph P. Harris, New York, 1959; BERTHA MOSER HAINES/

nor a list of fundamental rights in its text. This circumstance was essentially due to slavery and the reluctance of Southern States to admit restrictions on slave trade, as well as the fact that the declarations of rights set forth in state Constitutions were then considered enough[121]. However, the revolutionary movement and the subsequent 1776 Declaration of Independence encouraged the emergence of several Constitutions in most federal states between 1776 and 1780. Some of them had separate Declarations of Rights, while others included the citizens' fundamental rights in their texts. From then on, the reaffirmation of equality between men was acknowledged as irreversible.

The principle of equality is reaffirmed in the 1776 *Declaration of Independence*, where it is stated that "*all men are created equal, that they are endowed by their Creator with certain unalienable rights that among these are life, liberty and the pursuit of happiness*". Furthermore, the 1776 *Bill of Rights*,

CHARLES GROVE HAINES, *The Constitution of the United States, F.S. Crofts & Co.*, New York, 1933; GEORGE BACROFT, *History of the Formation of the Constitution of the United States of America*, Vol. 2, 1889. Concerning Portuguese speaking authors, see JORGE BACELAR GOUVEIA, *Manual de Direito Constitutional*, Volume I, 5th edition, Almedina, Coimbra, 2013, p. 259 et seq.; ANSELMO PRIETO ALVAREZ/WLADIMIR NOVAES FILHO, *Constituição dos EUA, Annotated*, 2nd edition, LtR, São Paulo, 2008; THOMAS M. COOLEY, *Princípios Gerais de Direito Constitucional nos Estados Unidos da América*, Ed. Russel, Campinas, 2002; ANA MARIA GUERRA MARTINS, *As origens da Constituição Norte-Americana, uma lição para a Europa*, Lex, Lisboa, 1994; NUNO ROGEIRO, *Constituição dos EUA – Anotada e seguida de estudo sobre o sistema constitucional dos EUA*, Gradiva, Lisboa, 1993.

[121] In any case, it should be noted that the inclusion of fundamental rights in the U.S. Constitution occurred with the approval of the first ten constitutional amendments, on 25 September 1789, and their further ratification on 15 December 1791, which led to the 1791 U.S. Bill of Rights. *Amendment I* introduced the freedom of religion and belief, the freedom of speech and of the press, the freedom of peaceful assembly and the freedom of petitioning for a governmental redress of grievances; *Amendment II*, the right to keep and bear arms; *Amendment III*, the prohibition of quartering of soldiers in private homes without the owner's consent, during peacetime; *Amendment IV*, the prohibition of unreasonable searches and seizures; *Amendment V*, the right to a due process and to private property; *Amendment VI*, the procedural guarantees of defense in criminal proceedings; *Amendment VII*, the right of trial by a jury; *Amendment VIII*, the prohibition of imposing excessive bail or fines, and the prohibition of inflicting cruel punishments; *Amendment IX*, protects other fundamental rights, even if not listed in the Constitution; and *Amendment X*, reinforces the principle of federalism by stating that the Federal Government possesses only those powers delegated to it by the States or the people through the Constitution.

approved separately from the Constitution on 12th June by the State of Virginia, as well as the 1780 Massachusetts Constitution, are also emblematic. Virginia's *Bill of Rights*, or *The Virginia Declaration of Rights*, written by GEORGE MASON, was the first legislative act of its kind and became a national model – on the principle of equality, it stated that *"all men are by nature equally free and independent and have certain inherent rights"*[122]; on the other hand, the *Constitution of the Commonwealth of Massachusetts* adopted a clearer and more universal formula, establishing that *"All men are born free and equal, and have certain natural, essential, and unalienable rights"*[123]. In fact, this was the formula accepted in the 1789 French *Déclaration des Droits de L'Homme et du Citoyen* – *"les hommes naissent et demeurent libres et égaux en droits"*. From then on, the principle of equality was included in the constitutions of most modern States, illustrating the importance of the United States of America in reaffirming equality on a global scale.

Since then, the principle of equality no longer ceased to be reaffirmed. As stated by STEFAN GOSEPATH, *"At least since the French Revolution, equality has served as one of the leading ideals of the political body"*, in such a way that *"The principle of equal dignity and respect is now accepted as a minimum standard throughout mainstream Western culture"*[124].

As pointed out by AMARTYA SEM, the concept of equality arises from the idea of Justice – one of John Rawl's principles on justice is precisely based on the idea that opportunities should be available to all, *"without someone being excluded or hampered, for example, on the basis of race or religious, ethnic and caste*

[122] The full text provided as follows: *"Section 1. That all men are by nature equally free and independent and have certain inherent rights, of which, when they enter into a state of society, they cannot, by any compact, deprive or divest their posterity; namely, the enjoyment of life and liberty, with the means of acquiring and possessing property, and pursuing and obtaining happiness and safety"*, available at http://www.archives.gov/exhibits/charters/virginia_declaration_of_rights.html, access in August 2015.

[123] The full text provided as follows: *"Article I. All men are born free and equal, and have certain natural, essential, and unalienable rights; among which may be reckoned the right of enjoying and defending their lives and liberties; that of acquiring, possessing, and protecting property; in fine, that of seeking and obtaining their safety and happiness"*. Available at https://malegislature.gov/Laws/Constitution, access in August 2015.

[124] See STEFAN GOSEPATH, "Equality", *The Stanford Encyclopedia of Philosophy* (Spring 2011 Edition), Edward N. Zalta (ed.), available at:http://plato.stanford.edu/archives/spr2011/entries/equality/ (access in 20 September 2013), p. 1 and 8.

origin"[125]. And as RICHARD ARNESON recalls, in this Rawlsian perspective, equality is seen in substantive terms (*substantive equality of opportunity*), as the power granted to all citizens to access the same opportunities, based on their merits and abilities[126].

It is in this context that the 1964 Civil Rights Act should be understood in the United States of America.

II. The importance of the U.S. 1964 Civil Rights Act is well known: it consisted of a milestone in the legal framework on civil rights for the United States of America – *"the constitutional canon of the civil rights revolution"*[127] – signed by President Lyndon B. Johnson on 2 July 1964[128, 129].

The 1964 Civil Rights Act was a determinant milestone – the so-called *"historic enactment of the Civil Rights Act of 1964"*[130] – which then represented a very significant civilizational progress on equality and non-discrimination, contributing greatly to fight discrimination on the basis of race, color, religion, sex and nationality, in various areas and domains of social life[131].

Covering a very broad range of matters, in particular the fight against racial segregation in the right to vote, access to education and *"public*

[125] See AMARTYA SEN, *A ideia de justiça*, Coimbra, Almedina, 2012, p. 106.

[126] See RICHARD ARNESON, "Equality of Opportunity", *The Stanford Encyclopedia of Philosophy* (Fall 2008 Edition), Edward N. Zalta (ed.), available at http://plato.stanford.edu/archives/fall2008/entries/equal-opportunity/, access in 27 September 2013), p. 8.

[127] BRUCE ACKERMAN, *We The People, 3, The Civil Rights Revolution*, cit., p. 56.

[128] On the historical background and the events surrounding the adoption of this legislative framework, in particular the speech of President L. Johnson in the Congress (whose most remarkable statement was as follows – *"The Members of the Congress, and the many private citizens, who worked to shape and pass this bill will share a place of honor in our history, for this one act alone (...). So, we will move step by step – often painfully but, I think, with clear vision – along the path toward American freedom"*), see BRUCE ACKERMAN, *We The People, 3, The Civil Rights Revolution*, cit., pp. 98 et seq.; HUGH DAVIS GRAHAM, *The Civil Rights era: Origins and Development of National Policy 1960-1972*, Oxford University Press, 1990, in particular pp. 89 et seq. President Kennedy mentioned the *Civil Rights Act* as a *"second Emancipation Proclamation"*.

[129] The original text of the 1964 *Civil Rights Act*, including *Title VII* above mentioned, is available at http://www.gpo.gov/fdsys/pkg/STATUTE-78/pdf/STATUTE-78-Pg241.pdf, access in August 2015.

[130] See ALAN FREEMAN, "Antidiscrimination Law: The View from 1989", *Race and Equality Law*, cit., p. 272.

[131] See GUILHERME DRAY, *The Influence of the United States of America on Reaffirming the Principle of Equality in Employment in Portuguese Speaking Language Countries*, cit., pp. 34 et seq.

accommodations", the 1964 Civil Rights Act also dedicated its Title VII to the subject of equality and non-discrimination on access to employment and at work – equal employment opportunities – being a pioneer in this subject.

As GEORGE A. RUTHERGLEN AND JOHN J. DONOHUE III underline, the commonly called Title VII was decisive in the fight for equality, not only regarding access to employment but in general, widening *Brown* case doctrine in several dimensions: "*from discriminating by government to discrimination by private employers; from discriminating on the basis of race and national origin to discrimination on the basis of sex; and from intentional discrimination to neutral practices with discriminatory effects*"[132]. On the first case, the extension required Title VII to go beyond the state action doctrine, which limited discrimination to Government actions, and in the field of public employment; on the second case, the Congress started acting by prohibiting sex-based discrimination, given that until then no constitutional provision did so; on the third case, *disparate treatment* was extended to *disparate impact*, and although the effects were hardly visible when Title VII was approved, they were clear when the Supreme Court started interpreting this legal provision. Case *Griggs v. Duke Power* (1971) should be mentioned in this regard. The Supreme Court held in this decision that "*Title VII prohibits examinations and other employment qualifications based on race and that may have a 'disparate impact', even if such practices had no discriminatory intent*"[133].

In fact, it was based on the Supreme Court interpretation of Title VII, and the decisions of that Court, that the Congress followed this Court's case law and started legislating on the subject of equality and non-discrimination, inverting the U.S. model of checks and balances. As these authors recall, "*Even when the Congress contributes to the meaning and implementation of the Constitution, the Supreme Court always has the last word in deciding issues of constitutionality. In employment discrimination law, with its basis in statutes like Title VII, these institutional roles are reversed. Much of the interest of the subject lies in precisely how Congress has responded to judicial decisions seeking to implement the statutory prohibitions that it has enacted*"[134].

[132] See GEORGE A. RUTHERGLEN/JOHN J. DONOHUE III, *Employment Discrimination*, cit., p. 2.
[133] See GEORGE A. RUTHERGLEN/JOHN J. DONOHUE III, *Employment Discrimination*, cit., p. 2.
[134] See GEORGE A. RUTHERGLEN/JOHN J. DONOHUE III, *Employment Discrimination*, cit., p. 5.

III. Title VII of the Civil Rights Act, included in *Sections §§ 2000e. of Subchapter VI, Chapter 21, Title 42* of the U.S. Code, prohibits any discriminatory practices regarding access to employment and at work, on the basis of race, color, sex, religion and nationality, covering several practices and entities: it is applicable to employers, employment agencies, labour organizations, businesses or enterprises with personnel qualified on the basis of religion, sex, or national origin; and to educational institutions with personnel of a particular religion. Furthermore, it contains provisions on training programs or on the burden of proof.

The prohibition of discriminatory practices is mainly focused on employer practices and is based on the following rule, provided for in *Title 42, Chapter 21, Subchapter VI, § 2000e–2 (Unlawful employment practices)*, of the U.S. Code:

> *"(a) Employer practices:*
> *It shall be an unlawful employment practice for an employer:*
> *(1) to fail or refuse to hire or to discharge any individual, or otherwise to discriminate against any individual with respect to his compensation, terms, conditions, or privileges of employment, because of such individual's race, color, religion, sex, or national origin; or*
> *(2) to limit, segregate, or classify his employees or applicants for employment in any way which would deprive or tend to deprive any individual of employment opportunities or otherwise adversely affect his status as an employee, because of such individual's race, color, religion, sex, or national origin"*[135].

IV. From then on, U.S. legislation against discrimination started becoming global and being applied to all States in a general and comprehensive way. Together with these changes , some Federal States currently have their own legislation against discrimination[136], either to protect groups of people who

[135] Available at https://www.law.cornell.edu/uscode/text/42/2000e%E2%80%932, access on August 2015.

[136] It should be recalled that Federal States generally also have specific local laws on equality and non-discrimination, the main references of which can be found in the *American Bar Association's Yearbook – Section of Labor and Employment Law,* called "*Employment at Will. A State-by-State Survey. 2014 Cumulative Supplement"*, Bloomberg BNA, Arlington, VA, 2014. To name some examples: in the State of Arizona there is the "*Arizona Civil Rights Act (ACRA)"*, although some cities on this State also prohibit discrimination on the basis of sexual orientation or gender identity or expression; in the State of California, the "*California Assembly Bill 1964 amended the Fair Employment and Housing Act (FEHA)"*; in the *District of Columbia*, the "*D.C.*

are not protected by federal law, as is the case of state or local legislation which prohibits discrimination *"based on sexual orientation"*, or to cover the actions of small employers who do not hire more than 15 employees, and are therefore excluded from the scope of federal legislation[137].

When so, *i.e.*, when both federal and state legislation against discrimination coexist, the employer must comply with both rules, as far as state law is consistent and in line with federal law.

V. As stated above, the concept of equal employment opportunities was always seen as an essential ingredient of the *"American Dream"*[138].

PATRICK CIHON and JAMES CASTAGNERA underline that *"Discrimination in employment, whether intentional or unintentional, has been a major concern of many people who believe that our society has not lived up to its ideals of equality of opportunity for all people"*. For that reason, these authors note, the essence of Equal Employment Opportunity Law lies in the following: ideally, employers should hire the best qualified workers for the type of work to be done; on the other hand, workers should ideally be chosen exclusively according to their

Human Rights Act"; in Hawaii, the *"Hawaii's* Employment *Discrimination Act"*; in the State of Louisiana, the *"Louisiana Equal Pay for Women Act"*; in *Louisiana*, the *"Louisiana Employment Discrimination Law Regarding Veterans"*; in *Maryland*, the *"Fairness to All Marylanders Act"*, who amended *"all laws dealing with discrimination in public accommodations, housing, and employment, to include a provision prohibiting discrimination on the basis of a person's gender identity"*; in *Massachusetts*, the *"Massachusetts's employment anti-discrimination law"*, which from 2012 on also included *"gender identity"*; in Missouri, the *"Missouri Humans Rights Act"*; in *Nebraska*, the *"Nebraska's Fair Employment Practices Act"* and the *"Nebraska Age Discrimination in Employment Act"*; in New Jersey, the *"New Jersey Conscientious Employee Protection Act"*; in *New York*, the *"New York City Human Rights Law"*, which in 2014 *"was amended to include expanded protections against discrimination for pregnant employees"*; in North *Dakota*, the *"North Dakota Statutes"*; in *Oklahoma*, the *"Oklahoma's Anti-Discrimination Act (OADA)"*; in *Puerto Rico*, the *Law no. 100*, according to which *"The dismissal of employees is prohibited because of age, race, color, sex (gender), sexual orientation, gender identity, social origin or condition, national origin, political or religious beliefs or affiliation, disability, marriage to an employee for the employer, being a victim or being perceived as a victim of domestic violence, sexual aggression or stalking"*; in *Texas*, the *Texas Civil Practice and Remedies Code;* and in Wisconsin, the *Wisconsin Fair Employment Act.*

137 See ALVIN L. GOLDMAN and ROBERTO L. CORRADA, *Labor Law in the USA, cit.* p. 185.

138 See ALVIN L. GOLDMAN and ROBERTO L. CORRADA, *Labor Law in the USA, Third Revised Edition,* Wolters Kluwer, Law and Business, The Netherlands, 2011, p. 184.

"ability to perform the job", and all discriminatory practices potentially harmful to human dignity should be banned[139].

The *Civil Rights Act* went in the same direction: the legislative act "*was intended to eliminate discrimination in a number of areas in society: housing, public accommodation, education and employment*". Title VII of the Civil Rights Act was particularly dedicated to "*discrimination in employment, creating the foundations of the modern federal equal employment opportunity law*"[140].

However, this does not mean that considering the U.S. legal system of safeguards there are no workers hired or fired for good or bad reasons, or for no reason, especially in the private sector. What does matter is that such reasons are not prohibited. "*The most important prohibitions contained in U.S. employment law are those that prohibit employers from making employment decisions on the basis of race, sex, color, religion, nationality, age or disability*"[141]. And precisely because such prohibitive rules do exist, the best way to prevent its violation by employers is through the adoption of a *"policy of fair treatment for all employees"*.

Similarly, Title VII does not prohibit the Federal Government from promoting affirmative action programs seeking to benefit a traditionally disadvantaged group[142, 143], provided that such actions do not cause *"a disproportional harmful effect on a different racial group"*[144].

[139] See PATRICK J. CIHON/JAMES OTTAVIO CASTAGNERA, *Employment & Labor Law*, Sixth Edition, South-Western Cenage Learning, 2008, Mason, p. 42.

[140] See PATRICK J. CIHON/JAMES OTTAVIO CASTAGNERA, *Employment & Labor Law*, cit., p. 43.

[141] See ALVIN L. GOLDMAN and ROBERTO L. CORRADA, *Labor Law in the USA, cit.* p. 184.

[142] On this subject, see PAUL JOSEPH WALKOWSKI, *Affirmative Action*, Branden Publishing Company, Boston, MA, 1999. See, in particular, the analysis of the first cases regarding *affirmative action* on access to employment decided by the *Supreme Court*, cases *Griggs v. Duke Power Company* (1971) and *Steel-workers v. Weber* (1979).

[143] On the measures adopted regarding affirmative actions based on racial origin and access to college and university, see PETER ACIDIANO/ESTEBAN AUCEJO/ANDREW HUSSEY/KENNETH SPENNER, "Racial Segregation Patterns in Selective Universities", *The Journal of Law & Economics*, The University of Chicago Press, Vol. 56, number 4, November 2013, pp.1039 et seq. The authors note that in the United States of America, "*The use of racial preferences in college and university admissions has been one of the most fiercely debated issues in higher education in the past decade*" and that "*U.S. Supreme Court admitted the constitutionality of the affirmative action admissions*" (p. 1039).

[144] In this regard, see JULIA KOBICK, *Discriminatory Intent Reconsidered: Folk Concepts for*

In any case, and as a rule, Title VII prohibits both the cases of *disparate treatment* and the cases of *disparate impact*. However, it considers certain distinctive practices as lawful, depending on the employer's good faith – the so called *bona fide occupational qualification* –, also allowing for such affirmative actions[145].

VI. For instance, regarding the concept of *disparate treatment*, the U.S. Supreme Court decided that a policy ban implemented by the employer to exclude women in childbearing age was discriminatory and therefore illegal.

In the *International Union, UAW* v. *Johnson Controls* (1991) the Supreme Court hold and addressed the issue of fetal hazards. In this case, the employer barred women of childbearing age from certain jobs due to potential harm that could occur to a fetus. The Court ruled that the employer's restriction against fertile women performing "dangerous jobs" constituted sex discrimination under Title VII. The Court further ruled that the employer's fetal protection policy could be justified only if able to bear children was a *bona fide occupational qualification* (BFOQ) for the job. The fact that the job posed risk to fertile women does not justified barring all fertile women from the position. In this case we are talking about a plant that fabricates batteries.

According to their medical services, the tools and the process of fabrication of those batteries could be harmful for pregnant women and any fetus carried by a certain female employee. As a consequence, the plant created a hiring ban policy, barring all fertile women, except those whose infertility was medically documented. Petitioners, a group of women affected by that fetal-protection policy, filed a class action in the District Court against the corporation (the defendant), claiming that the policy constituted sex discrimination ans such violated Title VII of the Civil Rights Act of 1964. The District Court granted summary judgment for the respondent and the Court of Appeals confirmed this decision, saying that the corporation acted

Intentionality and Equal Protection Jurisprudence, Harvard Civil Rights – Civil Liberties Review, Harvard Law School, Vol. 45, No. 2, Summer 2010, pp. 517 et seq.

[145] See Guilherme Dray, *The Influence of the United States of America on Reaffirming the Principle of Equality in Employment in Portuguese Speaking Language Countries*, cit., pp. 63 et seq.

under a *Bona Fide Occupation Qualification*, since its "fetal-protection policy" is reasonably necessary to further the industrial safety concern that is part of the essence of the respondent's business.

Contrarily, the Supreme Court held that by excluding women with childbearing capacity from lead-exposed jobs, the corporation created a facial classification based on gender and explicitly discriminated against women on the basis of their sex. Moreover, in using the words "capable of bearing children" as the criteria for exclusion, the policy classified based on potential for pregnancy, which must be regarded in the same light as explicit sex discrimination.

The Supreme Court also held that the Court of Appeals erred in assuming that the policy was facially neutral because it had only a discrimination effect on women's employment opportunities, and because it's asserted purpose in protecting women was benign. The Supreme highlighted that the policy is not neutral, because it does not apply to male employees in the same way that it applies to females, despite evidence on the debilitating effect of lead exposure on the male reproductive system. Also, the absence of malevolent motive does not convert a facially discriminatory policy into a neutral policy with a discriminatory effect.

The BFOQ allows an employer to discriminate on the basis of sex "*in those certain instances where sex is a reasonable element necessary to the normal operation of a particular business*". In this case, the Supreme held that unless pregnant employees differ from others in their ability or inability to work, they must be treated the same as other employees for all employment-related purposes. The legal framework prohibits an employer from discriminating against a woman because of her capacity to become pregnant unless her reproductive potential prevents her from performing the duties of her job. The so-called safety exceptions to the BFOQ are limited to instances in which sex or pregnancy actually interfere with the employee's ability to perform in activities that clash with the essence of the particular business. Respondent cannot establish a BFOQ. Fertile women participate in the manufacture of batteries as efficiently as anyone else. Moreover, respondent's professed concern about the welfare of the next generation does not suffice to establish a BFOQ of female sterility. Title VII mandates that decisions about the welfare of future children be left to the parents who conceive rather to the employers who hire those parents or the courts. Besides, the incremental cost of employing members of one sex cannot justify a discriminatory refusal to hire members of that gender[146].

VII. About voluntary and private *affirmative action* plans, the Supreme Court held that Title's VII prohibition against racial discrimination does not condemn all private, voluntary and race-conscious affirmative action plans[147].

In United Steel Workers of America v. Weber (1979),the Supreme Court held that private sector employers and unions may lawfully implement voluntary affirmative action plans to remedy past discrimination. The Court additionally held that an employer and union do not violate the law by reserving through a collectively bargained agreement 50 percent of the slots of a training program in a traditionally segregated industry for black employees. The program is lawful because it does not "unnecessarily trammel the interests of white employees," nor does it "create an absolute bar to the advancement of white employees," and is "a temporary measure not intended to maintain racial balance, but simply to eliminate a manifest racial imbalance."

In this case, the petitioners, United Steelworkers of America and Kaiser Aluminum Chemical Corporation entered into a collective agreement (a single-undertaking agreement) covering terms and conditions at 15 Kaiser plants. Until 1974, Kaiser only hired as craft workers for its plant in Gramercy persons with prior craft experience. Because African Americans had long been excluded from craft unions, few were able to present such credentials. Therefore, to tackle this status quo, the agreement included an affirmative action plan designed to eliminate conspicuous racial imbalances in Kaiser's which worked almost exclusively in benefit of white craft work forces. The plan reserved for black employees 50% of the openings in plant training programs until the percentage of black craft workers in the plant is commensurate with the percentage of blacks in the local labour force. This litigation arose from the operation of the affirmative plan at one of Kaiser's plant where, prior to 1974, only 1.83% of the skilled craft workers were black, even though the local workforce was approximately 39% black.

[146] See Guilherme Dray, *The Influence of the United States of America on Reaffirming the Principle of Equality in Employment in Portuguese Speaking Language Countries*, cit., pp. 59 et seq.
[147] See Guilherme Dray, *The Influence of the United States of America on Reaffirming the Principle of Equality in Employment in Portuguese Speaking Language Countries*, cit., pp. 63 et seq.

In this context, Kaiser, rather than continuing the practice of hiring trained outsiders, established a training program to train its production workers to fill craft openings, selecting trainees on the basis of seniority, with the provision that at least 50% of the trainees were to be black until the percentage of black skilled craft workers in the plant approximated the percentage of blacks in the local labour force. During the plant's first year of operation, 7 black and 6 white craft trainees were selected from the plant's production workforce, with most senior black trainees having less seniority than several white production workers whose bids for admission were rejected. Weber, a white employee, claimed and alleged that, because the affirmative action program, junior black employees were receiving training in preference to senior white employees, and therefore the respondent was being discriminated in violation of the provisions of the Civil Rights Act of 1964.

The Supreme held that the Title's VII prohibition against racial discrimination does not condemn all private, voluntary, race-conscious affirmative action plans.

An affirmative action plan voluntarily adopted by private parties to eliminate traditional patterns of racial segregation is lawful.

Historically speaking, Title VII was conceived and addressed to open opportunities for blacks in occupations which have been traditionally closed to them. The principal aim of Title VII was to invite employers and unions to self-examine and to self-evaluate their employment practices in order to eliminate, so far as possible, the last vestiges of an unfortunate and ignominious page in U.S. history related to the segregation doctrine.

This plan was therefore lawful based on its purpose, content and temporary validity.

The purpose of the plan was benign – it was designed to break down old patterns of racial segregation and hierarchy and open employment opportunities for blacks in occupations which had been traditionally closed to them.

In terms of content, the plan did not trammel the interest of white employees, neither required the discharge of white workers and their replacement with new black hires, nor created an absolute bar to the advancement of white employees, since half of those trained in the program were still caucasian.

Finally, the plan was a temporary measure, not intended to maintain racial balance, but simply to eliminate a manifest racial imbalance.

The affirmative action plan collectively bargained by an employer and a trade union, that reserved for black employees 50% of the openings in an in-plant craft training program, was therefore legal and lawful, since Title VII does not prohibit such race-conscious affirmative action plans.

7.
Parental protection rights

7.1. General overview

The basic idea underlying the legal regime regarding maternity and paternity is to protect parents, especially pregnant, puerperal and nursing women, as well as to guarantee the conciliation between private life and family life and above all to protect children. The idea is simple: when it comes to raising children, family is better at doing so than the Government. Therefore, the State must create the conditions for it by promoting parental rights and empowering parents, through the establishment of a wide range of parental entitlements.

The Portuguese legal framework considers family and parental rights as fundamental rights.

As a matter of fact, article 67.th of the Portuguese Constitution states that as a nuclear element in society, family is afforded the right to protection by the State and to the effective implementation of all the conditions needed to enable family members to achieve personal fulfillment. Moreover, on fatherhood and motherhood, article 68.th of the Portuguese Constitution declares that in performing their irreplaceable role in relation to their children, particularly as regards to children's education, fathers and mothers have the right to be protected by society and the State altogether with the guarantee of their own professional fulfillment and participation in civic life. As a consequence, motherhood and fatherhood constitute eminent social values and women have the right to special protection during pregnancy and following childbirth. That same legal provision states that working women also have the right to an adequate period of leave from work without loss of remuneration or of any privileges. The Constitution expresses that ordinary law shall regulate the attribution to mothers and fathers the right to an adequate period of leave from work, in accordance with the interests of the child and the needs of the household. That law referred in the Constitution is the Portuguese Labour Code[148].

Following the same token and granted maternity and paternity are considered as "*eminent social values*" (article 33.rd of the Labour Code), the Portuguese Labour Code contains a broad range of parental rights[149]. These rights were reinforced through the Law n.º 90/2019, September 4.th, which amended the Labour Code. Under the new article 35.º-A, it becomes clear that any form of discrimination on the basis of exercise by the workers of their maternity and paternity rights shall be prohibited. The prohibition includes, in particular, wage discrimination relating to the award of attendance and productivity benefits, as well as discriminations regarding the career progression.

7.2. Parental rights in the Labour Code

I. Generally speaking and breaking down these rights, we may find five main groups of legal rules expressed in our Labour Code regarding parental rights: rules about absences from work (articles 35.th et seq. and article 65.th); about working time entitlements (articles 54.th to 60.th); about the reinstatement of the mother after childbirth (article 61.st); about safety and health regarding the protection of the mother and the foetus (article 62.nd); and about the protection against dismissal of pregnant and puerperal (article 63.rd).

In brief, these rights are aimed at guaranteeing that pregnant women will not be discriminated for being pregnant, puerperal or breastfeeding.

[148] See JORGE MIRANDA/RUI MEDEIROS, *Constituição Portuguesa Anotada*, cit., notes on article 67.th.

[149] See GUILHERME DRAY, *Código do Trabalho Anotado*, cit., notes on article 33.rd of the Portuguese Labor Code, pp. 197 et seq.

Article 36.th of the Labour Code[150] defines the concepts of pregnant, puerperal and breastfeeding employee, attaching the use of parental benefits with the provision of the right information to support it. As a matter of fact, if an employee wants to benefit from parental rights he/she has to inform the employer about his/her own situation. To be considered a pregnant employee, women must inform the employer about her pregnancy, by presenting a medical certificate. The same occurs after the birth of a child, to be considered under the status of puerperal or a breastfeeding employee. Puerperal employee is a mother within the period of 120 days after childbirth. To be considered a puerperal employee and to benefit from its correspondent rights she has to inform the employer about the birth of the baby by submitting the birth certificate of the child. Finally, a breastfeeding employee is one which breastfeeds or nurses the baby and informs the employer about this situation, by sending him/her a medical certificate.

II. In the first group of rules, related to absences from work, the Labour Code presents a long list of parental leaves, justified absences and releases from service. They are all listed in article 35.th and their legal effects are expressed in article 65.th [151]. Generally speaking, parental leaves and justified absences count as time of service for all the working effects, save for the payment of salary. That means that they are relevant, for example, for seniority counting and for job promotions, but the employer doesn't have to pay the salary to the mother or the father that benefits from a parental leave during this period. These payments, as we will see further on, are made by the State (article 65.th, n.er 1). Contrarily, the release of services, namely for antenatal care, to see a doctor or to attend prenatal classes, or for breastfeeding or nursing the baby, are seen as working time even with regards to the payment of salaries. That means that the employer has to pay the entire salary, for example, even when a mother is entitled to a working release to go to an antenatal medical consultation (article 65.th, n.er 2).

Regarding parental leaves, the Labour Code contains and lists several types of them in article 35.th: a parental leave before childbirth in case of

[150] See Guilherme Dray, *Código do Trabalho Anotado*, cit., notes on article 36.th.of the Portuguese Labor Code, pp. 202 et seq.

[151] See Guilherme Dray, *Código do Trabalho Anotado*, cit., notes on articles 35.th .and 65.th of the Portuguese Labor Code, pp. 200 et seq. and 240 and seq.

a risky pregnancy; a leave to travel the hospital unit located outside the island of residence to childbirth; a leave for the interruption of a pregnancy; an initial parental leave; a parental complementary leave; a leave in case of adoption; a parental leave to assist a child under the age of 12 years old; or a parental leave to assist a handicaped child or a child with oncological disease. All these parental leaves are subsequently ruled in articles 37.th et seq. of the Labour Code.

The most used parental leave is the initial parental leave.

Under article 40.th of the Labour Code, in case of childbirth, employees (mother and father) are entitled to an initial parental leave of 120 or 150 consecutive days. That means that they can opt between a 120 or a 150 days parental leave and they can also choose between sharing or not sharing this leave. The option is based on the time they want to be with the baby, on one hand, and on the payment of the subsidies they will receive from the Portuguese Social Security, on the other. These payments and subsidies are stipulated in the Decree-Law 91/2009, from 9 of April, that regulates social protection in case of maternity and paternity. If the parents choose a parental leave of 120 days, the Social Security pays a subsidy corresponding to 100% of the salary; if their option is for a leave of 150 days, they will only receive an allowance equivalent to 80% of the salary (article 30.th of Decree-Law 91/2009).

Parents can share the parental leave, but the law imposes a mandatory initial parental leave exclusively for the mother, corresponding to a six-week period after childbirth (article 41.st of the Labour Code). On the other hand, the employee who becomes a father is entitled to take a paid leave of 20 working days during the first six weeks after the childbirth, 5 of which must be consecutive and taken immediately after the birth of the baby. After the enjoyment of the referred leave, the father is also entitled to 5 working days of leave, followed or interpolated, provided that he enjoys it simultaneously with the leave of the mother.

The law also states that after the first 120 days and until the end of the 150 day's period, parents can use the initial parental leave simultaneously. That means that if they chose to benefit from a parental leave of 150 days, they can use it at the same time during the last 30 days. In that case, the date in which the parental leave ceases will come earlier. For example: if, on 30.th June, they already used 120 days of the initial parental leave and decide to use the remaining 30 days simultaneously, the leave will end on 15.th July, since each of them took 15 days at the same time. On the contrary, if only the mother uses the last period of 30 days of the initial parental leave, then the leave will end later, on July 30.

In this first group of rules we may also find justified absences, namely to give assistance to a child under the age of 12, if he or she is sick (article 49.th), or to give assistance to a grandson or a granddaughter, in case he or she is a son or a daughter of a youngster under the age of 16 (article 50.th).

During pregnancy, the Labour Code also contains the rights to paid service releases to attend prenatal medical appointments whenever it is necessary, including antenatal classes (46.th). The worker is also entitled to three work releases to attend medical appointments for medically assisted procreation (46.th – A). These releases are paid but the law establishes that medical consultations must be attended by the pregnant women out of their working hours whenever possible. The Code also asserts that the breastfeeding employee is entitled to service releases to feed and nurse the baby, having the right to benefit of two breaks during the working day (47.th). Both the antenatal medical consultations to attend medical appointments for medically assisted procreation, and the releases to breastfeeding and nurse the babies must be paid by the employer (article 65.th, n.^{er} 2)[152].

III. On the topic of entitlements regarding work time, the Labour Code expresses that in order to guarantee the protection of the pregnant women, the puerperal or breastfeeding mothers, they are exempt to work in adaptability schemes, hour banks or concentrated working schedules (58.th). They are also exempt to provide overtime work (59.th) or to work at night, namely through night shifts (60.th).

IV. The Portuguese Labour Code also contains rules to guarantee the return and the reinstatement of the puerperal employee after the use of the parental leave. The basic rule is that the employer must reinstate the mother into her old job. The employee is entitled to come back to exactly the same job with the same role that she used to play before entering into parental leave. Otherwise, if she is impaired because of her maternity, namely in

[152] See Guilherme Dray, *Código do Trabalho Anotado*, cit., notes on articles 46th to 47th of the Portuguese Labor Code, pp. 215 et seq.

terms of career promotions or salary rights, we may have a discriminatory practice, forbidden under articles 23.rd et seq.

Besides that, in order to guarantee that the return of the mother is peaceful and that she was not impaired due to her long absence from work, article 61.st states that the employer must provide the employee, after the leave to assist a child or to provide assistance to a disabled person or someone with a chronic illness, the participation in training and professional up-dating actions, in order to promote their full reintegration.

V. In addition, in order to protect the pregnant woman and the fetus, the Labour Code stipulates specific rules on health and safety, stating that in case employees' work duties entail clinical risks to a pregnant employee or to her unborn child, the employer must either provide the pregnant employee with alternative working conditions; send the employee to a workplace compatible with her pregnant condition; or avoid the pregnant employee's exposure to risks for as long as necessary (article 62.nd)[153].

VI. Finally, the Code regulates the dismissal of a pregnant, puerperal or breastfeeding employee, by creating a specific protection against dismissal. Considering that there are employers that don't want to cover maternity leaves and deal with employees with family responsibilities, the legislator created a specific regime against the unlawful dismissal of pregnant women because of their pregnancy.

Basically, article 63.rd of the Labour Code[154] states that the dismissal of a pregnant, puerperal, or nursing woman requires a prior and statutory legal opinion from the State Agency that stands up for pregnant women – the Commission for Employment Equality (*Comissão para a Igualdade no Trabalho e no Emprego – CITE*) – 63.rd, n.er 1 PLC. If the legal opinion of this Agency (CITE) is against the dismissal, then the employer cannot dismiss the pregnant employee, unless he/she initiates legal action in the courts in order to achieve a judicial certification that confirms the existence of a just cause for dismissal (article 63.rd, n.er 7).

[153] See Guilherme Dray, *Código do Trabalho Anotado*, cit., notes on article 62nd of the Portuguese Labor Code, pp. 232 et seq.

[154] See Guilherme Dray, *Código do Trabalho Anotado*, cit., notes on article 63rd of the Portuguese Labor Code, pp. 233 et seq.

Moreover, before the Labour Code, the dismissal of a pregnant, puerperal or breastfeeding employee is presumed to be without just cause and therefore unlawful and null. That means, in brief, that the law creates a reversion of the burden of proof (article 63.rd, n.er 2). Consequently, in case of a dismissal of a pregnant woman, she can initiate a lawsuit and must only state she was dismissed while pregnant. In that case, it's up to the employer to prove that there was a just and legal cause for the dismissal and that the termination of the contract was unrelated to the pregnancy.

On the other hand, if the dismissal is declared illegal and the employee requires her reintegration in the corporation, the employer cannot refuse the reinstatement of the pregnant, puerperal or breastfeeding employee (63.rd, n.er 8). If, alternatively, instead of resuming to work the employee chooses to receive a severance compensation, then the amount of this compensation will be higher than usual – she will be entitled to receive a severance compensation between 30 and 60 days of salary for each year of seniority, instead of the general compensation applied for the generality of employees, which is between 15 and 45 days for each year of seniority (articles 63.rd, n.er 8, and 392.nd, n.er 3).

8.
Formation of the employment contract

8.1. General overview

I. To have an employment contract we must have a mutual agreement between the employer and the employee[155]. Usually, that agreement is a result of a bargain process that includes necessarily two manifestations of willingness: the offer and acceptance[156].

The offer is a manifestation of willingness to enter into a bargain process; the acceptance is an unconditional willingness to be bound by that offer and therefore to sign a contract and make a deal.

The Portuguese Labour Code does not regulate those two manifestations of willingness and their effects. As a consequence, to find legal rules regarding the formation of a contract and the declarations of willingness we must resort to the Portuguese Civil Code, which contains several provisions on offer, acceptance and the conclusion of a private contract[157].

Regarding the declarations of willingness, article 217.th of the Portuguese Civil Codes states that the negotiating declaration may be expressed or implied: it is expressed, when was written or has any other direct means of expressing such will; it is tacit when it results from facts that, in all likelihood, reveal it. Moreover, article 224.th regulates the effectiveness of

[155] See João Leal Amado, *Contrato de Trabalho*, cit., pp. 153 et seq.

[156] See Maria do Rosário Ramalho, *Tratado de Direito do Trabalho – Parte II*, cit., pp. 142 et seq.

[157] See Pedro Romano Martinez, *Direito do Trabalho*, cit., pp. 429 et seq.

business declarations, stipulating that the business declaration that has a recipient becomes effective as soon as it comes to his/her power or is by him/her known; the offer that doesn´t have a recipient becomes effective as soon as the will of the declarant is manifested in an appropriate manner. It is also considered effective the declaration which was not timely received by the recipient because of his/her own fault.

Regarding the duration of the contract proposal, article 228.th of the Civil Code expresses that the proposed contract requires the following from the applicant: a) If it is stipulated by the offeror or agreed by the parties a deadline for the acceptance, the tender is valid until its defined term; b) If there is no fixed term but the offeror asks the tenderer immediate response, the tender is valid until, under normal conditions, the offer and the potential acceptance reach their destination; c) If no deadline was fixed and the proposal is addressed to a missing person or, in writing, to a person that is not present, the acceptance will remain for five days after the deadline.

Finally, the Civil Code states that acceptance must be unconditional – under article 232.nd the contract is not complete until parties have agreed on all the terms which any of them deems necessary for the agreement; complementarily, article 233.rd states that acceptance with modifications, additions, limitations or other modifications accounts to a rejection of the proposal; nevertheless if the amendment is sufficiently precise, then we´ll have a new proposal, so long as no other meaning can be found in this declaration.

To sum up, to have a contract the parties must agree on everything. They must be "on the same page". If so, then we have a mutual agreement and the formation of a contract took place. That is also the case with the employment contract[158].

As referred above, the Labour Code does not contain specific provisions on offer, acceptance and the formation of the contract, but it nevertheless regulates some specific issues about the elements of the contract. For instance, the Labour Code establishes principles that shall apply in a negotiation process; the capacity of a minor to enter into an employment contract; some specific assumptions for the employment contract; the proper form of this

[158] See Luís Menezes Leitão, *Direito do Trabalho,* cit., pp. 197 et seq.

contract; some specific rules on the preliminary employment contract; and the employment contract of adhesion.

II. The principles that must be accomplished in an employment negotiation process are basically the freedom or liberty of contract; equality in the access to employment; and the *bona fide* principle during the negotiation of the contract.

Firstly, the formation of an employment contract must respect the liberty and freedom to negotiate and to enter into a contract. That means that the employee is free to choose his/her own profession, to enter into an employment contract and that servitude and slavery are forbidden. Because of its importance, this liberty is enshrined in article 47.th of the Portuguese Constitution. On the other hand, the employer is also free to choose the employee he/she wants to hire, under his/her private autonomy, expressed at article 405.th of the Portuguese Civil Code[159].

Secondly, as we already analyzed, the employer must follow the principle of equality on the access to employment. Therefore, he/she cannot discriminate a job applicant based on his or her gender, race, color, religion, nationality, filiation, sexual orientation, etc. The provisions on this principle are expressed in articles 23.rd et seq. of the Labour Code, as referred above. In the event of an illegal discrimination, the employer incurs in liability (article 28.th of the Labour Code).

Finally, under article 102.nd of the Labour Code, both the employer and the employee that negotiate to conclude an employment contract shall, in the primary process and in its formation, proceed according to the rules of good faith. As a consequence, the one who breaches the bona fide rules may incur in a penalty or liability for damage caused to the other party. That includes the respect and compliance with duties of information and duties of loyalty. In the first case, the employer has the duty to inform the employee about the relevant aspects of the employment contract, its functions and insertion in the organizational framework. The information must be in written form (107.th Labour Code) – that is what is usually called as a "Statement of Particulars". This statement must at least cover the information listed in article 106.th, n.er 3, of the Labour Code, namely as follows: identification

[159] See Pedro Romano Martinez, *Direito do Trabalho*, cit. pp. 429 et seq.

of both parties; place of work; job description; the date in which the employment contract enters into force; the duration of the contract in case it is a non-permanent contract; the duration of holidays; the prior notices duration to terminate a contract; the amount and periodicity of the salaries; the daily and weekly working time period; the description of the insurance against labour accidents; the collective agreement applicable, when it exists, etc. Others may be added, such as the possibility of being insolvent or punctually failing to pay the salary. On the opposite side, the employee shall inform the employer of any circumstance that might affect the exercise of these functions. This information must be provided in the period preceding the conclusion of the contract.

The duty of loyalty, on the other hand, forbids an unjustifiable breach of negotiations that may cause damages to the other parties. For instance, if after a tender process to hire an employee the employer convinces the job applicant to give notice of dismissal from his/her previous job and then breaches the negotiations without any plausible reason, he/she may incur in liability and can be ordered to pay a compensation to the job applicant to compensate him/her for any damages incurred. The same occurs inversely if, for example, the candidate to an employment position, knowing in advance that he/she does not want to be hired, doesn´t reveal it immediately to the employer, only revealing it after a long and costly tender process organized and financed by the employer during which several candidates were interviewed and excluded. By acting like that, he/she may cause significant damages to the employer and therefore may be held liable for it[160].

8.2. Minors and capacity

I. Legal capacity to enter into an employment contract is a requisite to have a valid contract[161].

Regarding the capacity to enter into an employment contract, the Labour Code contains specific rules related to minors and youngsters that

[160] See Pedro Romano Martinez, comments to article 106.º of the Labor Code, at *Código do Trabalho Anotado*, cit., pp. 309 et seq.
[161] See Alvin L. Goldman and Roberto L. Corrada, *Labor Law in the USA*, cit., p. 92.

complement the legal regime of capacity expressed in articles 122.nd et seq. of the Portuguese Civil Code.

Under the Civil Code, the general rule is that a person has the capacity to freely and autonomously exercise his/her own rights and duties and to enter into contracts after reaching the age of 18 years old. Under the Labour Code, the rules differ. The legislator admits that a minor provides an activity as an employee before reaching 18 years old, even while he/she is a minor. The reason is straight forward: following the international rules and standards on this issue, the lawmaker admits that sometimes it is better to have a minor working than to have someone without any sources of income. Work can be a necessity to some minors and an alternative to poverty. As a consequence, the lawmaker decided to authorize work provided by a minor, under certain conditions and guarantees. In this case, the law imposes specific requirements and assignments in order to protect the minor and his/her physical, moral and educational development[162].

Bearing that in mind, underlying article 66.th of the Labour Code, the legislator states that the employer must provide to the minor employee good working conditions, adequate to his or her age, as well as to protect his or her health, safety, physical and moral development, education and training, preventing any risk that results from his or her lack of seniority and experience or from detrimental working conditions[163].

As a consequence, article 68.th, n.[er] 1, imposes three assumptions for the hiring of a minor:

(i) Minimum age for admission to work;
(ii) Conclusion or the attendance of compulsory schooling that goes until the end of 12th year of school; and
(iii) Physical and moral capacity to provide that specific activity.

The same provision declares that the minimum age to provide an activity as an employee is 16 years old (68.th, n.[er] 2).

As a consequence, and as a general rule, a minor with 16 years old that is attending compulsory school can enter into an employment contract, if the

162 See Guilherme Dray, *Princípio da Proteção do Trabalhador,* cit., pp. 733 et seq.

163 See Maria do Rosário Ramalho, *Tratado de Direito do Trabalho – Parte II,* cit., pp. 112 et seq.

employer creates conditions to guarantee the minor's physical, moral and educational development[164].

II. Despite these general rules, the Labour Code admits two types of exceptions, in order to lighten the system.

The first, states that a minor younger than 16 years that has already concluded or is attending compulsory school may provide light work as an employee. In this case, he/she can only provide simple and non-harmful activities that cannot jeopardize his or her physical and mental development integrity and school attendance (68.th, n.er 3). Moreover, he or she shall also attend complementary educational training (article 69.th, n.er 1, first section).

The second exception is intended minors above 16 years old but that have not yet completed compulsory schooling. In this case, the law imposes the attendance of complementary educational training (article 69.th, n.er 1, second section)[165].

Besides the rules on the capacity of minor's to provide an activity as employees, the Labour Code also regulates their competence to sign and autonomously enter into an employment contract, establishing an exception to the Portuguese Civil Code by allowing minors to sign the contract themselves.

If the minor is a 16 years old youngster and he/she is attending compulsory schooling, he/she can sign freely and autonomously the contract and this contract is lawful, unless his or her legal representatives are opposed to in writing the celebration of such contract (article 70.th, n.er 1).

If the minor hasn't reached the age of 16 years old or if he or she is not attending compulsory schooling, then the contract must be authorized by his or her legal representatives to be lawful. Without such authorization the contract is unlawful and void (article 70.th, n.er 2).

In addition, the law provides that the minor employee is entitled to receive directly his or her salary paid by the employer (article 70.th, n.er 3).

[164] See Guilherme Dray, comments to articles 66th – 83.rd of the Labor Code, at *Código do Trabalho Anotado*, cit., pp. 242 et seq.

[165] See Guilherme Dray, notes on articles 69.th – 71.st of the Labor Code, at *Código do Trabalho Anotado*, cit., pp. 242 et seq.

III. Finally, under the law, the employer must ensure specific safety working conditions for minors, providing them with medical exams to certify his or her physical and moral capability to perform the job (article 72.nd). The same provision also affirms that the legislator can legally identify specific activities prohibited or conditioned for minors (article 72.nd, n.er 2). Minors are exempt to work more than 8 hours a day and 40 hours a week, and if they are under the age of 16 years old they cannot work more than 7 hours a day and 35 hours a week (article 73.rd). They are also exempt to perform in flexible working time schedules such as adaptability, hour banks or in the regime of concentrated working time (article 74.th), as well as to provide overtime working (article 76.th) or night shifts, between 8 p.m. and 7 a.m. (article 76.th). Minors are entitled to a daily breaking periods between 1h to 2h a day (article 77.th) and a rest period between two working days of 14 hours if he/she is below the age of 16 and 12 hours if he/she is 16 or older (article 78.th). The minor is also entitled to have a weekly rest period of 2 days (article 79.th).

The use of child labour in violation of article 68.th, n.er 1, or in violation of article 72.nd, n.er 2, is considered a crime and shall be punished with imprisonment for up to two years or with a penalty of up to 240 days if a more severe penalty is not provided for in another provision. In case the minor has not completed the minimum age of admission, has not completed compulsory schooling or is not enrolled and attending school at the secondary level of education, the limits of penalties can double those listed. In case of reoccurrence, the minimum limits can be tripled (article 81.st).

8.3. Legality of the object and the purpose

I. With regards to the contract and besides the questions regarding the capacity of the parties, the law also requires the legality of the object and of the purpose of the contract[166, 167].

The contract must be sufficiently determinable, physically and legally possible to execute (article 280.th of the Civil Code). For instance, I cannot hire an employee to provide all kinds of activities in my corporation, without

[166] See MARIA DO ROSÁRIO RAMALHO, *Tratado de Direito do Trabalho – Parte II*, cit., pp. 135 et seq.

[167] See JOÃO LEAL AMADO, *Contrato de Trabalho*, cit., pp. 160 et seq

determining the specific activities he/she was hired to provide for. In this case there would be a lack of determinability. On the other hand, the contract must be physically possible. This means that I cannot hire someone to bring me the moon to the earth. Thirdly, the object and the purpose of the contract must be lawful (articles 280.th and 281.st of the Portuguese Civil Code). Under these provisions, I cannot hire an employee as a hit man or a killer or to be a drug dealer because the object is unlawful. Besides, I cannot hire him/her as a car mechanic (a legal object) if to help me prepare and execute assaults and robberies (illegal purpose). If the contract infringes the provisions of articles 280.th and 281.st of the Civil Code, i.e., if it is a legally or physical impossible contract, or if its purpose is unlawful, the contract is considered null and ineffective (articles 121.st et seq. Labour Code).

II. Moreover, regarding some specific job activities, the Labour Code states that if and when the law requires a specific job title issued by an administrative agency or a bar association to provide a professional activity, then the contract is null if the employee doesn't fulfil that requirement (117.th)[168].

8.4. Proper form: freedom of form and exceptions

I. With regards to the proper form of the contract, the Labour Code states as a general rule that the employment contract is free to follow or not to follow a strict form and does not require a specific written document[169]. Hence the employment contract, or better referenced, the open-ended employment contract, can be an oral contract and doesn't require any specific form. The absence of a written form can bring some advantages. Freedom of proof allows greater hiring speed and better protection of the employee who starts the activity without any document, which allows him/her to prove the existence of this contract even without a written basis[170].

[168] See Pedro Madeira de Brito, notes to article 107.th of the Labor Code, at *Código do Trabalho Anotado*, cit., pp. 329 et seq.

[169] See João Leal Amado, *Contrato de Trabalho*, cit., pp. 176 et seq

[170] See Maria do Rosário Ramalho, *Tratado de Direito do Trabalho – Parte II*, cit., pp. 191 et seq.

That's why we have a general rule, comprised in article 110.th of the Labour Code, that is equivalent to the rule expressed in article 219.th of the Portuguese Civil Code[171].

II. Despite this rule, the referred provision adds that the law can require a specific form for specific employment contracts. This is the case with non-permanent employment contracts or those with specific characteristics. For specific contracts, listed following, the Labour Code requires a written form:

a) Employment contract with foreign workers (article 5.th, n.er 1);
b) Employment contract with a plurality of employers (article 101.st, n.er 2);
c) Preliminary Employment contract (article 103.rd, n.er 1);
d) Term employment contract (article 141.st, n.er 1);
e) Part-time employment contract (article 153.rd, n.er 1);
f) Intermittent employment contract (article 158.th, n.er 1);
g) Teleworking contract (article 166.th, n.er 4).

III. Contracts in which a written form is required must be signed by the parties. Usually, when there is a violation of the law that imposes written form, the legal consequence is the conversion of the specific type of employment contract into a traditional open-ended employment contract. This is, once again, a distinguished consequence created by the legislator when compared with the consequences expressed in the Portuguese Civil Code. Under article 220.th of the Civil Code, the contract which violates the form required by law is null. Under the Labour Code, the consequence is different, in order to protect the employee. If the consequence was the invalidity of the contract, the activity had to cease, and the employee would lose his/her employment. To avoid this, the law imposes the conversion of that specific form of contract into an open-ended employment contract. That is the consequence expressed in article 147.th, n.er 1, subparagraph c), of the Labour Code, with regards to the unwritten fixed-term contract – the law imposes the conversion of this non-permanent employment contract

[171] See Pedro Romano Martinez, notes to article 110.th of the Labor Code, at *Código do Trabalho Anotado*, cit., pp. 312 et seq.; Luís Menezes Leitão, *Direito do Trabalho*, cit., pp. 217.th et seq.

into a permanent employment contract which is beneficial to the employee. As a result of the disrespect of the rule that imposes written form (article 141.st) the contract becomes an open-ended contract.

8.5. Invalidity of the contract

I. If the employee doesn't have the capacity to enter into an employment contract or the contract endorses an unlawful object, the employment contract is null and therefore invalid[172].

Regarding the invalidity of the employment contract, article 122.nd of the Labour Code prescribes a specific consequence different from the general consequence of the invalidity of contracts expressed in the Portuguese Civil Code.

Under article 289.th of the Portuguese Civil Code, both the declaration of invalidity and annulment have retroactive effects and therefore all that was supplied should be reimbursed or, if restitution in kind is not possible, a pecuniary amount should be paid. On the contrary, in the Labour Code, article 122.nd contains a fiction of legality until the declaration of invalidity is stated and does not provide a retroactive effect of this declaration. Article 122.nd expresses that the employment contract declared null and void shall produce effects as if it was valid in relation to the time in which it was executed. The reason, once again, is related with the protection of the employee. Under this rule, despite the invalidity of the contract, the employee is protected and does not have to refund or to payback the salaries received for the activity provided. Under the Labour Code, there's no refund obligation applicable to the received salaries or other values received by the employee[173].

[172] See ALVIN L. GOLDMAN and ROBERTO L. CORRADA, *Labor Law in the USA*, cit., p. 94.

[173] See GUILHERME DRAY, comments to articles 66th- 71.st of the Labor Code, at *Código do Trabalho Anotado*, cit., pp. 347 et seq.; LUÍS MENEZES LEITÃO, *Direito do Trabalho*, cit., pp. 221 et seq.

9.
Performance and content of the employment contract

9.1. Object

I. By entering into an Employment Contract, the employee undertakes to provide an activity in exchange for remuneration and under the authority of the employer[174].

The activity he/she undertakes to provide is defined by the contract under article 115.th of the Labour Code, which states that it is a competence of the parties to determine by agreement the activity assigned to the worker. This implies that the activity provided by the employee must be described within the employment contract. That is what we usually call the object of the contract. Under that same legal provision, the determination referred in the contract may be made by reference to the category of the instruments of collective labour regulation or internal rules of business, i.e., by remission to one of those two instruments. That same article 115.th also affirms that when the nature of the activity involves the practice of legal business, the contract of employment shall be deemed to grant the employee the necessary powers, unless the law requires a special instrument to do so[175].

In brief, the object of the contract is determined by the employment contract and the activities the employee undertakes to provide are those

[174] See JOÃO LEAL AMADO, *Contrato de Trabalho*, cit., pp. 236 et seq

[175] See PEDRO MADEIRA DE BRITO, *Código do Trabalho Anotado*, cit., notes on article 115.th, pp. 347 et seq.; LUÍS MENEZES LEITÃO, *Direito do Trabalho*, cit., pp. 160. et seq.

expressed in the contract. Generally speaking, these are the core functions that the employee must provide.

II. That same idea is also confirmed by article 118.th, n.er 1, of the Labour Code, that states that the employee must, as a rule, perform duties corresponding to the activity for which he was hired, and the employer shall assign to it, within the scope of that activity, the functions most appropriate to the employees skills and professional qualification.

Nevertheless, the scope of activities that must be provided by the employee can be enlarged under article 118.th, n.er 2. Actually, in order to provide flexibility to the management, the Labour Code enlarges the object of the contract, adding that the functions required to the employee must also cover the activities that are similar or linked to the core functions the employee promised to provide since he/she has the skills to practice those. Indeed, the referred article 118.th, n.er 2, affirms that the contracted activity, although determined by reference to a professional foreseen in the instrument of collective bargaining regulation or the internal rules of business, shall include the functions related or functionally linked to the activities determined under article 115.th, whenever the employee has the adequate skills and qualifications to perform them and if the new activities do not imply professional devaluation. That means, for example, that if a corporation hires a driver, it can require him/her, besides the core activity he/she was hired for, to wash and clean the vehicle once a week. Although the contract only says that he was hired to drive people (core functions) these activities are linked to the driving activity (similar functions) and can be required from the driver, as they are connected to the designated ones and he/she possesses the skills to perform them and they don't imply a professional devaluation. In another example, the employee who was hired as a personal Secretary can be ancillary required to help the telephone operator[176].

III. In order to fall under the concept of the activities related to or functionally linked to the core activities, article 118.th, n.er 3, states that without prejudice to the collective labour regulation, are considered to be related or functionally linked, in particular, the functions that belong to the

[176] See Pedro Madeira de Brito, *Código do Trabalho Anotado*, cit., notes on article 118.th, pp. 329 et seq.; Luís Menezes Leitão, *Direito do Trabalho*, cit., pp. 164. et seq.

same group or professional career. Number 4 of this provision adds that whenever the exercise of ancillary functions requires special qualifications, the worker is entitled to vocational training of not less than 10 hours a year.

IV. In line with the goal of flexibility and the freedom of the management the law gives the employer the power to require from the employee the practice of activities that go beyond the object of the contract and that are neither the core functions nor the similar functions expressed respectively in articles 115.th and 118.th, n.er 2, of the Labour Code.

Actually, before the current article 120.th of the Labour Code, under the title "*functional mobility*", the law stated that the employer may, when there is an interest of the company to do so, require the employee to temporarily perform duties not included in the contracted activity, as this does not entail a substantial change in the position of the worker. The order of amendment shall be justified by mentioning the reason why this enlargement is necessary and by indicating its expected duration, that shall not exceed two years. This provision also clarifies that the enlargement of the object and the new activities practiced by the employee may not imply a reduction of his/her salary and that the employee is entitled to benefit from the most favorable working conditions inherent to the new functions performed, namely regarding wages.

Moreover, unless otherwise is agreed, the employee does not acquire the job title corresponding to the new functions temporarily exercised. For example: under this provision, an employer may require a mechanic to temporarily provide functions as a driver, if the original driver of the company is sick. In this case, the order is objectively justified and despite knowing that the new activity is beyond the core functions usually provided by the employee (article 115.th) and that it is not directly linked to them (article 118.th, n.er 2), the employer may request the employee to perform them, since there is an objective interest and the change is only temporary. In order for this to be feasible, the mechanic should know how to drive and have a valid driver's license. In this case, the wages of the mechanic could not be reduced and if the salary paid to the driver was higher than the mechanic's the later should benefit from it during the time he/she worked as a driver. At the end of this temporary situation, when the original driver returns to work, the mechanic should also return to his/her original duties and cannot demand the reclassification of his/her professional category as a driver.

This regime is also known by the Latin verbatum, as "*ius variandi*", or "right to change"[177].

Functional mobility and the power to require new functions to the employee that are beyond the object of the contract is lawful so long as all legal requirements are met: the change must be based on an objective interest of the corporation; the *ius variandi* must be temporary; the change cannot imply a substantive modification of the employees position and a reduction of his/her salary. Contrarily, if the new functions are better paid, the employee is entitled to receive the new salary during the time he/she performs these new activities.

Finally, article 120.th, n.er 2, adds that the parties may extend or restrict the power conferred on this provision by agreement which shall expire after two years if it has not been applied.

9.2. Duties and responsibilities

I. Labour Law is essentially based on employees' rights and freedoms, due to the fact that in an employment relationship we face an unbalanced relation, from both an economic and a legal standpoint.

Nevertheless, an employment relationship is a two-way street involving duties and responsibilities for both parties. A responsibility is a duty or something one should do. In the context of an employment relationship, the employee is entitled to several rights but must also comply with a wide number of duties.

The main or principal duty of the employee is to provide the activity he/she undertook to offer under the employment contract. Besides that duty, he/she must also fulfil secondary duties, i.e., duties that complement the principal duty expressed in the law (article 128.th, Labour Code), as well as ancillary duties, based on the bona fide principle (article 126.th of the Labour Code)[178].

[177] See Pedro Romano Martinez, *Direito do Trabalho*, cit., pp. 499 et seq.; Pedro Madeira de Brito, *Código do Trabalho Anotado*, cit., notes on article 120.th, pp. 336 et seq.; Luís Menezes Leitão, *Direito do Trabalho*, cit., pp. 164. et seq.

[178] See Pedro Romano Martinez, *Direito do Trabalho*, cit., pp. 502 et seq.; Pedro Romano Martinez/Pedro Madeira de Brito/Guilheme Dray, *Código do Trabalho Anotado*, cit.,

The legal duties of the employees that constitute his/her secondary responsibilities are enshrined in article 128.th of the Labour Code. Some of them are directly attached to the main duty as they are only required during the time the employee is providing his/her main activity. For example, the duties of punctuality, attendance or even obedience. These duties are not applicable if, for instance, the employee is benefiting from a parental leave or if he/she is enjoying a holiday leave period. Contrarily, we have a plethora of secondary duties which are autonomous from the main duty. For exemple, the duties of respect and courtesy, loyalty or even custody, this one if the employee takes with him tools or instruments of the employer during the period he or she is on leave. That means that the autonomous duties are expected to be respected even when the employee is not working. The idea behind these autonomous duties is easy to strike: the fact that the employee is not working doesn't give him the right to offend, defame or insult the employer or the right to damage the corporation's image, interests, tools and instruments.

II. The duties expressed in article 128.th are the following:

a) Respect and courtesy;
b) Punctuality and attendance;
c) Care and diligence;
d) Diligent participation in vocational training actions provided by the employer;
e) Obedience;
f) Loyalty;
g) Custody;
h) Promotion of the company's productivity improvement;
i) Prevention and promotion of health and safety conditions at the workplace;
j) Compliance with health and safety rules[179].

notes on articles 126.th – 128.th, pp. 352 et seq.; Luís Menezes Leitão, *Direito do Trabalho*, cit., pp. 229. et seq.

[179] See Pedro Romano Martinez/Pedro Madeira de Brito/Guilherme Dray, *Código do Trabalho Anotado*, cit., notes on article 128.th, pp. 360 et seq.

Under the duty of respect and courtesy the employee shall respect and behave towards the employer, hierarchical superiors, colleagues and people who relate to the corporation with civility and probity (article 128.th, 1, subparagraph *a)*).

Within the scope of the duty of attendance and assiduity the employee shall attend the job with assiduity and punctuality. He/she cannot be absent from work or show up later, disrespecting the working schedule (article 128.th, 1, subparagraph *b)*).

The duty of care and diligence means that the employee shall perform his/her work with zeal and diligence, doing the best he/she can to achieve good results and to promote the company's productivity (article 128.th, 1, subparagraph *c)*).

The employee shall also attend diligently vocational training provided by the employer (article 128.th, 1, subparagraph *d)*).

The duty of obedience entails that the employee complies with the orders and instructions given to him/her by the employer regarding the execution of work or safety and health conditions at work, so long as they are not contrary to his rights or guarantees (article 128.th, 1, subparagraph *e)*). The duty of obedience comprises the employer's orders or instructions directed to the employee by a hierarchical superior of the worker, within the powers that were assigned to him/her (article 128.th, n. 2).

Under the duty of loyalty the employee shall be loyal to the employer, in particular by not negotiating on his own account or with the competition or by disclosing information regarding his/her organization, production or methods or businesses (article 128.th, n. 1, subparagraph *f)*).

The duty of custody of labour instruments entails that the employee shall ensure the conservation and good use of work-related assets entrusted to him by the employer (article 128.th, 1, subparagraph *g)*).

The employee also has a duty to promote the improvement of productivity of the company. That means that he/she has to do his/her best in order to promote the corporation and all its stakeholders, including customers, shareholders and the entire community (article 128.th, 1, subparagraph *h)*).

Finally, regarding health and safety, he/she has to cooperate in the improvement of occupational safety and health, in particular through the representatives of the workers elected for that purpose (article 128.th, 1, subparagraph *i)*), as well as to comply with occupational safety and health requirements that emerge from a legal or collective Instrument of regulation (article 128.th, 1, subparagraph *j)*).

III. If the employee violates one of these duties, he/she incurs in a disciplinary infraction. His/her misconduct can lead to the exercise of the disciplinary power by the employer (articles 98.th and 328.th et seq.) towards the application of a disciplinary sanction or penalty (article 328.th). If the misconduct is not serious, the sanction should be a conservative one amongst the list of potential sanctions provided by the referred article 328.th of the Labour Code, for example, a mere reprehension or a pecuniary penalty; if the sanction is serious, the employer can ultimately dismiss the employee for just cause and without any compensation (article 351.st). The idea is that the sanction applied by the employer should abide by the principle of proportionality: if the employee's misconduct is serious, the penalty should also be serious; contrarily, if the offense committed by the employee is not serious, the sanction should only be preventive not leading to the termination of the employment relationship (article 330.th). The right to exercise disciplinary power when a misconduct occurs shall expire one year from the offense, or within the limitation period prescribed by criminal law if the infraction is also considered a crime (article 329.th, n. 1). Disciplinary proceedings must start within 60 days following knowledge of the infraction by the employer or his/her hierarchical superior doted with disciplinary competence (article 329.th, n2)[180].

9.3. Workplace

I. The workplace is the physical place where the worker performs his/her activity and is available to the employer[181]. The workplace and its potential relocation is a very important issue since generally, the employee organizes his/her own life and his/her family's life based on the place he/she works. For instance, the choice of the family's house and the children's school are usually made on the basis of the selected workplace. As a consequence, the

[180] See Pedro Romano Martinez, *Código do Trabalho Anotado*, cit., notes on articles 328.th – 329.th, pp. 758 et seq.

[181] See João Leal Amado, *Contrato de Trabalho*, cit., pp. 242 et seq

lawmaker tries to avoid unilateral and arbitrary transfers of the workplace by the employer[182].

As a general rule, the worker must carry out the activity in the workplace contractually defined, being nevertheless subjected to movements inherent to his or her functions or indispensable to his or her professional training (article 193.rd).

Because of the importance of the workplace to the employee's personal life, the law states that once it is defined, the worker shall not be moved from his/her workplace (129.th, n.1, subparagraph f)). This is commonly known as a guarantee of immobility or immovability. That means that generally, the transfer from the original workplace depends on a mutual agreement between the employer and the employee.

However, in some cases, the transfer determined by the employer is authorized, even without the employee's consent. Under the law, we may distinguish two possibilities of unilateral displacement determined by the employer: the collective transfer and individual transfer. The first is the transfer based on a total or partial change or extinction of the establishment. The latter is a transfer of a single employee. Using other criteria, the transfer can also be qualified as temporary or definitive. A temporary transfer is a transfer of up to 6 months (194.th, n. 3) and the definitive transfer is one which is made without a fixed term. Both the collective and the individual transfer, as well as the definitive and temporary transfer are regulated in article 194.th of the Portuguese Labour Code. In both cases the employer must fulfill specific requirements to transfer the employee to another workplace[183].

II. A collective transfer results from a total or partial change or extinction of the existing establishment. Under article 194.th, n.[er] 1, subparagraph a), of the Labour Code, a collective transference is allowed if the company's place of work is to be completely or partially replaced. When it happens, the employer may impose a transfer of the employee's workplace. For example: if a company operates in Lisbon and wants to transfer its headquarters to Sintra, then the employer can require all employees to start working in Sintra considering the existing workplace will be closed. The change of workplace

[182] See Menezes Cordeiro, *Direito do Trabalho, II,* Almedina, Coimbra, 2018, pp. 492 et seq.

[183] See Maria do Rosário Ramalho, *Tratado de Direito do Trabalho – Parte II,* cit., pp. 359 et seq.

can be total if we deal with the transference of the whole corporation, or partial if only a specific part of the business is transferred. If the change is partial, the transfer of the employee is only allowed if he works in the part of the establishment that will be transferred. In case of a definitive collective transfer, the employee cannot refuse to obey and cannot state he/she wants to stay at the original workplace since this place of work will be closed. Nevertheless, if the transfer causes serious harm to the employee he/she can terminate the contract, receiving a compensation calculated under article 366.th of the Labour Code (article 194.th, n.er 5). This implies that the existence of a serious harms to a specific employee is not an obstacle to the change of the corporation's headquarters or units, but if an employee proves that the change of his/her workplace causes him/her a serious harm, then he/she will be entitled to terminate the contract for just cause and receive a severance compensation[184].

III. The individual transfer occurs when the employer wants to change the workplace of a specific employee. In this case, it is not a collective transfer of all the employees, but only an intention to transfer a specific employee from a workplace to another. The individual transfer depends on specific and more demanding requirements, in order to avoid retaliation or orders aimed at jeopardizing a specific worker. Under article 194.th, n.er 1, subparagraph b), the individual transfer is only allowed when there is a justifiable interest of the company and if the employee is not seriously harmed as a result of that transfer. That implies that the individual transfer determined by the employer depends on an objective interest of the company. A simple decision of the employer is not sufficient, having to add a business justification of a technical, productive or organization character. Moreover, this displacement shall not cause serious damage to the worker. That means that the transfer shall not imply an excessive modification in the organization of working time, rest or life habits of the worker, being weighted factors such as the residence, location of the employee's family, the employee's health and social life or the living costs. Both case law and legal doctrine are very stringent when dealing with the concept of serious harm. By serious harm, we may understand not only a mere inconvenience

[184] See Pedro Romano Martinez, *Direito do Trabalho*, cit., pp. 534 et seq.

but rather something more serious that can really affect the employee. For instance: it is considered that a change in the workplace that only implies more time using public transportation is not sufficient to sustain serious harm. To spend an additional 30m or even 1h in public transports is not considered serious harm, but only a mere inconvenience. Contrarily, if the change of workplace involves the need of relocation of the employee's residence or his/her children's school or if the employee needs to remain working in a big city to get medical assistance due to a chronic disease, then we can have a serious harm that prevents the individual transference of the workplace. If these requirements are not fulfilled then the employee can refuse to be transferred and remain working at the same workplace. If the employee is a worker's representative, then the individual transfer is only allowed if the employee gives his own permission. That's the rule stated in article 411.th of the Labour Code, aimed at preventing retaliation against worker's representatives.

IV. Both in the case of a collective or an individual transference, the law states that the employer must cover the expenses of the employee arising from increased travel costs and relocation or, in the event of a temporary transfer, accommodation (article 194.th, n.er 4)[185].

In both cases the employer must previously inform the employee of the transfer, in writing, 8 or 30 days in advance, depending on whether it is a temporary or definitive transfer. The communication shall refer the reasons on which it is based and its duration (article 196.th).

V. Although the transfer of the workplace is usually made by the employer in the interest of the company, the law also regulates a specific situation in which the transfer is based on the interest of the employee.

Under article 195.th of the Portuguese Labour Code, the worker that is a victim of domestic violence may ask to move to another corporate establishment. In order to do so, the worker must satisfy two requirements: filing a criminal complaint against the spouse and depart the family home at the time of transfer. When that happens, the employer must, by default, accept the transfer. He/she can only postpone the transfer on the basis of

[185] See Pedro Madeira de Brito *Código do Trabalho Anotado*, cit., notes on articles 194.th – 196.th, pp. 504 et seq.

overriding requirements relating to the company or service, or until there is an available workstation. In this case, the employee is entitled to suspend the contract immediately until the transfer is finalized. The change of workplace based on a case of domestic violence should be confidential – unless the employee authorizes, the employer cannot disclose information regarding the new workplace to where the employee was transfered to (195.th, n.[er] 4).

9.4. Work time

I. The topic of work time and the establishment of working hour limits is part of the Employment Law History and evolution[186].

Since its inception, the imposition of thresholds to the working hours was a major concern and a fundamental issue under Employment Law, in order to guarantee a conciliation between family and professional life and to provide periods of r est to the employee.

The definition of working time and periods of rest is a matter of dignity at work and citizenship. The inexistence of limits on working time could lead us towards a sort of slavery or to the destruction of the employee's private life. Nowadays, time is one of the most priceless values of our society[187].

That is the reason why we find in several international treaties and fundamental laws numerous provisions regarding the working day and the fundamental right to rest. For example: the ILO's Convention n.[er] 1 (1919) regulates "Hours of Working", stating that the working hours of persons employed in any public or private industrial undertaking or in any branch thereof, other than an undertaking in which only members of the same family are employed, shall not exceed eight hours in a day and forty-eight hours in the week[188].

This is also prescribed by the Portuguese Constitution – article 59.th, n.[er] 1, subparagraph d), states that regardless of age, sex, race, citizenship, place of origin, religion, political and ideological convictions, every worker has the

[186] See Menezes Cordeiro, *Direito do Trabalho*, II, cit., pp. 499 et seq

[187] See João Leal Amado, *Contrato de Trabalho*, cit., pp. 259 et seq.

[188] See ILO's Convention n.[er] 1 at https://www.ilo.org/dyn/normlex/en/f?p=NORMLEXPUB:12100:0::NO::P12100_ILO_CODE:C001

right to rest and to leisure time, a maximum limit on a working day, a weekly rest period and periodic paid holidays[189].

The Portuguese Labour Code goes further on this, creating a legal framework based on the concepts of work time, normal period of time, period of operation and work schedule. The Code also contains rules regarding the working day limits, as well as rules concerning some type of flexible working time, such as adaptability, a bank of hours, concentrated schedule, exemption from work schedule or overtime work.

Let's analyse these closely.

II. Starting with the basic concepts, we have to highlight the concepts of work time, the normal period of time, the period of operation and the work schedule.

The *work time* is the time during which the employee performs his/her activity or is available to work altogether with some interruptions or small breaks (197.th, n.er 1,). Under the law, work time is the period during which the employee is effectively working, comprising some periods of inactivity (interruptions or small breaks) for justifiable reasons. These interruptions which count as work time are all those referred to in article 197.th,, n.er 2, of the Portuguese Labour Code, namely breaks taken by the employee to go to the restroom, breaks for technical or cleaning reasons, for meals, etc[190].

The second basic concept is the concept of a normal period of work.

The *normal period of work* is the length of time during which the employee undertakes to perform his/her activity under the authority of the employer. It is a quantifiable concept, measured in numbers of hours, per day and week (198.th). Under Portuguese Law, there is a maximum threshold of 8 hours a day and 40 hours a week (203.rd), which means that as a general principle the employee cannot work more than that. Additionally, the employee shall not work more than 5 consecutive hours a day and is entitled to have a daily break between 1h to 2h (213.rd) during his/her working day.

The third basic concept is the concept of period of operation.

[189] See Jorge Miranda/Rui Medeiros, *Constituição Portuguesa Anotada*, ci., notes on article 59th of the Portuguese Constitution.

[190] See Luís Miguel Monteiro *Código do Trabalho Anotado*, cit., notes on article 197.th, pp. 519 et seq.

The *period of operation* is the daily period during which the corporations may operate. It can be the "shop business hours" if it concerns the opening and closing hours of a shop, or the "industry hours" if it refers to the period of operation of a factory or plant (201st). Finally, we have the concept of work schedule.

The *work schedule* often called in the Anglo-Saxon countries as a "Rota", is the distribution of the working hours during the day, by respecting the limit of hours of the normal period of work, the requirement of a daily break and the period of operation of the corporation, respectively. Basically, the work schedule indicates the time when the employee must show up to start working, the time he/she leaves, and the daily breaks he/she may take, namely for lunch.

That means that while under a work schedule, the employer must respect the limit of 8h of work per day, the period of operation of the corporation and the need to provide the employee a break for lunch. For instance: if we consider a factory with a period of operation from 7 a.m. to 10 p.m., the employer can create a schedule under which a specific employee works from 9 a.m. to 1 p.m. (4 hours), can benefit from one hour lunch (from 1 p.m. to 2 p.m.) and resumes work again from 2 p.m. to 6 p.m (4 hours). By defining the schedule this way, the employer is simultaneously respecting the limit of 8 hours of the normal period of work (198.th,), the corporation's period of operation (201.st) and the employee's daily break between 1h to 2h (213.rd).

Under the Portuguese Labour Code, the definition of a work schedule is an exclusive competence of the employer (212.nd) and during the process of creating a work schedule, the employer shall balance the needs of the corporation and the needs of the stakeholders, such as employees and customers. The employer shall, for instance, take into account the needs of safety and health conditions at the workplace, as well as to create conditions so the employee can conciliate his professional life with his family life and can also attend educational training or courses (212.nd, n.er 2). Before organizing and setting the schedule, the employer shall consult the employees working committee or, in case this council doesn't exist, the trade union representatives existing at the firm. They have a say regarding scheduling but their opinion is not binding for the employer (212.nd, n.er 3). The scheduling, as referred, is an exclusive competence of the employer.

All the same, under article 217. th, n. er 1, of the Labour Code, the change of the work schedule is up to the employer and it's his/her own competence unless the employer has individually agreed on a specific schedule with the employee. In this case, since the schedule was individually agreed with the employee, a change requires another agreement and the authorization of the worker (217.th, n.er 4). Nevertheless, as a principle, the employer may unilaterally change the work schedule, since it is not a substantive change. For example: it is not permitted to the employer to unilaterally change a day's working schedule to a night working schedule, since the change is substantial and could create serious harm to the employee. But he/she can change a work schedule that starts at 9 a.m and runs until 6 p.m. to another that starts at 8 a.m. and ends up at 5 p.m.

The law also states that if the change of the schedule causes damage or additional expenses to the employee, the employer must compensate him/her in that same amount (217.th, n.er 5)[191].

III. At the inception of the employment market, everyone used to work together, confined to the same workplace under a rigid work schedule. That was what was commonly referred to as the Taylorism model.

With the dislocation of corporations, the creation of new areas of activity, the use of Technologies of Information and Communication and the globalization, the employment market developed and changed, and the employers required more flexibility namely regarding the management of the work time.

The demand was simple: the employers wanted new tools to attach the work schedules with the need of the consumers, the suppliers and the market as a whole. For instance: in some seasons, when the demands of the consumers are higher, the employees must work more; in others, there´s no need of such increased hours of work time, and so they can work less.

With that in mind, the legislator drafted, especially since early 21st century, several types of flexible models. We are here referring to flexible models of work time comprised in the Portuguese Labour Code: are the adaptability, the bank of hours, the concentrated schedule and exemption of work schedule.

[191] See Luís Miguel Monteiro *Código do Trabalho Anotado*, cit., notes on articles 212nd – 217th, pp. 560 et seq.

Let's take a glance at them.

The *adaptability* is expressed under articles 204.th to 207.th of the Labour Code[192].

Under the adaptability regime, the normal period of work may be set in average terms, within a period of reference. That means that during some days and weeks the employee works more and in other days and weeks he/she works less. At the end of the reference period, the average must correspond to 8 hours a day and 40 hours a week. The reference period is stated in article 207.th, as follows: it has a maximum limit of 12 months and it must be set by an instrument of collective labour regulation (ICLR). If it is not set under an ICLR, the law states that the reference period, by default, corresponds to 4 months. At the end of that period the employee should have worked an average of 8 hours a day and 40 hours a week. During some weeks and months, he/she may work more since in the following ones he/she is to work less.

Under the law, the adaptability model can be defined by collective agreement or by an individual agreement[193].

Under the *adaptability by collective agreement* (204.th), the daily limit of working hours can go up to 12 hours with the weekly maximum limit of 60 hours. This means that in some days the employee can work 12 hours and in some weeks 60 hours as long as the employer compensates him/her with less work in other days or weeks (for instance, 4h a day and 20 hours a week). At the end of the reference period, the number of hours worked by the employee on average must correspond to 8 hours a day and 40 hours a week.

Under the *adaptability by individual agreement,* which must be in written form, the employee can work up to 10 hours a day and 50 hours a week (205.th). The system is similar to the *adaptability by collective agreement,* but with less increased hours. Nevertheless, if an employee works 10h a day and 50 hours a week during a certain week or month, the employer must compensate him/her with less work in the subsequent days or weeks. For example: he/she may work 10h a day and 50 hours at a specific week, and 6 hours a day and 30 weekly hours at the following week. What matters is

[192] See Luís Miguel Monteiro *Código do Trabalho Anotado,* cit., notes on articles 204th – 206.th, pp. 532 et seq.

[193] See Pedro Romano Martinez, *Direito do Trabalho,* cit., pp. 539 et seq..

that at the end of the reference period the average of hours corresponds to 8h a day and 40 hours a week.

Finally, we have the *group adaptability* (206.th). It is a model created by the legislator to complement and extend the adaptability by collective agreement or the adaptability by individual agreement in case they are not applicable to the generality of employees. It means that if the adaptability by collective agreement applies to at least 60% of the employees, then the employer can extend that regime to other employees, even if they are not organized in unions. It would be, in that case, an exception to the principle of affiliation (article 496.th). Also, if the employer reaches a number of individual agreements applied to at least 75% of the employees, then he/she can extend the effects of the individual adaptability to the remaining workers, even without their agreement. To sum up, group adaptability is a mechanism created by the legislator to extend the effects of the adaptability and to create an harmonized regime in the same corporation, even when the collective or the individual agreement does not cover all the workers.

The *bank of hou*rs is also a mechanism to measure the normal period of work on average terms within a certain period of reference. The difference is based on the fact that, in this case, the employer can compensate the employee for the extra time of work whether by reducing the number of working hours (like in the adaptability) or by paying an extra salary or giving him/her more holidays. The bank of hours can be defined by collective agreement (208.th), or by the law (208.th-B). Under the bank of hours established by collective agreement, the normal working hours may be set in average terms and the daily limit can go up to 12 hours and the weekly limit corresponds to 60 hours (208.th). Just like we saw with group adaptability, the legislator also accepts group bank of hours (208.th – B), using the same requirements expressed in article 206.th above referred to the group adaptability, as follows: if the bank of hours by collective agreement bounds at least 60% of the employees then the employer can extend that regime to the other employees, even if they are not organized in unions; the employer may also organize and submmit the bank of hours to a referendum that must be approved by at least 65% of the employees.[194].

[194] See Luís Miguel Monteiro *Código do Trabalho Anotado*, cit., notes on articles 208th – 208.th-A, pp. 546 et seq. Until the approval of the Law n.º 63/2019, September 4th, there was also the "individual bank of hours". This regime was revoked by the referred Law n.º 63/2019.

The *concentrated work schedule* is enshrined in article 209.th of the Labour Code. Under this regime, the work schedule can be concentrated by letting the employee work more 4h a day than usual, up till the limit of 12 hours a day, so he/she can concentrate the schedule during 3 or 4 days a week, depending on the way in which their agreement was reached. The agreement can be set by collective agreement or by individual agreement between the employer and the employee. If the concentrated work schedule is agreed individually, then the work can be concentrated within 4 days a week; if it comes from a collective agreement, then it can be concentrated in 3 days a week[195].

The idea is simple: to work more in two or three days of the week and therefore not to work during one or two working days of the same week. For example, the employee may work more from Monday to Wednesday and therefore be released from work on Thursday and Friday. It's only a question of concentrating the work schedule in fewer days than usual. The law also states that one cannot simultaneously use the adaptability regime and the concentrated work schedule (209.th, n.er 2).

In the regimes of adaptability, bank of hours and concentrated work schedule, the employer does not have to pay an additional salary to the employee unless he/she chooses to do it under the bank of hours to compensate the extra number of hours made by the employee. The basic idea is that the employer doesn't have to pay more than usual, since at the end of the reference period the employee works on average 8 hours a day and 40 hours a week.

Finally, the Labour Code contains the *exemption of work schedule* (articles 218.th and 219.th)[196].

This regime cannot be used by all the employees. Under article 218.th, which contains the conditions for the application of the exemption from working schedule, this model of work time depends on the signature of a written agreement drafted by the employer and the employee in one of the following situations:

[195] See Luís Miguel Monteiro *Código do Trabalho Anotado,* cit., notes on article 209th, pp. 553 et seq.

[196] See Pedro Romano Martinez, *Direito do Trabalho,* cit., pp. 548 et seq.

a) The exercise of administration or direction functions, or functions of trust, supervision or support, to the holder of these positions;
b) Carrying out preparatory or supplementary work which, by nature, can only be carried out outside the limit of working hours;
c) Telework and other cases of regular exercise of activity outside the establishment without immediate control by a hierarchical superior.

The Instrument of collective labour regulation may provide for other situations of admissibility of exemption from working hours.

Regarding the type and effects of the exemption of a working schedule model, article 219.th of the Labour Code states that the parties may agree on one of the following exemptions from working hours:

a) Non-compliance with the maximum limits of the normal period of work (total exemption), which means that the employee may work 9h, 10h, 11h, 12h or even 13h a day while respecting the daily period of rest of 11 consecutive hours between two working days (article 214.th);
b) The possibility of a certain increase of the normal period of work, per day or per week (partial exemption), which means that employer and employee may agree in setting for example that the employee may work 11h hours a day and no more than that;
c) Observation of the agreed normal working period, which means, in this case, the employee shall respect the limit of 8h a day and 40 hours a week, without having a rigid work schedule (flexible work schedule).

In the absence of specific stipulation by the parties, the law states that the provisions of subparagraph *a)* of article 219.th (total exemption) shall apply, as the default model[197].

The law also clarifies that the exemption from working is not detrimental to the right for a weekly (mandatory or complementary) rest day, neither the right to holiday or to benefit from daily rest (article 219.th, n.er 3).

In case the employee works under the exemption from working hours, the employer shall, in this case, pay him a special subsidy, expressed in article 265.th of the Labour Code, as follows: if the employee works under one of the

[197] See Luís Miguel Monteiro *Código do Trabalho Anotado*, cit., notes on article 219th, pp. 576 et seq.

items *a)* (total exemption) or *b)* (partial exemption) of article 219. th, then the employer shall pay him a subsidy corresponding to an additional hour per day, which amounts to 5 extra hours per week; if he/she works under item *c)* (flexible work schedule) thus respecting the limits of 8h a day and 40 hours a week, he/she is entitled to receive a minor subsidy, corresponding only to two 2 extra hours per week.

9.5. Right to rest

I. Under the law, everyone has the right to rest and leisure, including the right to a reasonable limitation of working hours and periodic holidays with pay[198].

This entitlement is provided in the Universal Declaration of Human Rights (article 24.th) as well as in the European Union Charter of Fundamental Rights (article 31.st), under which every worker has the right to a limitation of the maximum working hours, to daily and weekly rest periods and to an annual period of paid leave.

The same idea is expressed in the Portuguese Constitution (article 59.th, n.er 1, subparagraph d)), that states that every worker has the right to rest and leisure time, a maximum limit on the working day, a weekly rest period and periodic paid holidays.

The periods of rest can be divided into daily, weekly and annual rest.

The Portuguese Labour Code comprises the right to rest and to leisure time and specifies its amount and ways of enjoyment.

II. Under article 213.rd of the Labour Code, every full-time employee who works 8 hours a day is entitled to a meal break after working 5 hours in a row. If the normal working period is more than 10h a day, then the break must start after 6 hours of consecutive work. The meal break has a minimum of 1 hour and a maximum of 2 hours.

Moreover, every employee is entitled to a minimum daily break of 11 hours between two working days (article 214.th). That means that if the employee leaves work at 7 p.m., for example, he/she cannot show up before

[198] See Menezes Cordeiro, *Direito do Trabalho II*, cit., pp. 568 et seq.

6.a.m of the following day. The law contains some exemptions to this rule, such as for directors and board member or whenever extra work is required in case of major force or to minimize the employer's losses (article 214.th, n.er 2). However, the general rule is that the employee is entitled to a minimum daily rest period of 11 hours between two working days[199].

The law also governs holidays.

On a first level, we have public holidays. Secondly, the law imposes paid holidays.

III. The mandatory public holidays are those listed in article 234.th of the Labour Code[200].

Under article 234.th, the legislator states the following public holidays: January 1; Holy Day (Easter Friday); Easter Sunday; April 25.th (Freedom Day); May 1.st (Workers Day); Body of God; June 10 (Day of Portugal); August 15.yh; October 5 (Day of the Republic); November 1.st, December 1 (Restoration or Independence Day); December 8.th; and December 25.th (Christmas Day). The Holy Friday holiday can be observed on another day with local significance in the Easter period[201].

In addition to mandatory holidays, the law also adds that by instruments of collective labour regulation or employment contract the days of Carnival Tuesday, and the municipal holiday, can also be qualified as public holidays. These are known as optional public holidays (article 235.th). The parties – employer and employee – may agree on replacing one of these optional public holidays for another holiday.

Finally, the law states that this regime is imperative – in the days considered as mandatory holidays, corporations must terminate or suspend the operation of all activities that are not allowed on Sundays and the legal regime cannot be displaced either by individual or collective agreement. Since public holidays regard the enjoyment of some cultural or historic

[199] See Luís Miguel Monteiro *Código do Trabalho Anotado*, cit., notes on articles 213.rd -214.th–, pp. 562 et seq.

[200] See Maria do Rosário Ramalho, *Tratado de Direito do Trabalho – Parte II*, cit., pp. 441 et seq.

[201] See Luís Menezes Leitão, *Direito do Trabalho*, cit., pp. 275.

event defined by the State, the instruments of collective regulation may not establish holidays other than those indicated in the law (article 236.th)[202].

Regarding the payment of these days, the law states that public holidays are paid. The worker is entitled to the daily salary corresponding to the holiday, without the employer being able to compensate that payment with supplementary work. The worker who provides normal work on a holiday in a company that is not obliged to suspend the operation on that day is entitled to compensatory rest for the duration of half the number of hours provided, or to an increase of 50% of the corresponding remuneration (article 269.th).

IV. The annual vacation days are governed by articles 237.th – 247.th of the Portuguese Labour Code[203].

Under the law, employees are entitled to a paid holiday period for each year of the calendar. The right vests on January 1.st of each year and refers to the work provided in the previous calendar year but is not conditional on attendance or service effectiveness. The right to holiday leave cannot be waived and its enjoyment cannot be replaced, even with the agreement of the worker, by any compensation, economic or otherwise. The right to paid vacation must be exercised in such a way so as to provide the employee's physical and mental recovery, personal availability, as well as his/her participation in family, social and cultural life (article 237.th).

The annual holiday period lasts for a minimum of 22 working days. For holiday purposes, one must consider the days of the week, from Monday to Friday, with the exception of public holidays (article 238.th).

Considering the referred provisions, we may conclude that a worker who was hired in 2017 is entitled to enjoy 22 days of paid vacation in 2018 for the work provided in 2017; and 22 days in 2019 for the work performed in 2018. In both cases, this right becomes due in January 1 of each of these years.

The law establishes two exemptions regarding the year of hiring and the year when the employment contract terminates.

Article 239.th states that at the year of hiring, the employee is only entitled to 2 vacation days for each month of the duration of the contract,

[202] See Luís Miguel Monteiro *Código do Trabalho Anotado*, cit., notes on article 236th, pp. 612 et seq.

[203] See Menezes Cordeiro, *Direito do Trabalho II*, cit., pp. 576 et seq.

up to 20 days. That means for example, that if one's hired at May 1.st and works 8 months, he/she will be entitled to 16 days of annual leave. In the year of admission, the enjoyment of the working days of leave may only take place after six full months of performance of the contract. As a consequence, considering the above exemple, the vacation entitlement would be due on November 1st [204].

When the employment contract terminates, the employee is entitled to receive the vested rights regarding holiday days and holidays subsidy. For example, if the contract terminates on March 31.st and if he/she didn't have time to enjoy the 22 vacation days he/she was entitled to since January 1.st for the work provided in the previous year, then the employer must pay him/her those days. This is the first rule, provided at article 245.th, n.er 1, sub-paragraph a). Secondly, the law also states that the employee has the right to receive the proportional of holidays regarding the work he/she performed at the year of the contract's termination. Considering the same example, that means that he/she would be entitled to receive as well 3/12 as holiday days and holiday subsidy based on the work performed in the year of termination (article 245.th, n.er 1, sub-paragraph b))[205].

The scheduling of vacation days is based on an agreement between the employer and the employee. Whenever they don't reach a settlement on the scheduling it's up to the employer to organize the vacation calendar. For this purpose, the employer must consult the Worker's Commission, and the holidays should take place between May 1 and October 31, unless the instrument of collective labour regulation disposes otherwise (241.st).

If the employer violates the employee's entitlement regarding the enjoyment of an annual vacation, then the employer should pay him/her a compensation equivalent to the amount of three times the remuneration of the period at stake, which must comprise the period before April 30.th of the following calendar year (article 246.th). This violation is considered a serious administrative offense.

During the vacation days, the employee should not perform any other paid professional activity, except when he or she already exercises it cumulatively

[204] See Luís Miguel Monteiro *Código do Trabalho Anotado,* cit., notes on article 239.th, pp. 618 et seq.

[205] See Luís Miguel Monteiro *Código do Trabalho Anotado,* cit., notes on article 245.th, pp. 629 et seq.

or whenever the employer authorizes it. In case of violation of this rule, the employee may be subject to disciplinary liability and the employer is entitled to recover the remuneration corresponding to the leave and the respective allowance, half of which will revert to the department responsible for the financial management of social security (article 247.th).

9.6. Retribution

I. Retribution is an essential element of the employment contract[206].

As analyzed, the employment contract is one in which a natural person undertakes, through retribution, to provide his or her activity to another or other persons, within the organization and under their authority. That is the definition stated in article 11.th of the Portuguese Labour Code. The retribution is therefore an essential ingredient of the employment contract as this contract is necessarily onerous. The legal regime of retribution is enshrined in articles 258.th et seq. of the Labour Code[207].

Article 258.th indicates the general principles on retribution. Under this provision, it is considered retribution the benefit to which the worker is entitled in exchange for his or her work. This rule also established that the retribution comprises the basic remuneration and other regular and periodic benefits made directly or indirectly, in cash or in kind[208].

The non-pecuniary retribution (in kind) must be based in commodities useful to the personal needs of the worker or his/her family (article 259.th). Additionally, the value of non-pecuniary remuneration benefits may not exceed the part of retribution in money, except as provided in a collective regulation instrument of work. So, under this provision, the employer cannot, for example, pay the employee through napkins or cotton. He must pay him/her at least half of his retribution in cash and the remaining part can be paid in kind since commodities or goods are useful to the personal needs of the worker or his/her family.

[206] See Pedro Romano Martinez, *Direito do Trabalho*, cit., pp. 577 et seq.

[207] See João Leal Amado, *Contrato de Trabalho*, cit., pp. 296 et seq

[208] See Joana Vasconcelos *Código do Trabalho Anotado*, cit., notes on article 258.th 260.th, pp. 645 et seq.

The law also describes what shall not be considered as retribution[209].

Under article 260.th, n.er 1, the following shall not be considered as a retribution:

(a) The sums received by the employee concerning daily of daily subsistence allowances, travel allowances, transport costs, installation allowances and other equivalent charges due to travel, new facilities or expenses incurred in the employer's service, except where such travel or these sums, in so far as they exceed their normal value, have been provided for in the contract or are an integral element of the employee's remuneration;
(b) Any special allowances or benefits granted by the employer as a reward for the good results obtained by the company;
(c) Benefits arising out of events related to the performance or merit, as well as the assiduity of the worker, whose payment, in the respective reference periods, was not guaranteed in advance;
(d) The profit-sharing of the undertaking, since the employee is entitled by contract to receive a certain variable or mixed remuneration, adequate to his/her job.

Number 2 of article 260.th also indicates that the provisions of subparagraph *a)* of number 1 shall also apply in the event of subsistence or meal allowances. That means that by default these allowances shall not be considered as retribution.

Nevertheless, number 3 of article 260.th expresses that the provisions of number 1, subparagraphs *b)* and *c)* shall neither be applied to bonuses due under the contract even if their attribution is conditioned to the good services of the worker, nor to those components that, because of their importance and regular character must be considered as element or integral part of his or her remuneration; or to benefits relating to the results obtained by the undertaking when they are regular and permanently stable, regardless of the amount. In these cases, the payments shall be considered as a retribution, despite the text of article 260.th, n.er 1.

[209] See Maria do Rosário Ramalho, *Tratado de Direito do Trabalho – Parte II,* cit., pp. 503 et seq.

II. The law also admits different kinds of retribution.

Under article 261.st [210], the retribution can be fixed, variable or mixed. A fixed retribution is the one that is equally paid at the end of each month and based on work time. For example, if an employee receives 2000€ per month, we have a fixed retribution. A variable retribution is the one that depends on some results or the achievement of some goals, such as bonus for sales. For example, if in a specific month the employee receives an extra amount of 1500€ based on a bonus sales of 1% and the sales he/she promoted, we have a variable retribution, since we don't know if he/she will receive it again in the following month or which amount will he/she receive it. A mixed retribution is one that combines the latter, partly fixed and partly variable (n.er 1). The remuneration calculated according to working time is fixed (n.er 2) and simple to determine. In order to determine the value of the variable remuneration, which can be different from month to month, the law states that we must consider the average of the amount of benefits corresponding to the last 12 months, or the duration of the contract if it lasted for less than 12 months (n.er 3). For example: an employer can pay to the employee a single salary, based on the performed working time. In that case the retribution is fixed. But he/she can add to that basic salary a variable retribution, based on the amount of sales made by the employee, if he/she is a seller. In the last case the retribution will be mixed, based on a certain and a variable part. If the retribution contains a variable part and if we need to determine its amount without having a specific criterion for doing it, the law says we must calculate the average of the amounts received by the employee during the last 12 months or the duration of the contract if it is inferior to that. For instance, if the employee is hired on January 1st and if in the beginning of the holiday period (in August, for example) we need to calculate the value of the variable retribution to pay him the leave retribution, we have to find the average of the amounts paid during the last 7 months.

The calculation of supplementary benefits is also regulated by law.

Under article 262.nd of the Labour Code, where a legal or contractual provision does not provide otherwise, the basis for calculating the supplementary or ancillary benefits is constituted by the basic remuneration and the seniority payments. The legislator defines basic remuneration as the

[210] See Joana Vasconcelos *Código do Trabalho Anotado*, cit., notes on article 261.st, pp. 654 et seq.

benefit corresponding to the activity of the worker in the normal period of work; and seniority payment as the benefit of a salary to which the employee is entitled based on seniority. Therefore, the general rule states that only the basic retribution and the seniority payments are relevant for the calculation of supplementary benefits[211].

For example: article 263.rd states that the employee is entitled to a Christmas bonus of one month which must be paid by December 15 of each year. If the contract or the Instrument of Labour Regulation does not provide otherwise, we must apply the rule of article 262.nd: even if the employee receives several payments as a retribution (basic salary, seniority payments, productivity allowances, bonus for sales, other fringe benefits as the use of a vehicle, etc), only the basic salary and the seniority payments will be taken in account to calculate the amount of the Christmas bonus.

III. Regarding the form of payment, article 276.th provides that the pecuniary part of the remuneration may be paid by check, money order or deposit in the worker's bank account, and the employer must pay expenses incurred with the conversion of the credit claim into cash or withdrawal of retribution. The remuneration credit is due for certain and equal periods unless otherwise stipulated or used – weekly, every fortnight and/or the calendar month. About the place of fulfillment, the payment of the remuneration must occur in the workplace as a general rule (article 277.th, n.[er] 1). Payment can be made in another place previously agreed, or by check, postal order or deposit to the worker's order (articles 277.th, n.[er] 1, and 268.th, n.[er] 2, LC). Remuneration shall be paid on a working day, during the working period or immediately thereafter. In case of variable remuneration with a calculation period exceeding 15 days, the employee may demand payment in fortnightly installments. The amount of remuneration must be made available to the employee on the due date or on the previous business day (article 278.th)[212].

[211] See JOANA VASCONCELOS *Código do Trabalho Anotado*, cit., notes on article 262.nd, pp. 656 et seq.

[212] See JOANA VASCONCELOS *Código do Trabalho Anotado*, cit., notes on article 278.th, pp. 676 et seq.

IV. Following article 59.th of the Portuguese Constitution, the Labour Code also states the need for a minimum monthly retribution.

For that purpose, article 273.rd states that workers are guaranteed a minimum monthly remuneration, regardless of the practiced modality, whose value is determined annually by the Government through specific legislation, after consulting the Permanent Committee on Social Concertation. In determining the minimum guaranteed monthly remuneration, the workers needs, the increase of the cost of living and the evolution of productivity, among other facts, shall be considered, in order to be adequate to the criteria of income and price policy[213].

V. Because of its importance for the employee and his or her family, the retribution is also protected against unilateral reductions made by the employer.

Actually, under article 129.th of the Labour Code, the retribution and its stability are a guarantee of the employee, through the principle of the impossibility of wage reduction. Thus, the employer cannot make any unilateral reduction in the remuneration, except in cases legally established by law or Instruments of Collective Labour Regulation (article 129.th, n.^{er} 1 subparagraph *d)*). Generally speaking, the only cases provided by law in which a wage retribution is allowed to be reduced are the following: *a)* when the employee returns to the primitive activity, in the event of exercise of other functions under the *ius variandi* (120.th); *b)* when he/she returns to his/her primitive functions after the termination of the commission of services employment contract (article 164.th, n.^{er} 1, subparagraph *a)*); *c)* when the employee is placed in a lower category, with the agreement and the authorization of Labour Conditions Authority (article 119.th).

9.7. Powers of the Employer

I. In order to manage his/her corporation, the employer possesses several powers that are part of the freedom of management[214]. Generally speaking,

[213] See Pedro Romano Martinez, *Direito do Trabalho*, cit., pp. 608 et seq.

[214] See João Leal Amado, *Contrato de Trabalho*, cit., pp. 210 et seq

we have the power of direction, the regulatory power and the disciplinary power[215].

The Labour Code legalizes and regulates all of them[216].

II. Article 97.th regulates the power of direction, stating that it is for the employer to establish the terms under which the work is to be performed, within the limits of the contract and the rules that govern it. Basically, it is the power of direction that allows the employer to determine the place, the schedule and the way the employee shall provide his/her activity. The power of direction gives the employer the chance to instruct the employee about the manner he/she should work as well as to give him/her specific orders for doing it, within the limits of the contract and the law. When exercised, the power of direction is the basis of the duty of obedience of the employee, who has to obey the orders given by the employer or its representatives (article 128.th, n.er 1, subparagraph *e)*). The duty of obedience means that the employee shall comply with the orders and instructions given by the employer regarding the execution of the contract or safety and health conditions at work, whenever they are not contrary to his/her rights or guarantees. The duty of obedience respects either the employer's instructions or instructions given to him/her by the hierarchical superior of the worker, within the powers that were assigned to him/her (article 128.th, n.er 2)[217].

III. Article 98.th contains the rule on disciplinary power, stating that the employer has disciplinary power over the employee at his/her service, while the employment contract is in force. This means that if the employee disobeys the employer's orders or has been accused of professional misconduct basd on a legal or contractual violation the employer can impose on him/her a penalty under the exercise of a disciplinary proceeding. The law also indicates the type of penalties that may be imposed by the employer[218].

[215] See Luís Menezes Leitão, *Direito do Trabalho,* cit., pp. 313 et seq.

[216] See Maria do Rosário Ramalho, *Tratado de Direito do Trabalho – Parte II,* cit., pp. 549 et seq.

[217] See Pedro Madeira de Brito, *Código do Trabalho Anotado,* cit., notes on article 97.th, pp. 286 et seq.

[218] See Pedro Madeira de Brito, *Código do Trabalho Anotado,* cit., notes on article 98.th, pp. 287 et seq.

Under article 328.th of the Labour Code, in the exercise of disciplinary power, the employer may apply the following sanctions:

a) Reprehension;
b) Recorded reprehension;
c) Penalty payment;
d) Loss of holidays;
e) Suspension of work with loss of remuneration and seniority;
f) Dismissal without compensation.

The instrument of collective labour regulation may list other disciplinary sanctions, provided that they do not affect the rights and guarantees of the worker.

Basically speaking, the reprehension means that the employer explains the worker that his or her behavior represents a violation of a duty, and that if it is to be repeated he/she may face more serious consequences. The recorded reprehension is the one that is recorded in the disciplinary books of the employee, highlighting the violation of the employment relationship. The penalty payment consists of a pecuniary amount awarded as a consequence of the infraction that is discounted in the employee´s remuneration. The employer can also apply as a penalty the loss of holidays. In this case, the application of this penalty cannot harm more than 20 useful days of holiday. The suspension of work with loss of remuneration and seniority constitutes a particularly serious sanction affecting the rights of the worker to effective occupation, remuneration and seniority. All these penalties are usually titled as conservative penalties, since by using them the employer doesn´t terminate the employment contract. Otherwise, the dismissal without compensation is a termination penalty as it ceases the employment relationship, by terminating the contract with just cause. This is the most serious and harmful penalty and as a consequence must be articulated with article 351.st of the Labour Code, that contains the concept of just cause, and the subsequent article 352.nd and others, which regulate a specific disciplinary procedure for the dismissal of the employee with just cause.

The exercise of the disciplinary power depends on the implementation of a specific procedure – the so called "disciplinary procedure", whose regime is expressed at the Labour Code.

Under article 329.th, the right to exercise disciplinary power shall lapse one year after the commitment of the offense, or within the limitation period under criminal law if it is also a criminal offense. Disciplinary proceedings must begin within 60 days after the date in which the employer, or the hierarchical superior with disciplinary jurisdiction, become aware of the offense. The disciplinary procedure shall expire one year after the date of the misconduct if within that timeframe the worker is not notified of the final decision. Once the disciplinary procedure has begun, the employer may suspend the employee if the employee's presence is inconvenient, while maintaining the payment of the salary.

The exercise of the disciplinary power shall also respect a principle of proportionality when deciding which penalty will be applied against the employee.

On this topic, article 330.th states that the disciplinary sanction must be proportionate to the seriousness of the offense and guilt of the offender, and the employer can not apply more than one by the same infringement.

The application of the penalty shall take place within three months. The employer shall deliver to the department responsible for financial management of the social security the amount of the penalty payment applied.

Finally, article 331.st, n.^{er} 1, foresees the abusive application of penalties, expressing that the disciplinary sanction is considered abusive if the worker:

a) Legitimately claimed bad working conditions;
b) Refuses to comply with an order to which he/she must not obey, in accordance with article 128.th, n.^{ers} 1 and 2;
c) Applies for the exercise of functions in a collective representation of workers;
d) Exercised, has exercised or intends to exercise or invoke his/her rights or warranties.

The dismissal or other sanction applied is presumed abusive under article 331.st, n.^{er} 2, when it takes place:

a) Up to six months after any of the facts mentioned above;
b) Up to one year after the denunciation or other form of exercise of rights of equality, non-discrimination and harassment.

The employer who imposes an abusive sanction must compensate the employee in general terms (article 331.st, n.er 3). In case of dismissal, the employee has the right to choose between the reintegration and compensation calculated in accordance with article 392.nd, n.er 3. In the case of a financial penalty or suspension of work, compensation shall not be less than 10 times the amount of the remuneration lost (article 331.st, n.er 5). The employer who imposes an abusive sanction in the case provided for in article 331.st, n.er 1, shall compensate the worker in the following terms:

a) The minimum amounts referred to in the preceding paragraph will be doubled;
b) In the event of dismissal, the compensation shall not be less than the value of the basic remuneration and seniority payments corresponding to 12 months (article 331.st, n.er 6)[219].

IV. Finally, the regulatory power is expressed in article 99.th of the Labour Code. It means that the employer may draw up internal rules of organization and discipline of work. In drafting the internal rules to be applied in a specific undertaking, the employer shall consult the Worker's Commission, or, failing this due to the fact that there's no commission in that corporation, the employer shall consult the inter-union commissions, the union commissions or the trade union delegates.

The rules of procedure shall take effect after the publication of the respective content, by posting at the registered office of the workplaces, so as to enable them to be fully known by the workers.

The elaboration of internal rules may be taken as mandatory by a regulatory instrument of collective labour regulation[220].

[219] See Pedro Madeira de Brito, *Código do Trabalho Anotado*, cit., notes on article 98.th, pp. 287 et seq.
[220] See Pedro Madeira de Brito, *Código do Trabalho Anotado*, cit., notes on article 99.th, pp. 289 et seq.

10.
Special contents

10.1. Limitations on the freedom to non-compete agreement, pacts of permanence and exclusivity

I. Under the principle of private autonomy, employer and employee may stipulate special clauses regarding specific aspects of the employment contract. Among these specific issues, those related to the freedom of work can be subject to special clauses or pacts. It is the case of the non-compete agreement (article 136.th), the permanence pact of (article 137.th), and the pact of exclusivity.

These pacts, as we will explain further on, are exceptions to a broader principle expressed in the Portuguese Constitution: the principle of the freedom to work (article 47.th)[221].

II. Under article 47.th of the Portuguese Constitution, everyone has the right to choose a profession or a type of work, freely and every citizen has the right to access to public service, under equal conditions, through a competitive selection process. The Fundamental Law retrieves the freedom to work from the wider category of citizen's liberties – the constitutional principle of freedom to work.

Under this principle, a person is free to work for anyone, cannot be forced to work for someone (article 47.th of the Constitution), and cannot be discriminated in access to employment (articles 13.th and 59.th of the

[221] See PEDRO ROMANO MARTINEZ, *Direito do Trabalho*, pp. 651 et seq.

Constitution). When someone is not bound by an employment contract or is unemployed, he/she is totally free to choose his/her employment.

This freedom suffers restrictions when someone enters into an employment contract.

III. After the conclusion of an employment contract, the freedom to work is narrower as the employee has a duty of loyalty to the employer.

Under article 128.th, n.^{er} 1, subparagraph *f)*, during the execution of the employment contract the employee shall be loyal to the employer, particularly by not negotiating on his/her own account or in competition with the employer and should not disclose information regarding his/her organization, production methods or business secrets (article 128.th, n.^{er} 1, subparagraph *f)*). Therefore, during the execution of the employment contract, the employee's freedom of work is compressed in the name of the duty of loyalty and in the interests of the company. That is to say, during the execution of the contract the employee cannot work for another entity that competes with the employer, nor can he/she negotiate on his/her own or in competition with the employer. That doesn't mean that the employee is forbidden to work for another beneficiary or that he/she cannot develop another activity. He/she can still do it, since one can work simultaneously for several employers. Nevertheless, he/she cannot act in competition with his/her employer. In order to better understand the concept of competing activity, Portuguese jurisprudence of higher courts affirms that an activity that conflicts or competes with the employer's interests is one that can be harmful to him/her. The deviation does not even have to be effective, the potential for such in itself is sufficient.

IV. The breach of the duty of loyalty, within the scope of the prohibition of non-competition, does not require the effectiveness of losses to the employer, or the effective diversion of customers. A "potential deviation" is sufficient. For this reason, for example, the Portuguese Supreme Court decided that there was just cause for dismissal because of the breach of the prohibition of non-competition in a case in which "*the employee (...) became a member of a commercial company with a corporate purpose similar to that of the employer*"[222].

[222] See court decision issued at September 9, 2015, by the Portuguese Supreme Court, available at www.dgsi.pt.

In short, in order to violate the duty of loyalty it is not necessary to prove an effective competition with effective losses to the employer. It is enough to have create a situation of danger by simply allowing the occurrence of a customer deviation. It is not necessary to materialize into a real damage.

With the termination of the employment contract, the duty of loyalty, as well as all the other duties expressed in article 128.th, also cease. They no longer produce any effects due to the termination of the contract. Therefore, the employee's freedom to work reappears.

V. After the termination of the employment contract, the employee is free, in business terms, to work to whoever he/she wants and whichever way he/she wants. He/she may start a new activity, even a competing one to his/her former employer or initiate a new employment relation with his/her competitor. The employee may also use the experience, knowledge and skills acquired during the performance of the employment contract. This position is strongly supported by the Portuguese legal doctrine since the 50's of last century. For example, according to the prominent author, RAÚL VENTURA, it would not make sense to impose on the employee a duty "*not to use the acquired technique to the service of any company, since the professional preparation of the worker constitutes the basis of his life, which cannot be withdrawn for any purpose*"[223]. In that sense, if no non-compete pact has been concluded, the employee's freedom to work tends to be in its fullest expression, and he/she may take advantage of the entrepreneurial know-how he/she acquired at the service of his/her past employer. He/she can use the knowledge of specific markets and even the portfolio of contacts and clients he/she acceded during his/her stay in the previous company. This, moreover, has also been the understanding endorsed by Portuguese higher courts, which have argued that "*After the termination of the employment relationship, the freedom of employment and work of the employee are restored and he's totally free to engage in any activity, even if it competes with the former employer*"[224].

[223] See RAÚL VENTURA, "Extinção das relações jurídicas de trabalho", at *Review of the Portuguese Bar Association*, 1950, n.er 1 e 2, p. 358.

[224] See decision n.er 256/2004 of the Court Appeals of Oporto, December 16, 2015, disposable at www.dgsi.pt. The Court also stated that although the reborn of the freedom to work, "II – *The freedom of competition reacquired by the employee with the termination of the employment relationship, if not restricted by the non-compete pact, is even though subject to certain limits. (...) we have*

The only way restrictions to this freedom may be imposed is through the signature of a non-compete pact or agreement.

10.1.1. Non-compete agreement

I. Article 136.th, n.er 2, of the Labour Code, admits under some conditions the validity of an agreement that limits the activity of the worker after the termination of the employment contract. It is the case of the non-compete clauses or pacts.

Under the above referred article 136.th, n.er 2, it is the limitation of the activity of the employee is lawful during the maximum period of two years after the termination of the employment contract, under the following conditions: a) Is embodied in a written agreement,, namely in an employment contract or in a revocation agreement; b) If it is an activity whose exercise may cause harm to the employer; c) If there is of a compensation to the employee during the period of limitation of the activity, which can be reduced when the employer has incurred substantial expenditure on his/her professional training[225].

The non-competition pact is, therefore, an agreement to limit the freedom of post-employment, which is based on the freedom of negotiation of both parties: the employer and the employee. It is a legal and authorized limitation that can have a broader or more stringent object – the pact can either inhibit the exercise of a certain activity, either as a dependent or an independent employee, or ban a particular provision of goods or services to certain competitors.

II. Because it contains a compression of the liberty to work, the legal regime of the non-compete agreement was scrutinized by the Portuguese Constitutional Court, which looked into the constitutionality in order to assess whether it violated the referred article 47.th of the Constitution. The Court's decision n.er 256/2004, of April 14 th, 2004, stated that there was no unconstitutionality, based on two main reasons. The first, related to the need

the limits of unfair competition (articles 317.º, 318.º and 331.º of the Industrial Property Code), as well as breaches of secrets protected by criminal law (articles 195.º and 196.º of the Penal Code".

[225] See Joana Vasconcelos, *Código do Trabalho Anotado*, cit., notes on article 136.th, pp. 375 et seq.

to combine conflicting interests; the second, based on the free revocability by the employee of the non-compete agreement. To sustain the first reason and recalling the teachings of MONTEIRO FERNANDES[226], the Constitutional Court recalled the need to reconcile the interests at stake: on one hand, the interests of the employer, wishing to "*preventing a competitor to use information, knowledge or resources (such as the clientele) to which the worker had access because of the special position he/she had in the company from which he/she now departs* "; on the other, the interests of the employee to guarantee his/her freedom to work. For this last reason, the conclusion of the agreement is only allowed when the activity may cause harm to the employer, if the employee is economically compensated for the celebration of this agreement and if the limitation of the freedom to work is temporary. Secondly, the Court sustained the constitutionality of the legal regime based on the free revocability of the non-compete pact. For this purpose, the Court recalled author PEDRO ROMANO MARTINEZ, who argues that "*the pact of no competition, while limiting freedom to work, cannot be regarded as unconstitutional, because it restricts justifiably a freedom and, in addition, the limitation is not absolute, because, under article 81, n.er 2, of the Portuguese Civil Code, the employee may at any time disassociate from this agreement as long as he/she compensates the employer for the inherent losses*"[227].

In short, the Constitutional Court did not consider the non-compete agreement unconstitutional, since the compression of a constitutional freedom respects the principles of necessity and proportionality provided for in article 18.th of the Constitution.

The limitation can only be accepted under the above referred legally expressed conditions which can be grouped into a time frame, formal, substantive, patrimonial, and geographic requirements.

The time frame requirement determines that the limitation of worker activity shall not be longer than 2 years following the termination of the contract. In specific cases, when there is a special relationship of trust or when the employee had access to particularly sensitive information the limit can go up to 3 years (article 136.th, n.er 5). The formal requirement imposes a written form to the non-compete agreement, which can either integrate the initial clauses of the contract, be concluded during the course of the contract, or in the context of a termination agreement of the contract (article 136.th,

[226] See MONTEIRO FERNANDES, *Direito do Trabalho*, cit., pp. 610-613.

[227] See PEDRO ROMANO MARTINEZ, *Direito do Trabalho*, cit., p. 656.

n.^{er} 2, a)). The substantive requirement is the following: the agreement is only justified to limit an activity, after the termination of the employment contract when its exercise may cause prejudice to the employer, that is, when we are dealing with what the case-law has called "differential competition". Differential competition is a particularly dangerous competition for the employer due to the access the worker previously had to clients, suppliers, know-how and information related to the business model (article 136.th, n.^{er} 2, subparagraph *b*)). The patrimonial requirement prescribes that post-employment limitation is valid if it is paid to the employee, during the activity limitation period, a compensation that can be reduced when the employer has incurred in substantive training expenses that benefited the employee (article 136.th, n.^{er} 1, subparagraph *c*)). Finally, some authors sustained that the validity of the agreement depends on its geographical or spatial limitation, in close correspondence with the geographical area of the employer[228].

IV. In case of violation of the non-compete agreement, the employee must compensate the employer for damages he/she incurred. Basically, if the employee violates the agreement, he/she incurs in liability under article 758.th of the Portuguese Civil Code. Nevertheless, the validity of the new employment contract, even if concluded with a competitor of the former employer, and thus in violation of the non-compete agreement, is not questionable.

The new contract will remain valid.

10.1.2. Pact of Permanence

I. Under article 137.th, n.^{er} 1, of the Labour Code, parties may agree that the employee undertakes not to terminate the contract of employment for a period not exceeding three years as compensation for the employer's heavy expenses incurred with the employee's professional training. In sum, speaking, under this agreement, the employee renounces to terminate the contract under article 400.th of the Labour Code. He/she can still terminate the contract with just cause (article 394.th, n.^{er} 1) and the employer also

[228] See Joana Vasconcelos, comments to article 136.th of the Labor Code, at *Código do Trabalho Anotado*, cit., pp. 362 et seq.

terminate the contract with just cause under the legal requirements (article 351.st.), so long as the employee renounces to cease the contract without just cause[229].

Since it is a limitation to the freedom to work principle, the employee may release himself/herself from the fulfillment of the agreement. To quit from, the employee must pay back the above referred expenses made by the employer in his/her benefit.

II. The validity of the permanence pact depends on the existence of heavy expenses made by the employer in the employee's training. For example, if an employer pays a two years' Master Business Administration (MBA) to his/her employee to be attended abroad, paying the tuition fees and all the expenses related to the travel, there is a tremendous expense made by the employer in the training of his/her employee. It is reasonable, in such case, that the employer obtains the outcome of that investment at the end of the MBA. The key point is the type of investment made. Only exceptional expenses made by the employer justify the permanence pact. The regular training expenses legally binding under article 127.th, n. er 1, subparagraph *d),* and 130.th et seq., do not justify the celebration of a permanence pact. On the other hand, during the execution of the permanence pact the employee is free to revoke it under the freedom to work. In this case, under article 137.th, n.er 2, the employee is bound to pay the employer a compensation for the damages caused to the employer, by reimbursing the amount corresponding to the expenses incurred by the employer.

III. The permanence pact must be in written form. It can be included in the employment contract or at an autonomous agreement, during the execution of the contract. After the termination of the employment contract, the pact of permanence also[230].

[229] See Pedro Romano Martinez, *Direito do Trabalho*, cit., p. 656 et seq.

[230] See Joana Vasconcelos, comments to article 137.th of the Labor Code, at *Código do Trabalho Anotado*, cit., pp. 379 et seq.

10.1.3. Exclusivity pact

I. As a general rule and so long as the employee does not violate the duty of loyalty (article 128.th, n.er 1, subparagraph *f)*), the employee can have more than one job and can work for several employers under his/her freedom to work. "Multi-employment" is lawful. Its limitation derives from the referred duty of loyalty. Outside of the scope of that duty, the employee can work for more than one employer.

An exception is admitted if the employee agrees to conclude a pact of exclusivity with the employer.

II. The exclusivity pact is an agreement concluded between the employer and the employee by which the worker undertakes to work exclusively for his/her employer, renouncing to work for someone else during the execution of the employment contract[231].

The exclusivity pact is not addressed in the Labour Code, but the Portuguese legal doctrine admits its conclusion under the general principle of private autonomy. Moreover, this possibility is stated in specific legislation regarding employment contracts for workers in artistic performances (Law n.er 4/2008 of February 7.th).

As a matter of fact, article 11.th, n.er 5, of the referred Law n.er 4/2008, states that "*The parties may establish, in writing, that the employee carries out his artistic activity exclusively for the employer, by setting adequate compensation for the work on an exclusive basis*".

In a nutshell: the exclusivity pact is possible and legally valid, so long as there is an objective reason to sustain it.

Nevertheless, even bound an exclusivity pact, the employee is free to deliver notice of termination of the employment contract under general terms (article 400.th) and therefore to offer his/her activity to a new employer upon the termination of the previous employment contract.

[231] See PEDRO ROMANO MARTINEZ, *Direito do Trabalho*, cit., p. 658 et seq.

10.2. Non-permanent contracts

10.2.1. General *overview*

I. One of the main issues of modern employment law is the division between permanent and non-permanent jobs. Permanent jobs are those that are not limited regarding its duration. Non-permanent jobs are those the duration of which is limited. Usually, permanent jobs are open-ended employment contracts, and the non-permanent jobs are fixed and unfixed-term contracts, on one hand, and a temporary employment contract, on the other.

Traditionally, people used to work their whole life in the same corporation and be bound by the same employment contract, but this traditional work model is changing. The Taylorism model is outdated. The conclusion of open-ended employment contracts for life is almost in extinction, giving leeway to new types of non-permanent jobs and atypical employment contracts.

In the gig economy, workers will, likely, have many gigs over the course of their careers, which meaning they will have to be lifelong learners. Currently, almost 2 billion people are working in the informal sector, totally unprotected by stable wages, social safety nets, or the benefits of education and lifelong training. There are more and more cases of work on call, zero-hour contracts, self-employment, fake independent employment, volunteer work, work named collaborative/cooperative, and gig work, among other atypical contracts.

Gradually, through different management models, self-employment or independent work is increasing worldwide.

Agencies of temporary employment, outsourcing and digital platforms are some converging examples of this new paradigm, that can create new risks to workers.

In a context of high unemployment and a shortage of new job offers, the so-called digital platforms follow business models with maximum profit and minimum costs of massified labour relations. At the same time, awareness grows because the gains to the economy from this type of company seem to be worthless.

Even within the formal economy, the non-permanent jobs are gradually increasing by comparison with permanent jobs.

II. Despite some recovery in recent years, the Portuguese labour market continues to show high levels of segmentation, with the third highest: number of non-permanent contracts of the European Union, considering total employed population (around 22%) and the fourth highest among young people. The excessive incidence of precarious employment weakens stability and job security, the prospects of progression and earnings of workers, especially younger employees, and ultimately affects the competitiveness and productivity levels of each company, as well as the financial sustainability of the Social Security.

That is the reason why the Portuguese National Assembly recently approved a new legislation – Law n.º 93/2019, of September 4th, that amended the Portuguese Labour Code, aimed at promoting stability in work and tackling the precariousness at the labour market.

III. Under the Portuguese Constitution, the model employment contract is the open-ended employment contract. This is the rule that arises from the principle of job security enshrined in article 53.rd of the Fundamental Law[232].

As a consequence, the main model of employment contract is based on permanent jobs and stability at work. Usually, whenever an employee is hired, he/she begins to work under a permanent contract. Moreover, based on the job security principle, the employer cannot dismiss the employee without just cause. Dismissal without just cause is null and void and we do not apply in Portugal the "employment at will doctrine", under which both parties (including the employer) can quit from the employment contract for any reason and without the need for payment of any severance compensation.

This is the reason why non-permanent contracts, such as a term contract (fixed-term or unfixed term) and temporary contract are exceptions to the general rule. Consequently, they are only allowed in specific situations and limited by restrictive rules expressed in the Labour Code.

In sum, the term employment contract is the contract in which the parties stipulate a term and its duration is limited. Under a term contract, the contract terminates when the term is verfified, i.e., when a specific event previously announced occurs. This means that the contract terminates by expiration. If the term is linked to an event that will certainly occur in the future, such as

[232] See Jorge Miranda/Rui Medeiros, *Constituição Portuguesa Anotada*, cit., notes on article 53.rd of the Portuguese Constitution.

a specific date, the term is a fixed term. For instance, if I hire an employee on January 1.st stating that the contract will last until June 30.th, that means that we have a fixed term employment contract, since I know by advance that the contract will last for six months and will terminate by expiration at the end of June. If, contrarily, one says the contract is temporary because it will last for a limited period, but we don't know in advance the specific moment in which it terminates, then we have an unfixed-term contract. For example, if I hire an employee to replace a permanent worker who is sick and temporarily prevented from working, I may employ a replacement based on an unfixed-term contract grounded on a specific need for replacement. One knows the contract is limited in time since it will terminate with the reinstatement of the worker who is replaced, but no one knows how long it will last because no one knows in advance when will the permanent worker recover and resume work.

As we'll see further on, the Portuguese Labour Code (articles 139.th and seq.) governs the fixed and unfixed term employment contract by imposing specific requirements for its celebration and validity, such as the need for a specific motive, written form and limits regarding its duration[233].

IV. The temporary employment contract is different, because it involves three parties.

The temporary employment contract is the triangular employment relationship that involves a user-undertaking corporation, to whom the employee Is assigned to work during a temporary period of time; a temporary-work agency ("temp-agency"), that hires temporary work employees to assign them to undertaking-users; and a temporary work employee, who is hired by the temp-agency to be assigned to work temporarily under the supervision of the undertaking-user. In this case, we have three parties – the temp agency, the temporary worker, and the user undertaking – and two contracts – a temporary employment contract concluded between the temporary agency and the worker, and a provision of services contract celebrated between the temporary agency and the user undertaking, for whom and under the supervision and direction of whom a temporary employee works for a limited period of time.

[233] See Menezes Cordeiro, *Direito do Trabalho II*, cit., 609 et seq.

The Portuguese Labour Code (articles 172.nd and seq.) governs the temporary employment contract by imposing specific requirements for its celebration and validity, such as the need for a specific motive, written form and limits regarding its duration. Moreover, it also establishes a wide range of obligations for the activities of temporary agencies, in order to protect the term employees against default or insolvency of these agencies.

Let's analyze these two types of non-permanent employment contracts[234].

10.2.2. Term contract

I. Under the Portuguese Labour Code, the conclusion of a term contract depends on the fulfillment of three specific requirements: substantive requirements, regarding the motives that may be used to justify the conclusion of an employment term contract; formal requirements, related to the proper legal form; and temporary requirements, regarding its maximum duration[235].

In order to guarantee that the conclusion of these contracts is an exception to the open-ended contracts, the law establishes in article 139.th that the legal regime of the term contract is imperative and cannot be replaced by an instrument of collective labour regulation, except to further some motives regarding temporary needs of the employer for hiring term employees.[236] The core idea, as referred, is that by principle employment contracts are open-ended contracts. As a consequence, the use of non-permanent contracts, such as the fixed or unfixed term contract, is only allowed under restrictive rules[237].

II. The substantive requirement is very important. It is the requirement which establishes in which cases the fixed or unfixed term employment contracts are allowed. The underlying rule is: the conclusion of term

[234] See Pedro Romano Martinez, *Direito do Trabalho*, cit., pp.689 et seq.

[235] See Maria do Rosário Ramalho, *Tratado de Direito do Trabalho – Parte II,* cit., pp. 239 et seq.

[236] See João Leal Amado, *Contrato de Trabalho,* cit., pp. 89 et seq.

[237] See Luís Miguel Monteiro, comments to article 139.th of the Labor Code, at *Código do Trabalho Anotado,* cit., pp. 383 et seq.

contracts is only allowed if based in the events listed in the law – article 140.th of the Portuguese Labour Code. In light of this requirement, we will determine which situations legitimize the celebration of these contracts.

Generally speaking, we may have three groups of reasons that justify term contracts: motives regarding a corporation's temporary needs (article 140.th n.er 1 and 2); motives related to the need of reducing the business risk whenever a new company is set up (article 140.th n.er 4, sub-paragraph a)); and social motives regarding the very long unemployed people (article 140.th n.er 4, sub-paragraph b)).

The first group of cases is expressed in article 140.th n.er 1 and 2.

In light of said provisions, the fixed-term employment contract can only be concluded to satisfy temporary needs of the company and for the period necessary to satisfy this need (article 140.th n.er 1). To clarify which situations can be presented by the employer, number 2 of said provision sates that the following ate the temporary needs of the company:

a) Direct or indirect replacement of a worker who is absent or who is temporarily prevented from working for any reason;
b) Direct or indirect replacement of a worker whose dismissal is being assessed before the courts;
c) Direct or indirect replacement of a worker on leave without remuneration;
d) Replacement of a full-time worker who starts to work part-time for a specified period;
e) Seasonal or other activity the production cycle of wich presents irregularities due to the structural nature of the respective market, including the supply of raw materials;
f) Exceptional increase of the company's activity;
g) Execution of occasional tasks or determined service precisely defined and not lasting;
h) Execution of construction, project or other related temporary work including the execution, direction or supervision of construction works, public works, assemblies and industrial repairs, under contract or in direct administration, as well related projects and supervision activities.

Article 140.th n.er 3 states that while all the motives expressed in number 2 can justify a fixed term contract, only the ones that are expressed at subparagraphs a), b), c), e), f), g), and h) can ground the conclusion of an unfixed-term contract.

Moreover, beyond the motives expressed in number 1, a fixed term contract may also be celebrated for the launch of a new uncertain activity or at the beginning of a new establishment owned by a company with less than 250 workers, since the conclusion of the contract occurs at the maximum period of two years after each one of these events (article 140th, n.er 4, sub-paragraph a))[238. 239].

Finally, the term contract may also be concluded for hiring very long unemployed people (article 140th, n. 4, sub-paragraph a)).

III. Being a special content that differs from the open-ended contract, the fixed-term contract is subject to written form and must contain the following references (article 141.st)[240]:

a) Identification, signatures and domicile or headquarters of the parties;
b) Activity of the employee and corresponding remuneration;
c) Workplace and normal working hours;
d) Date of commencement;
e) Indication of the stipulated term and respective justification;
f) Dates of beginning of the contract and its termination.

In the absence of the reference required by subparagraph d) of the preceding paragraph, the contract shall be deemed to have commenced on the date of its conclusion. For the purposes of subparagraph e) of number 1, an indication of the motive justifying the term must be delivered expressly

[238] See Luís Miguel Monteiro, comments to article 140.th of the Labour Code, at *Código do Trabalho Anotado*, cit., pp. 385 et seq.

[239] Before the amendment of the Labour Code approved through Law n.º 93/2019, September 4.th, the term contract could also be concluded for other labor market reasons, namely to hire youngsters in their first employment or long term unemployed or in any other cases expressed in the employment legislation. That possibility was revoked by the referred Law, aimed at avoiding the conclusion of term contracts for permanent needs and thus reducing the precariousness of the employment contract.

[240] See Luís Miguel Monteiro, *Código do Trabalho Anotado*, cit., notes on article 141.st, pp. 394 et seq.

mentioning the facts that comprise it. The relationship between the justifications invoked and the stipulated term must be explained.

IV. The duration of the term contract depends on whether it is a fixed term contract or an unfixed-term contract, as well as on the grounds for conclusion.

Article 148.th states that the duration of the fixed-term contract shall not exceed 2 years (article 148.th, n.er 1) and the duration of an unfixed-term contract may not exceed 4 years (article 148.th, n.er 5). If the fixed term employment contract is based on the launching of a new uncertain activity or the beginning of a new establishment owned by a company with less than 250 workers (article 140.th, n.er 4), the contract cannot last more than two years from the inception of the motive that justifies its celebration (article 148.th, n.er 4).

On the other hand, the minimum threshold of duration is generally six months. A fixed-term employment contract may only be concluded for less than six months in a situation provided for in article 140.th, n.er 2 subparagraphs (a) to (g) and may not last less than the task or service to perform. In case of violation of this provision, the contract is considered to be concluded for a period of six months so long as it corresponds to the satisfaction of temporary needs of the company (148.th, n.er 2 and 3).

To assess the limit of two years of duration of the fixed-term contract one shall include the duration of fixed-term or temporary work contracts concluded between the employee and the same employer or companies which are in a control or group relationship or maintain common organizational structures, whose execution takes place within the same work post (article 148.th, n.er 6)[241].

V. By principle, the fixed-term contract may be renewed.

The parties may agree that the fixed-term employment contract is not subject to renewal (149th, n.er 1), but in the absence of that stipulation and of a declaration by any of the parties aimed at terminating the contract, the same will be renewed at the end of the term, for an equal period if no other is agreed by the parties (149th, n.er 2).For example, if I hire an employee for

[241] See Luís Miguel Monteiro, *Código do Trabalho Anotado*, cit., notes on article 148.th, pp. 408 et seq.

six months and if at the end of that period, neither the employer nor the employee declares his/her opposition to the renewal of the contract, the same will be renewed for more six months. Nevertheless, the renewal of the contract is subject to the confirmation of its admissibility and motives, in the terms foreseen for its conclusion, as well as to the same formal requirements in case of stipulating a different period (149.th, n.er 3). That means that if I hire someone, for example, to replace an employee who is under a parental leave, I cannot renew the fixed-term contract of his/her substitute if the employee that was using that leave resumes work, since in that case the motive ceases to exist. The law also establishes a maximum threshold for the renewals. Under the law, the fixed-term employment contract may be renewed up to three times and the total duration of renewals may not exceed that of the initial term of the contract (149.th, n.er 4).

VI. As already said, the legislator tries to avoid the generalization of the fixed-term contract, since the Portuguese Constitution gives prevalence to the open-ended employment contracts.

As a consequence, the Labour Code prohibits the succession of fixed-term employment contracts at the same work post.

Article 143.rd states that the termination of a fixed-term employment contract, for reasons not attributable to the employee, prevents re-admission or assignment of employees through a fixed-term contract, temporary work or provision of services contract if its execution takes place on the same job for the same purpose, concluded with the same employer or company which is in a control or group relationship, or maintains common organizational structures, before a period of time equivalent to one-third of the duration of the contract, including renovations.

This prohibition rule shall not apply in the following cases: a) new absence of the replaced worker, when the fixed-term contract has been concluded for his replacement; b) exceptional increase in the activity of the company after the termination of the contract; c) seasonal activity; d) a worker previously employed under such scheme is applying to be hired as a first time employee. The violation of these provisions constitutes a serious administrative offense[242].

[242] See Luís Miguel Monteiro, *Código do Trabalho Anotado*, cit., notes on article 143.st, pp. 396 et seq.

Also aiming at preventing the abusive use of term employment contracts, the lawmaker states that the employer must notify inspection authority of the Ministry of Employment, as well as the workers' committee and the trade union in which the worker is affiliated, about the conclusion of a fixed-term contract, stating the reasons for it, as well as the termination of the contract, within five working days (144.th, n.^{er} 1 and 2). Again, but in this case to prevent discriminatory practices, the employer must communicate, within five working days, to the administrative agency (CITE – Comissão Para a Igualdade no Trabalho e Emprego) with competence in the field of equal opportunities between men and women the reason for not renewing a fixed-term employment contract of a pregnant, puerperal or breastfeeding employee (144.th, n.^{er} 3).

Finally, regarding the duty of information, the law states that the employer must inform the employees regarding the existence of permanent jobs that are available in the company or establishment.

Also to promote the open-ended employment contract over the term contract, the Labour Code establishes that within 30 days after the termination of the term contract, the employee has, on equal terms, a preference for the conclusion of an open-ended contract, whenever the employer processes an external recruitment to perform the same functions for which the employee was hired. In the event of violation, the employer must compensate the employee in a value which corresponds to three months of basic pay (145.th).

VII. Bearing in mind that the conclusion of employment term contracts is only allowed through the fulfillment of strict requisites – substantive, formal, and temporal – the law establishes that in case of violation of those the term contract should be considered as an open-ended contract.

Article 147.th n.^{er} 1 states that the term employment contract shall be deemed to be an open-ended contract in the following cases:

a) When the stipulation of a term is intended to circumvent the provisions governing the term employment contract;
b) If the contract is concluded outside the cases provided for in article 140.th;
c) When the term contract is not in written form, or if it lacks the identification or signature of the parties, or of the dates of conclusion

of the contract and of commencement of work, as well as the date in which it is signed and the references to the term and justification;

d) If the term contract is concluded in violation of article 143.rd, regarding the prohibition of succession of term contracts.

The same provision (article 147.th n.[er] 2) also establishes that a term employment contract becomes an open-ended employment contract if:

a) The renewal of the term contract was made in violation of the provisions of article 149.th;
b) The period of duration or the number of renewals referred is exceeded;
c) As an unfixed term contract, the worker remains in activity after the expiry date indicated in the employer's notice or, failing that, 15 days after verification of the term.

In both situations (article 147.th n.[er] 1 and 2), the seniority of the worker shall be counted from the commencement of work, except in a situation which involves the violation of article 143.rd – in this case one shall include the time of work performed in pursuance of successive contracts[243].

VIII. The expiration of a fixed or an unfixed-term employment contract is not automatic.

Regarding the expiration of the fixed-term contract, article 344.th states that the term contract expires at the end of the stipulated period, or term of renewal, provided that the employer or the employee reports to the other party the wish to do so, in writing, respectively, 15 or 8 days before the deadline expires.

In the event of expiration of a fixed-term employment contract resulting from a declaration of the employer, or if parties stated in the contract that the same would not be renewed, the employee is entitled to compensation corresponding to 18 days of basic salary and seniority payment for each full year of seniority, calculated in accordance with the formula expressed at article 366. The only situation in which the employee is not entitled to a

[243] See Luís Miguel Monteiro, *Código do Trabalho Anotado*, cit., notes on article 147.th, pp. 404 et seq.

compensation is whenever the contract expires due to the employee's own initiative.

Considering the expiration of an unfixed-term contract, article 345.th states that the unfixed-term employment contract expires when, foreseen the occurrence of the term, the employer notifies the termination of the contract with a minimum previous notice of 7, 30 or 60 days, depending on whether the contract has lasted up to six months, to two years, or for a longer period.

In the situation provided for in article 140.th n.er 2, sub-paragraphs e) or h), which gives rise to the hiring of several workers, the communication made by the employer shall be made successively from the gradual decrease of their occupation, as a result of the normal activity, task or work for which they were hired.

In the absence of this communication the employer shall pay to the employee the amount of remuneration corresponding to the due period of prior notice.

In the event of expiration of an unfixed-term contract, the worker is entitled to compensation corresponding to the sum of the following amounts: a) 18 days of basic and daily remuneration for each full year for the first three years of the contract; b) 12 days of basic and daily remuneration for each full year after the previous three years of performance of the contract.

The compensation shall be set in accordance with the formula expressed in article 366.th.

10.2.3. Temporary contract

I. Temporary work is the triangular employment relationship that involves user-undertaking-corporations ("user-undertaking"), for which the employee will be assigned to work during a temporary period of time; a temporary-work agency ("temp-agency"), that hires temporary work employees to assign them to undertaking-users; and a temporary employee, which is hired by the temp-agency to be assigned to work temporarily under the supervision of the undertaking-user[244].

[244] See Menezes Cordeiro, *Direito do Trabalho II*, cit., pp. 669 et seq.

It is striking that in this setting the position of the employee is very weak: he/she works for an undertaking (the user-undertaking) wich is not his/her employer, and he/she concludes an employment contract with a corporation (the temp-agency) for whom he/she will not work. He/she works under the supervision of a corporation (user-undertaking) that did not hire him/her and is under the disciplinary power of a corporation (temp-agency) for whom he/she doesn't work ([245]). Moreover, the duration of the contract is limited and the law – as we will see further on – imposes less restrictions regarding the number of renewals than in the legal regime of the fixed-term employment contract.

In a nutshell, temporary work is one of the most precarious types of work admitted in our law.

For this reason, the Labour Code imposes some limits to the celebration of these contracts and establishes specific requirements for their validity, in order to avoid the use of the temporary employee as a commodity.

II. The Portuguese Labour Code (articles 172.nd et seq) describes three contracts that may be concluded under this relationship, as the following[246]:

a) Temporary employment contract is a fixed-term employment contract concluded between a temporary-work agency ("temp-agency") and a worker, whereby the latter undertakes, by way of remuneration, to provide employment to undertaking-users, while remaining bound to the temp agency;
b) Open-ended contract to temporary agencies means an open-ended employment contract concluded between a temp-agency and a worker, whereby the latter undertakes, by way of remuneration, to provide temporary employment to users, while remaining bound to the temp agency;
c) Contract of services for the use of temporary work is a contract concluded by a user undertaking and a temp agency by which the latter undertakes, by way of remuneration, to provide one or more temporary employees to that user.

[245] See JOÃO LEAL AMADO, *Contrato de Trabalho,* cit., pp. 123 et seq.

[246] See GUILHERME DRAY, *Código do Trabalho Anotado,* cit., notes on article 172.th, pp. 464 et seq.

Besides, one may also use the concepts of "User undertaking", as a corporation for which and under the supervision and direction of which a temporary agency employee works for a short period of time; "Temporary-work agency"("Temp Agency"), which means to a corporation which, in compliance with national law, concludes contracts of employment or relationships with temporary employees in order to assign them to user undertakings to work temporarily under their supervision and direction; and "Temporary agency employee", which refers to an employee with a contract of employment or an employment relationship with a temp-agency, with a view, to be assigned to a user undertaking to work temporarily under its supervision and direction.

III. As we saw above regarding the term employment contract, both the contract of services for the use of temporary work and the temporary contract depends on the fulfillment of three types of requisites: substantial, regarding the motives for its celebration; formal, regarding the proper form; and limitation on its duration.

The substantive requirements for the celebration of a contract of services for the use of temporary work are expressed in articles 175.th to 179.th

Following article 175.th, that rules the substantive requirement, the contract of services for the use of temporary work, which is a provision of services contract concluded between a user-undertaking and a temp-agency, is only allowed in the same situations provided for in the fixed term contract and expressed in article 140th, ner 2, subparagraphs a) to g), as well as in the following situations[247]:

a) Job vacancy when the recruitment process takes place for its completion;
b) Intermittent labour demand, determined by fluctuation of the days or parts of the day, provided that the use does not exceed half of the normal working hours practiced by the user;
c) Intermittent need to provide direct family support, during days or parts of the day;

[247] See GUILHERME DRAY, *Código do Trabalho Anotado*, cit., notes on article 175.th, pp. 472 et seq.

d) Realization of a temporary projects namely set up or restructuring of a corporation or an establishment, or industrial repairs.

Moreover, the duration of the contract shall not exceed the period strictly necessary to satisfy the user's need (175.rd, n^{er} 3) and it is up to the user-undertaking to prove that the substantive requirement is fulfilled and the contract was concluded within the cases provided for in article 175.rd, n^{er} 1 (176.rd, n^{er} 1). The contract concluded out of the situations provided in article 175.rd, n^{er} 1, is null (176.^{r}, n^{er} 2). When this happens, the law considers the employee as a permanent employee of the user-undertaking, under an open-ended employment contract (176.rd, n^{er} 3). Alternatively, the employee may opt for a severance compensation up until 30 days after the beginning of his/her performance, calculated under article 366.th of the Labour Code (173.rd, n^{er} 6).

The formal requirement is expressed in article 177.th. Under this provision, the contract must be written and drafted in two copies and contain several references such as the identification of the parties, the motive that justifies the contract, the characterization of the job, the workplace, the normal period of work, the salary, as well as the duration of the contract and its commencement (article 177.th, n.^{er} 1). The user-undertaking must indicate every little detail that justifies it, in order to make clear that there is a reason to conclude this contract. If the contract is not written, then it will be null and the law considers the employee as a permanent employee of the user-undertaking, under an open-ended employment contract (177.rd, n.^{ers} 4 and 5)[248].

The duration of the contract of services for the use of temporary work is limited. Following article 178.th, the contract cannot last more than 2 years, or more than 6 months, in the case of job vacancy when the recruitment process takes place, or 12 months, if the motive is an exceptional increase of the user-undertaking activity (178.rd, n^{ers} 2 and 5). It is considered as a single contract the one that was subject to renewal. If the temporary worker remains at the user's service 10 days after the termination of the contract of services without the conclusion of a new contract, it is considered that the

[248] See Guilherme Dray, *Código do Trabalho Anotado*, cit., notes on article 177.th, pp. 475 et seq.

work is provided to the user on the basis of an open-ended contract (178.rd, n.[er] 3 and 4).

If the maximum duration of the contract for the use of temporary work has been completed, the continuation in the same job of a temporary worker or fixed-term employee can only take place after a period of time equal to one third of the duration of the contract, including renovations (article 179.th)[249].

IV. The same type of requirements – substantive, formal and regarding a maximum duration – are applicable to the temporary employment contract.

Following article 180.th, temporary employment contracts can only be concluded for a fixed or unfixed term in the situations listed for the conclusion of a contract of services for the use of temporary work (article 180.th, n.[er] 1). That means that the motives that ground the contract of services for the use of temporary work are the same motives that must be used to conclude a temporary employment contract. The term stipulated in violation of this rule is null and void. In that case, the law considers the work performed by the employee as a work under an open-ended contract for the temporary employment agency. Alternatively, the employee can choose to receive a severance compensation until 30 days after the beginning of its performance, calculated under article 366.th of the Labour Code (articles 180.[th,] n[er] 2, and 173.rd, n.[er] 6)[250].

If the nullity of the temporary employment contract is simultaneous with the nullity of the contract of services for the use of temporary work, the law considers that the employee should be seen as a permanent employee of the user-undertaking, under an open-ended contract (article 180.[th,] n.[er] 3). The choice made by the lawmaker is easy to understand: the employee worked at the user-undertaking and this entails that the corporation ultimately has work to provide him/her.

The temporary employment contract must be written.

In light of article 181.st, the temporary employment contract shall be in written in two copies and shall contain several references, such

[249] See Guilherme Dray, *Código do Trabalho Anotado*, cit., notes on articles 178.[th,] – 179.[th,] pp. 478 et seq.

[250] See Guilherme Dray, *Código do Trabalho Anotado*, cit., notes on article 180.[th,], pp. 481 et seq.

as the identification of the parties, their addresses or headquarters, the reasons justifying the conclusion of the contract, the job description, the workplace, the normal period of time, the salary, the date of commencement of work, the term of contract and the date of its conclusion.

In the absence of a written document or in case of omission of the references imposed by the law, the contract is null and the law states that the worker should be considered a permanent employee and that the work is provided to the temporary employment agency under an open-ended contract. Again, the employee is entitled to opt for a severance compensation under article 173.rd n.er 6, instead of remaining as a permanent worker.

V. The duration of the temporary employment contract may not exceed that of the contract of services for the use of temporary work.

The duration of the fixed-term temporary employment contract, including renewals, may not exceed 2 years, or the limit of 6 months, in the event of a job vacancy in which the recruitment process takes place, or 12 months, if the motive is an exceptional increase of the corporate activity.

Temporary fixed-term employment contracts are not subject to the limits of duration of article 148.th n.er 2 and may be renewed up to 6 times (article 182.nd n.er 1, 2 and 3)[251].

The unfixed-term temporary contract lasts for the time necessary to satisfy the temporary need of the user and cannot exceed the duration limits mentioned in the previous paragraph.

At the expiration of the temporary employment contract, the provisions of article 344.th or 345.th shall be applied and the temporary employee will be entitled to receive a severance compensation, depending on whether it is a fixed-temporary contract or an unfixed-temporary contract.

VI. Finally, the law also governs the open-ended temporary employment contract for temporary assignment (article 183.rd and 184th)[252].

[251] See Guilherme Dray, *Código do Trabalho Anotado,* cit., notes on article 182.th, pp. 484 et seq.

[252] See Guilherme Dray, *Código do Trabalho Anotado,* cit., notes on article 183.th – 184.th, pp. 485 et seq.

It is an open-ended contract concluded between the temp-agency and the temporary worker, under which the employee is hired to be assigned to user-undertakings.

The difference, regarding the fixed-term and the unfixed-term temporary contract, is that with the open-ended contract the employee is a permanent worker of the temp-agency, hired to be permanently transferred to other users whenever they need his/her expertise.

During the period in which the employee is not assigned, he/she may provide his/her activity to the temp-agency. In that case, if the employee doesn´t perform any activity to the temp-agency, he/she will be entitled to receive a compensation provided for in the collective labour regulation, or two-thirds of the last remuneration or the minimum monthly salary guaranteed, whichever is the most favorable.

If the employee performs an activity for the temp-agency, he/she will be entitled to receive the remuneration corresponding to the activity performed.

The open-ended temporary employment contract for temporary assignment must be written, in duplicate and shall contain several references, such as the identification of the parties, signatures, domicile, number and date of license of the temporary employment agency, express mention to the assent of the worker to be assigned to user-undertakings, the general description of the duties to be performed, the minimum remuneration during assignments, etc (article 184.th).

In the absence of a written document the employee will be considered as a regular and permanent worker of the temp-agency under a normal open-ended contract, under which the employee cannot be assigned.

VII. During the assignment, the employee is subject to the power of management oh the user-undertaking, regarding the type, place, duration of work and suspension of the employment contract, as well as to the rules regarding occupational safety, health and access to social rights. The user-undertaking has the power to organize the work provided by the worker. Contrarily, the exercise of disciplinary powers remains at the temp-agency. That means that we have a split of the traditional employer´s powers: the management power belongs to the user undertaking, while the disciplinary power remains with the temp-agency (article 185.th n.^{er} 1-3) .

The temporary employee is entitled to the minimum remuneration of the collective labour regulation applicable to the user-undertaking that corresponds to his/her type of work, or to the greater salary that arises from equal salary for equal work.

The temporary employee is also entitled, in proportion to the duration of the respective contract, to paid holidays and christmas allowances, as well as to other regular benefits to which the user-undertaking's workers are entitled to.

The remuneration of the holiday period and christmas allowances of the employee temporarily assigned are calculated based on the average of the remunerations earned in the last 12 months, or in the period of performance of the contract, whichever is the lowest.

Moreover, the rules that arise from the instruments of collective labour regulation that bound the user-undertaking and its workers who perform the same functions as the temporary employee, are also applicable to him/her.

The user-undertaking must inform the temporary employee of the jobs available in the company or establishment for functions similar to those exercised by him/her, with a view to allow his/her application (article 185.th, n.er 4-11) [253].

10.3. Special contracts

10.3.1. Part-time contract

I. Besides the non-permanent contracts, the law also establishes specific contents within the permanent employment contracts. It is the case of the part-time contract, the intermittent contract, the commission of services contract, and the telework contract.

The part-time contract is the contract under which the employee works less than the full-time work (e.g. 4h a day and 20h a week) in a comparable

[253] See Guilherme Dray, *Código do Trabalho Anotado*, cit., notes on article 185.th, pp. 489 et seq.

situation. The legal regime is stated under articles 150-156 of the Labour Code[254].

The conclusion of this type of contract is based on the freedom of choice and this freedom cannot be excluded by a collective labour regulation instrument (article 152.nd)[255]. A part-time worker may work full-time or the reverse, either permanently or for a fixed period, with the written agreement of the employer. The employee may terminate the agreement referred by means of a written communication sent to the employer up to the seventh day after its conclusion, unless the agreement to modify the work period is duly dated and signed and the signatures are subject to notarial recognition in person. When the change of full-time work to part-time work occurs for a defined period, the worker is entitled to resume full-time work at the end of that period (article 155th).

The instruments of collective labour regulation should establish, for part-time admission, preferences in favor of a person with family responsibilities, with reduced working capacity, with a disability or chronic illness or who attends a school (article 153.rd).

The part-time contract is subject to written form and must contain several indications, such as the identification, signatures and domicile or headquarters of the parties; and the normal daily and weekly work period, with reference to full-time work.

When the written form is not observed, or in the absence of the indication of the period of time agreed by the parties, the contract is considered full-time (article 153.rd).

A part-time worker shall not be treated less favorably than the full-time worker in a comparable situation, unless a different treatment is justified by objective reasons, which may be defined by an instrument of collective labour regulation.

Under the law (article 154.th), the part-time worker is entitled to:

a) The basic remuneration and other benefits provided for by law or instrument of collective labour regulation, if more favorable, or to those benefits paid to a full-time worker in a comparable situation, in proportion to their normal weekly period work;

[254] See Pedro Romano Martinez, *Direito do Trabalho*, cit., pp. 550.

[255] See João Leal Amado, *Contrato de Trabalho*, cit., pp. 128 et seq.

b) The meal allowance in the amount provided for in an instrument of collective labour regulation or, if it is more favorable, in the company policy, except where the normal daily working time is less than five hours. In this case it is calculated in proportion to their normal weekly working period.

10.3.2. Intermittent contract

I. The intermittent contract is an open-ended employment contract under which the employee works during some months of the year and does not work in other months[256]. It is a special contract conceived to be used in enterprises that carry out activities with discontinuity or variable intensity. For example, a film production company may hire an actress to perform movies throughout the months of April to September, without the need for her performances in the other months of the year. Under such agreement, the company knows that every year they can count with those actresses' performance without having to conclude new annual contracts each year. On the other hand, she knows in advance that she will work every year for such company, which gives her some stability. Nevertheless, under the law, the intermittent employee must work at least 5 months a year, 3 of them consecutively. During the periods in which he/she is not working he/she has the right to receive a compensation for inactivity corresponding at least to 20% of the basic salary. The legal regime is stated under articles 157.th to 160.th of the Labour Code[257].

These contracts should be permanent. Therefore, the law states that the intermittent contract cannot be concluded as a fixed-term contract or a temporary employment contract (article 157.th). It is a permanent employment contract.

II. Being a special contract, the intermittent contract must follow a written form.

Article 158th states that the intermittent employment contract is subject to written form and must contain several references, such as the

256 See João Leal Amado, *Contrato de Trabalho,* cit., pp. 133 et seq.

257 See Pedro Romano Martinez, *Direito do Trabalho,* cit., pp. 558 et seq.

identification, signatures and domicile or headquarters of the parties; as well as an indication of the annual number of hours worked or the annual number of full-time working days.

When the written form is not observed, or in the absence of the indication of the number of hours worked, the lawmaker considers that the contract is concluded without a period of inactivity.

Moreover, the parties shall determine the duration of the work in a consecutive or interpolated manner, as well as in the beginning and end of each working period, or the employer's advance notice of the beginning of the work period, which shall not be less than 30 days if the employee is working to another employer during his/her period of inactivity, or 20 days in other cases (article 159.th)[258].

III. During the period of inactivity, the employee is entitled to compensation in the amount established in an instrument of collective labour regulation or, failing that, 20% of the basic remuneration payable by the employer with a periodicity equal to that of the remuneration (article 160.th, n.er 2). If he/she works for a different employer during the period of inactivity, the amount the employee receives from the other employer shall be considered and discounted on the amount of compensation payed by the employer with whom he/she signed an intermittent contract (article 160.th, n.er 3). Vacation and christmas allowances are calculated based on the average remuneration and compensation payments earned in the last 12 months or the actual duration of the contract if lasting less than 12 months. During the period of inactivity, the worker may carry out another activity, but the rights, duties and guarantees of the parties that do not presume effective work (such as the duty of loyalty and confidentiality) are maintained (article 160.th).

10.3.3. Commission of services contract

I. The commission of services contract is an employment contract concluded to hire employees that require a special relationship of trust, like board members, general directors or personal secretaries of these members.

[258] See Pedro Romano Martinez, *Direito do Trabalho*, cit., pp. 561 et seq.

Under this contract the employer may terminate the contract without just cause, if there is a breach in the trust relationship. To terminate the contract the employer must send an advance previous notice of 30 or 60 days, depending on the duration of the contract (less or more than 2 years). The legal regime is stated in articles 161.st to 164.th of the Labour Code[259].

Article 161.st states that it may be exercised in a commission of services contract the following activities: a management position or equivalent, a director or a management directly dependent on the administration or a director-general or equivalent, functions of personal secretariat of the holder of any of these positions, or others expressed in an instrument of collective labour regulation if the nature of it also involves a special relationship of trust.

The employer can hire under a commission of services regime either an employee of the company or another person especially hired for this existing.

In the event of admission of an external worker to perform a position in a commission of service, their stay in the company after the end of the commission period may be agreed.

II. The contract for the exercise of a position in the commission of service is subject to written form and must contain the identification, signatures and domicile or headquarters of the parties and the position to be performed, with an explicit mention to the commission of services regime. If the position is performed by an internal employee of the company, the contract must indicate if different what is the new activity that he/she will perform after the termination of the commission. In the event an external worker especially hired and is expected to remain in the company after the end of the commission of services, the contract must indicate the activity that he/she will perform after the commission ceases.

A contract that does not follow a written form or which lacks a mention to this specific regime is not considered as a commission of service (article 162).

III. Since the commission of services contract is based on a special relationship of trust, either party may terminate the contract without just

[259] See Luís Menezes Leitão, *Direito do Trabalho*, cit., pp. 432 et seq.; Guilherme Dray, *Código do Trabalho Anotado*, cit., notes on articles 161.st – 164.th, pp. 434 et seq.

cause, by giving at least 30 or 60 days of prior notice, in writing, depending whether the contract lasted for a period of up to two years or longer.

The lack of prior notice does not prevent the termination of the commission of service, but the defaulting party incurs in the obligation to compensate the counterparty under the terms of article 401.st of the Labour Code.

Under article 164.th, in case of termination of the commission of services contract, the employee is entitled to the following rights[260]:

a) If the employee was already working for the company and if he/she remains working there, he/she is entitled to carry out the activity performed before the commission of service, or the one corresponding to the category to which he/she was promoted or, also, the activity foreseen in the agreement referred to in article 162.nd;
b) If he/she doesn't want to keep his/her job at the company, he/she is entitled to terminate the employment contract within 30 days following the decision of the employer to terminate the commission of service contract, thus receiving a compensation calculated in accordance with article 366.th;
c) If an external employee was especially hired to work on a commission of service, and if these agreement terminates at the initiative of the employer without corresponding to a dismissal by just cause, the employee is entitled to a compensation calculated in accordance with article 366.th.

The periods provided for in the referred article and the amount of compensation may be increased by a collective labour regulation instrument or work contract.

10.3.4. Telework agreement

I. Finally, the law also contains the telework employment agreement[261].

[260] See Guilherme Dray, *Código do Trabalho Anotado*, cit., notes on article 164.th, pp. 446 et seq.

[261] See João Leal Amado, *Contrato de Trabalho*, cit., pp. 148 et seq.

Telework is the work performed usually outside the company using information and communication technologies. Basically speaking, the Portuguese regime was inspired by the Framework Agreement on Telework concluded on July 16th, 2002, between the European Trade Union Confederation (ETUC) and the European Trade Unions Confederations (UNICE, UEAPME, and CEEP). At that time, the Framework Agreement was seen as "*A good example of successful dialogue between employers and trade unions at European level*", aimed at modernizing work organization, reconciling work and social life, and encourage new forms of work organization within information society.

After the conclusion of the Framework Agreement, several Member-States started to enact legislation to promote this type of work. In Portugal, telework was adopted at the Portuguese Labour Code (articles 165.th to 171.st)[262].

II. Under Portuguese law, telework may be performed either by an employee of the company or another person especially hired to work in a teleworking model (article 166.th).

Telework is based on the freedom of choice and therefore depends on an agreement between employer and employee. Nevertheless, the law (article 166.th) states that in case of domestic violence (article 195.th) the employee has the right to start working on a teleworking basis, when this is compatible with the activity performed. Also, a worker with a child up to 3 years of age has the right to work in telework, when this is compatible with the activity performed and the employer has the resources and means to do so.

The telework contract is subject to written form and must contain several references, such as the identification, signatures, domicile or headquarters of the parties; the indication of the activity to be provided by the employee, with an explicit mention of the telecommuting system, and corresponding remuneration; the identification of the normal period of work; if the period for teleworking is shorter than the expected duration of the employment contract, contract, the indication of the activity to be performed after the end of that period; the ownership of the work tools as well as the person responsible for their installation and maintenance and payment of the respective consumption and use expenses; as well as the identification of

[262] See Luís Menezes Leitão, *Direito do Trabalho*, cit., pp. 435 et seq.

the establishment or department of the company in which dependence the worker is attached to, and also the employee at the headquarters he/she should contact in case of need.

If the worker who will work under a telework regime was already an internal employee of the company, the initial duration of the telework contract may not exceed 3 years, or the term established in an instrument of collective labour regulation. In this case, either party may deliver notice of termination of the contract during the first 30 days of its execution.

Terminating the contract, the employee resumes working as he/she did before the teleworking model, under the terms agreed or provided for in an instrument of collective labour regulation (article 167.th)[263].

III. The law regulates several aspects regarding telework, such as the property of the tools and equipment used by the teleworker, the principle of equality, the right to privacy and collective representation.

Regarding the tools and equipment, article 168.th provides that in the absence of a stipulation in the contract it is presumed that the instruments of work relating to information and communication technologies used by the employee belong to the employer, who must ensure the respective installation, maintenance and payment of the inherent expenses. The worker must obey the rules of use and operation of the instruments of work that are made available to him/her. Unless otherwise agreed, the worker must not give to the instruments of labour provided by the employer another use other than that inherent to the performance of his/her work.

Regarding the principle of equality, article 169.th states that teleworkers have the same rights and duties as other workers, in particular those concerned training and career promotion, limits on normal working hours and other working conditions, occupational safety, health and damages protection arisen from an accident at work or occupational disease. In the context of vocational training, the employer must provide the worker, if necessary, with adequate training on the use of information and communication technologies inherent to the exercise of his or her activity. The employer must avoid the isolation of the worker, especially guaranteeing regular contacts with the company and other workers.

[263] See Guilherme Dray, *Código do Trabalho Anotado*, cit., notes on articles 165.th . 171.st, pp. 450 et seq.

Regarding privacy, article 170.th states that the employer must respect the worker's privacy and the rest periods of the worker's family, as well as provide him/her with good working conditions, both physical and psychological. Whenever teleworking takes place at the employee's home, visits to the place of work should only concern the control of the work activity and the instruments of work and can only be carried out between 9am and 7pm, with the assistance of the worker or a person chosen by him/her.

Finally, regarding the collective employees representation, article 171.st states that the teleworker integrates the number of employees of the company for all purposes related to structures of collective representation and can apply for these bodies. The worker can use the information and communication technologies used to provide work to participate in a meeting promoted in the workplace by the structure of collective representation of workers. Any structure of collective representation of workers may use the technologies in order to communicate with the worker in telework, namely by disseminating information and communications regarding his/her activity[264].

[264] See Guilherme Dray, *Código do Trabalho Anotado*, cit., notes on articles 171.st, pp. 462 et seq.

11.
Modifications, change of circumstances & vicissitudes

11.1. General overview

I. After the conclusion of the employment contract and with the initiation of its performance, the contract will follow the initial contents and clauses agreed by the parties, namely regarding the workplace, working time, salary and the object of the contract.

Nevertheless, for different reasons the contract may sometimes face modifications or changes of circumstances. We usually use the overarching expression "vicissitudes" to refer to all those unpredictable phenomena that may occur during the execution of the employment contract[265].

Basically speaking, the vicissitudes that can affect the employment contract are as follows:

a) Contractual modifications;
b) Assignment of contract;
c) Transfer of undertaking;
d) Employee´s occasional transfer;
c) Reduction of activity and suspension of employment contract.

Let´s take a closer look at them.

[265] See Luís Menezes Leitão, *Direito do Trabalho*, cit., pp. 329 et seq.

11.2. Contractual modifications

I. Under the principle of private autonomy (articles 405.th and 406.th of the Portuguese Civil Code) contractors may mutually agree to amend the contract.

A contract modification may introduce or cancel specifications or terms of an existing contract, while leaving intact its overall purpose and effect.

Bilateral modifications are achieved through a supplemental agreement, also called contract amendment or modification of contract. At times during the execution of the employment contract, employer and employee modify the contract, whether under a formal or an informal non-written amendment.

II. For example: if the employer increases the employee's salary, there's a contractual modification. The acceptance can be implicit and there's no need for a written amendment.

11.3. Assignment of the contract

I. An assignment of contract occurs when one party of an existing contract (the "assignor") transfers the contract's obligations and benefits to another party (the "assignee").

Ideally, the assignor wants the assignee to step into his/her position and assume all of his/her contractual obligations and rights.

In order to do that, the other party to the contract (i.e. the employee, if it is an employment contract) must be properly notified and accept it.

That is the rule that arises from article 424.th of the Portuguese Civil Code, which states that in an agreement with mutual obligations either party may transfer to third parties his/her contractual position, provided that the other contractor, before or after the conclusion of the agreement, consents to the transmission.

If the consent of the other contracting party is prior to the assignment, it shall only take effect upon its notification or recognition.

II. In the event of an assignment of the employment contract, the contents of the contract will remain unaltered[266].

For instance: the job position, the salary and the working schedule defined in the employment contract will remain unaltered. The assignee must comply with all the employer's obligations stated in the contract.

The only consequence of the assignment is the transmission of the employer's position from the assignor to the assignee (article 427.th Portuguese Civil Code).

11.4. Transfer of undertaking

I. Under article 285.th of the Labour Code, if the owner of an undertaking sells the company, an establishment or a business unit to an acquirer, the position of the employer regarding the employment contracts is to have them transferred by law without the need of the employee's previous acceptance[267].

Aiming at the protection of employees, the European Union enacted Directive 2001/23/EC of 12th March 2001 regarding the safeguarding of employees' rights in the event of transfer of undertakings, businesses or parts of undertakings to another employer ("transferee") as a result of a legal transfer or merger. Under article 3.rd of said Directive, the transferor's rights and obligations arising from an employment contract or from an employment relationship existing on the date of a transfer shall, by reason of such transfer, be transferred to the transferee.

Member States may provide that, after the date of transfer, the transferor and the transferee shall be jointly and severally liable in respect of obligations which arose before the date of transfer from a contract of employment or an employment relationship existing on the date of the transfer.

II. Article 285.th of the Portuguese Labour Code endorses the rules of the Directive.

[266] See Romano Martinez, *Direito do Trabalho*, cit., pp. 767 et seq.

[267] See Luís Menezes Leitão, *Direito do Trabalho*, cit., pp.330 et seq.

Regarding the transfer of an undertaking or a business, the law states that in the event of transfer of ownership of an undertaking, a business or part of an undertaking or businesses which are part of an economic unit,

The employer's position in the employment contracts shall be transferred to the transferee, as well as the responsibility for the payment of penalties imposed to the transferor by an administrative agency for labour misconducts. For the purposes of this provision, the law defines an economic unit as a set of organized means with the purpose of carrying out a main or ancillary economic activity.

The transferor to be jointly or severally liable to the obligations matured up to the date of the transfer, in the year subsequent to it.

The same regime applies to the transfer, assignment or reversal of the holding of an enterprise, establishment or economic unit, which shall be jointly and severally liable, in case of a transfer or reversion.

Contrarily, these provisions shall not apply to the employee who, prior to the transfer, is transferred by the transferor to another establishment or economic unit, in accordance with the provisions of article 194.th regarding the transfer of workplace, keeping him/her as employee, except with respect to the liability for the payment of penalties: for a labour misconduct imposed by an administrative agency[268].

III. The law also imposes a duty of information and consultation of the workers' representatives. Under article 286.th, the transferor and the transferee shall inform the representatives of their employees or, if they do not exist, the employees themselves, of the date and reasons for the transfer, the legal, economic and social consequences for the employees involved and the measures envisaged in relation thereto. The information must be provided in writing, before transmission, in a timely manner, at least 10 days before the said consultation. The transferor and the transferee shall consult the representatives of their employees before transfer in order to reach an agreement on the measures they intend to apply to employees without prejudice to the legal and conventional provisions applicable to such measures.

[268] See Joana Vasconcelos, *Código do Trabalho Anotado*, cit., notes on articles 285.th-287.th, pp. 683 et seq.

The transfer shall not alter the contents of the employment contracts and, therefore, the employment relationship is not jeopardised, as the employee maintains his/her employment contract with the transferee. In order to avoid transfers of undertakings that could be harmful to the employee, the lawmaker created a mechanism – right to opposition – to defend the worker against such harmful transfers.

Under article 286. th-A, the worker may exercise the right to oppose the transfer of the employer's position in his/her contract of employment in the event the transfer, or reversal of an undertaking or establishment, or part of an undertaking or establishment constituting an economic unit, where it is likely to cause serious damage to him, in particular as a result of a manifest lack of solvency or a difficult financial situation of the potential transferee, or if its work organization policy does not instil confidence in him/her. The opposition of the employee prevents the transfer of the position of the employer in his/her contract of employment. In order to exercise this right, the employee must inform his/her employer in writing, mentioning his/her identification, the activity contracted and the basis and the motives for the opposition.

If the transfer takes place, the representation of the employees shall continue within the organization of the transferee.

IV. Article 287.th expresses that if the undertaking or establishment maintains its autonomy after the transfer, the status and function of the employees' representatives affected shall not change, provided that the necessary requirements for the establishment of the collective representation structure at stake is maintained. If the company, establishment or economic unit transfered is incorporated in the undertaking of the acquirer transferee and there is no corresponding structure of collective representation of employees provided by the law, the one existing in the merged entity remains in office for a period of two months from the date of transmission or until a new structure is elected and assumes its functions or for another two months if the election is annulled.

Finally, in the event of transfer, by any title, of the ownership of an enterprise or establishment or of part of an enterprise or establishment that constitutes an economic unit, the instrument of collective labour regulation binding the transferior shall apply to the purchaser transferee until the end of the period of validity of this instrument or at least 12 months from the date of the transfer, unless in the meantime another instrument of collective bargaining is applied to the acquirer. This rule also applies to the transfer, assignment or reversion of the operation of an enterprise, establishment or economic unit (article 498.th)[269].

11.5. Occasional transfer of the employee

I. The occasional transfer is the temporary assignment of an employee by the employer to provide work for another entity, to whose power of management the employee becomes subject, maintaining the initial contractual relationship[270].

Under article 289.th of the Labour Code, the occasional assignment of employees is lawful whenever the following conditions are cumulatively met:

a) The employee is bound to the assigning employer by permanent contract of employment;
b) The assignment occurs between affiliated companies, in relation to corporate ownership of mutual interests, ownership or group, or between employers having common organizational structures;
c) The employee agrees with the assignment;
d) The duration of the transfer does not exceed one year, renewable for equal periods up to a maximum of five years.

The conditions of the occasional assignment of an employee may be regulated by an instrument of collective regulation, but this does not dismiss the need of previous authorization by the employee. The employee must always agree with the occasional transfer[271].

II. The occasional assignment of an employee depends on an agreement between the assignor and the transferee, subject to written form, which

[269] See Luís Gonçalves da Silva, *Código do Trabalho Anotado*, cit., notes on articles 498.th, pp. 1058 et seq.
[270] See Romano Martinez, *Direito do Trabalho*, cit., pp. 767 et seq.
[271] See Guilherme Dray, *Código do Trabalho Anotado*, cit., notes on articles 289.th – 293.rd, pp. 700 et seq.

must contain several references, such as the identification, signatures and domicile or headquarters of the parties; the indication of the activity to be provided by the employee, the starting date and the duration of the transfer; as well as the declaration of agreement by the employee (article 290.th).

In the event of termination of the occasional assignment, the employee shall return to the transferor, retaining the rights he/she had before the transfer, the duration of which shall count for the purposes of seniority.

III. During the occasional assignment, the employee is subject to the working regime applicable to the transferee with regards to workplace, duration of work, suspension of employment contract, occupational safety and health conditions and access to social equipment. The transferee shall inform the transferor and the assigned employee of the risks to the health and safety inherent to the workplace to which he/she is assigned. The assignment of an employee to a job that is particularly dangerous for his/her safety or health is not permitted, unless he/she corresponds to this specific professional qualification (article 291.st).

Under the same provision, during the occasional transfer, the assigned employee has the right to:

a) A minimum remuneration which, by means of the instrument of collective regulation is applicable to the transferor or the transferee and corresponds to his or her functions, or to the remuneration paid by the transferee at the time of transfer, whichever is higher;
b) Holidays, vacation allowances and christmas allowances as well as other regular and periodic benefits to which the transferee's employees are entitled for the same work, in proportion to the length of the transfer.

IV. The occasional transfer of an employee outside the conditions and requirements in which it is admissible, or the lack of the employee's agreement, gives the assigned employee the right to choose to remain at the service of the assignee under an open-ended employment contract (article 292.nd). This right may be exercised until the end of the transfer, by notifying the transferor and the transferee by registered letter with receipt of acknowledgment.

11.6. Reduction of activity and suspension of the employment contract

I. Whenever there is a problem during the execution of the contract regarding the employer's economic situation or an employee's temporary impossibility to work, we may have a reduction of activity or the suspension of the employment contract[272].

Reduction of activity is the reduction of the normal working period. Suspension of the contract respects the temporary suspension of the contract, with the corresponding suspension of the rights and duties of the parties[273].

The Labour Code governs these two situations and comprehends general rules for these situations in articles 294.th and 295.th.

Under article 294.th, the temporary reduction of normal working hours or the suspension of the employment contract may be based on the temporary or total impossibility of rendering work by a fact regarding either the worker or the employer. With that in mind, reduction of the normal period of work or the suspension of the employment contract is possible when needed to ensure the viability of the company and the maintenance of jobs, in situations of business crisis, or where there is an agreement between the employee and the employer, in particular the pre-retirement agreement. Suspension of employment contract may also occur by initiative of the employee, based on a lack of timely payment of salaries by the employer.

II. Article 295.th states that during reduction or suspension, the rights, duties and guarantees of the parties that presuppose effective work are suspended. For example, the duties of assiduity, punctuality or obedience are suspended. Contrarily, those that do not presume these rights and duties are maintained, such as the duties of loyalty and confidentiality. The time of reduction or suspension is considered for purposes of seniority and reduction or suspension shall have no effect for the purposes of expiration of a fixed-term contract, nor shall prevent either party from terminating the contract under general terms. After the reduction or suspension period the

272 See Pedro Romano Martinez, *Direito do Trabalho*, cit., pp. 760 et seq.

273 See João Leal Amado, *Contrato de Trabalho*, cit., pp. 336 et seq.

rights, duties and guarantees of the parties resulting from active work are reestablished (article 295.th)[274].

The law then rules two different situations: reduction or suspension based on facts regarding the employee (articles 296.th – 297.th) and reduction or suspension based on a business crisis caused by the employer (articles 298.th – 305.th).

III. The suspension of the contract for causes regarding the employee can occur whenever there is a temporary obstacle by facts concerning the employee that are not his/her responsibility but last for more than a month, namely illness, accident or fact arising from the application of the law of military service. Even before the period of 30 days, the employee can immediately suspend the employment contract in case of domestic violence (article 195.th) where there is no other establishment of the undertaking to which the employee may request transfer; or when it is foreseeable that the impediment will last longer than that period, namely in case of illness. The suspended contract of employment expires when it is certain that the impediment is definitive (article 296.th). On the day immediately following the termination of the impediment, the worker must present himself/herself to the employer to resume activity (article 297.th)[275].

IV. Regarding the employer's impediment, article 298.th states that the employer may temporarily reduce normal working hours or suspend employment contracts for market, structural or technological reasons, catastrophes or other occurrences which seriously affect the normal activity of the undertaking, provided that such action is indispensable to ensure the viability of the company and the maintenance of the jobs.

The reduction may include one or more normal working hours, daily or weekly, and may relate to different groups of workers; the decrease in the number of hours can correspond to the normal daily or weekly working perio.

[274] See JOANA VASCONCELOS, *Código do Trabalho Anotado*, cit., notes on article 295.th, pp. 709 et seq.
[275] See JOANA VASCONCELOS, *Código do Trabalho Anotado*, cit., notes on article 296.th – 296.th, pp. 711 et seq.

The reduction or suspension scheme shall apply to cases where such a measure is determined in the context of a business declaration in a difficult economic situation or, with the necessary adaptations, in the process of recovery of an undertaking.

The company that makes use of the reduction or suspension regime must have its tax situation settled before the tax administration and social security, in accordance with the legislation in force.

The reduction or suspension shall not exceed six months or, in the event of a disaster or other occurrence which has seriously affected the normal activity of the undertaking, one year (article 301.th).

V. Under article 305.th, during the period of reduction or suspension, the employee is entitled[276]:

a) To receive, on a monthly basis, a minimum amount equal to two thirds of his/her normal gross remuneration or the value of the minimum monthly guaranteed salary corresponding to his/her normal working hours, whichever is higher;
b) To maintain the social benefits or benefits of social security to which he/she is entitled as the respective basis of calculation is not altered by the effect of the reduction or suspension;
c) To engage in another paid activity.

VI. Contrarily, article 309.th states that in the event of temporary closure or temporary reduction of activity of an enterprise or establishment that is not caused by a situation of business crisis, the employee is entitled to[277]:

a) When due to unforeseeable circumstances or force majeure – 75% of the remuneration;
b) When attributable to the employer or because of his/her interest, the entire remuneration.

[276] See JOANA VASCONCELOS, *Código do Trabalho Anotado*, cit., notes on article 305.th, pp. 726 et seq.

[277] See JOANA VASCONCELOS, *Código do Trabalho Anotado*, cit., notes on article 309.th, pp. 734 et seq.

The value of remuneration is deducted to what the employee receives during the period at stake by performing another activity that he or she has taken to exercise by the effect of the closure or reduction of activity.

Ultimately, the employer must inform employees whose activity is suspended or reduced of termination of reduction or suspension so as to enable them to resume work (article 310.th).

VII. The law also comprehends unpaid leave, under an employee's request and further to the employer's acceptance. Article 317.th states that the employer may grant the employee, at the latter's request, a license without remuneration. The employee is entitled to a leave without remuneration for more than 60 days for the attendance of a training course given under the responsibility of an educational institution or vocational training, or under a specific program approved by a competent authority and executed under its pedagogic control or to attend a course of study. In these cases, the employer must assent. Nevertheless, the employer may refuse to grant a license where, during the preceding 24 months for: adequate vocational training or leave for the same purpose has been provided to the employee; if it is a worker with less than 3 years of seniority; when the employee has not requested the license with a prior notice of 90 days before the start date; in the case of micro-enterprises or small enterprises, where adequate replacement if the employee is at managerial level or qualiffied staff and it is not possible to replace him/her during the leave period, without serious prejudice to the operation of the undertaking[278].

The license determines the suspension of the employment contract, with the effects foreseen in the referred article 295.th.

VIII. Additionally pre-retirement is allowed and governed by the Labour Code.

Article 318.th defines pre-retirement as the situation of reduction or suspension of work, consisting of an agreement between an employer and an employee with at least 55 years of age or over, during which he/she is entitled to receive from the employer a monthly cash benefit, known as pre-retirement.

[278] See Pedro Romano Martinez, *Direito do Trabalho*, cit., pp. 766.

The pre-retirement agreement is subject to written form and must contain the identification, signatures and domicile or headquarters of the parties; the date of commencement of the retirement agreement; the amount of the pre-retirement benefit; and the organization of working time, in case of reduction of the work performance[279].

[279] See Pedro Romano Martinez, *Direito do Trabalho*, cit., pp. 767; Joana Vasconcelos, *Código do Trabalho Anotado*, cit., notes on article 318.th, pp. 745 et seq.

12. Accidents at work

12.1. General overview

I. With the advent of the Industrial Revolution, accidents at work and professional diseases became more common due to the use of heavy machinery and the existence of bad working conditions[280].

The Industrial Revolution created new forms of work through the industrialization process and boosted the number of accidents at work, as unpredictable misfortunes that occur in the workplace and during the work time which cause injuries to the employee or even his/her death[281].

This situation, along with the exploitation of the workers by the employers and the flux of poor migration from rural areas to urban areas, led to the so called "Social Question"[282].

The incidence of accidents in the workplace and of professional diseases associated with long working hours, the commodification of the working force, including women and child labor, extreme poverty and bad working conditions created an unsustainable number of widows, disabled persons, and unattended elderly – without a primary breadwinner. As a consequence

[280] See Luís Menezes Leitão, *Direito do Trabalho*, cit., pp. 347 et seq.

[281] See Maria do Rosário Ramalho, *Tratado de Direito do Trabalho – Parte II*, cit., pp. 709 et seq.

[282] See Gustav Schmoller, *Die soziale Frage: Klassenbildung*, Arbeiterfrage, Klassenkampf, Duncker & Humblot, Munich,1918. See also Alvin L. Goldman and Roberto L. Corrada, *Labor Law in the USA, Third Revised Edition*, Wolters Kluwer, Law and Business, The Netherlands, 2011.

of the movement of trade unions, the collective demands of the workers and the inception of collective bargaining processes led to the situation in which employers created "employer plans" to compensate the diminished working capacity related to work-based accidents or old age. In the United States, for example, a small number of industries, notably in the railway and mining sectors, created the first private pension plans for their workers in order to compensate them. In the 19th Century, this trend was extended to some frontline companies, such as American Express, ATT, Carnegie Steel and Kodak[283]. Nevertheless, these plans were only addressed to certain employees and benefits were discretionary and financially precarious, given the fact that they depended on the company's future financial success. They were neither universalistic, nor secure. A new answer was necessary and required. That answer should be given by the State, even if as a complement to private systems[284].

II. In this context, some countries started to legislate on occupational injuries and pension systems mostly to guarantee the protection of injured workers and older civil servants against the loss of income after their retirement.

The British Government introduced civil-service pensions in 1834; the State of New York City began providing pensions for its servants in 1857.

Public pension systems soon spread from the public sector to the private sector, especially in the manufacturing industry. In 1881 Germany's Emperor, William the First, in a groundbreaking letter to the German Parliament, wrote that "*those who are disabled from work by age and invalidity have a well-grounded claim to care from the State.*" Finally, in 1889, Germany's Chancellor, Otto von Bismarck, launched the world's first universal pension-insurance system. Through this system, Germany became the first nation in the world to adopt a social insurance program, aimed at promoting the well-being of workers and at keeping the German economy operating at maximum efficiency. Politically speaking, the creation of this system was an answer to the labour workforce demands and thus a response to stave off calls for radical socialist alternatives. In other words, it was meant to stop the growth of labour and socialist movements. The German system provided contributory retirement and disability benefits as well. Participation in the

[283] Gøsta Esping-Andersen, *The Three Worlds of Welfare Capitalism*, cit., p. 91.
[284] See Pedro Romano Martinez, *Direito do Trabalho*, cit., pp. 821 et seq.

system was mandatory and contributions were taken from the employee, the employer and the government. O. Bismark adopted the age of 70 years old as the standard retirement age. Linked with the workers' compensation program established in 1884 and the "sickness" insurance enacted the year before, the Germans created a complete and comprehensive system of income security based on social insurance principles that would be enlarged in 1927 with insurance for unemployment.

From then on, all the Western countries started to create similar social insurance systems. Some of them based on public systems; others on private insurance systems; a third type, like the Portuguese, a hybrid: the accidents at work are covered by private insurance but professional diseases are covered by Social Security.

III. The increase of accidents at work also changed the liability regimes.

To protect the employees and overcome the problems regarding the burden of proof, as it was difficult for the employee to prove the employer's conduct was either negligent or intentional, lawmakers created the concept of objective liability.

Under objective liability, the employer is always liable if there is an accident at work that causes the employee's death or bodily injury resulting in reduction of working capacity or gain, even in the cases in which the employer complies with all the rules. The idea is simple: since the employer is the owner of the company in which the employees work, he/she should have the responsibility for all the accidents that took place in his/her undertaking under the idea of "enterprise risk".

Thus, when an accident at work occurs, the employer is liable and must compensate the employee, even if there is no employer's misconduct[285].

12.2. Legal framework

I. The Portuguese Labour Code lists some principles regarding health and safety in the workplace in articles 281.st et seq.

[285] See PEDRO ROMANO MARTINEZ, *Direito do Trabalho*, cit., pp. 836 et seq.

The legal system is aims at the prevention of accidents at work stating that the employer must issue rules regarding health & safety and the employee must comply with these rules.

The Labour Code adds that employees are entitled to be compensated in the event of an accident at work or a professional disease. Nevertheless, article 284.th of the Labour Code affirms the idea that accidents in the workplace must be subjected to specific legislation. As a consequence, the lawmaker issued specific legislation to regulate these matters: Law 98/2009, September 4.

Law 98/2009 of September 4, contains the legal regime of the accidents at work and professional diseases. Basically speaking, it is divided in IV chapters, as follows:

Chapter I regarding the scope of the law.
Chapter II regarding accidents at work
Chapter III regarding professional diseases
Chapter IV regarding the employee´s rehabilitation and resume of his/her work.

II. In relation to the personal scope, article 3.rd states that the law is applicable to the employees (3.rd, n.er 1); providers of services legally equivalent to employees as a result of economic subordination (3.rd, n.er 2); apprentices and trainees (3.rd, n.er 3); foreigner employees working in Portugal (5.th); and Portuguese or foreigner employees working abroad being employed by a Portuguese undertaking (6.th). This legal regime is also applicable to those that are volunteers– Law n.er 71/98 of November 3 (article 7.th, n.er 1, *f*)).

The concept of accident at work is enshrined in article 8.th [286].

An accident at work is an incident that occurs at the workplace and during the working time which results directly or indirectly in bodily injury, functional disturbance or a disease resulting in a reduction of work capacity or gain, or death (8.th, n.er 1)[287].

To enlarge the concept of accident at work and provide a broader protection to the employee the legislator created an overarching concept of "workplace" and "working time".

[286] See Pedro Romano Martinez, *Direito do Trabalho*, cit., pp. 846 et seq.
[287] See Luís Menezes Leitão, *Direito do Trabalho*, cit., pp. 351 et seq. 351.

Under Law 98/2009, "Workplace" means any place in which the worker is or should be addressed by virtue of his/her work and in which he/she is, directly or indirectly, subject to the employer's control (8.th, n.er 2, subparagraph *a)*).

That is to say, if the employee regularly performs deliveries out of office and suffers an accident while working outside, this accident will be considered as an accident at work, even if he/she is not working at the employer's headquarters or establishment.

Under Law 98/2009, "working time" includes the normal period of work as well as the period preceding its commencement, in acts of preparation or related, and the period that follows it, in acts related to its termination as well as normal or forced interruptions of work (8.th, n.er 2, subparagraph *b)*).

That is to say, if an employee suffers an accident during his/her break time or during a forced interruption for technical reasons, this accident will be considered as an occupational injury even if the employee is not working at his/her normal working period.

Under this concept, Portuguese courts decided that an employee who works at a brewery in shifts, from 6 pm to midnight, and is shot at 00:15 while cleaning the esplanade and arranging the tables and chairs so that the establishment could resume its activity for opening to the public, suffers an accident at work[288].

Because of the use of overarching concepts of "workplace" and "working time" the Law considers as a work accident the accidents *in itinere*, i.e., an incident you may have on your way to and from work, as well as accidents that in normal conditions should not be considered as work accidents.

III. Accidents *in itinere* are regulated in article 9.th, n.er 1, subparagraph *a)* and article 9.th, n.er 2[289].

Other accidents are regulated in article 9.th, n.er 1, subparagraphs *b)* to *h)*.

Accidents *in itinere* comprehend the following incidents:

a. From work to work if the employee has more than one job;
b. From the employee's residence to work and vice-versa;

[288] Decision by the Court of Appeals of Oporto (15.05.2017).

[289] See Pedro Romano Martinez, *Direito do Trabalho*, cit., pp. 857 et seq.

c. From any of the above-referred places and the place where the employee receives his/her salary;
e. From the workplace to the place he/she goes to have a meal and vice-versa;
f. From any place he/she goes to run a business errand (under the employer's request) to his/her normal workplace or his/her residence.

Under the concept of accidents *in itinere*, the Portuguese Courts decided that the employee who was attacked while going to the Mall where she was going to work, a result of which she was injured, suffered a work accident "in itinere"[290].

IV. The Law (article 9.th) also considers as a work accident the following cases:

a) Whilst the employee executes, on a voluntary basis, a task that can be profitable to the employer (article 9.th, n.er 1, subparagraph *b)*);
b) Whilst the employee is attending a trade union's meeting at or out of office, if he/she is at a meeting organized under the Labour Code (article 9.th, n.er 1, subparagraph *c)*);
c) Whilst the employee is attending a training session at or out of the workplace, when allowed by the employer (article 9.th, n.er 1, subparagraph *d)*);
d) At the place where the employee goes to receive his/her salary while staying there (article 9.th, n.er 1, subparagraph *e)*);
e) At the place where the employee goes to receive medical assistance due to a previous accident at work while staying there (article 9.th, n.er 1, subparagraph *f)*);
f) While searching for a job during the period in which he/she is allowed to do so as a result of a collective dismissal process (article 9.th, n.er 1, subparagraph *g)*);
g) Out of office while executing a business errand under the employer's request (article 9.th, n.er 1, subparagraph *h)*).

[290] Decision by the Court of Appeals of Oporto (02.03.2017).

12.3. Employee's entitlements

I. When there is an accident at work that causes injuries to the employee, he/she or his/her family, in the event of the employee's death, must be compensated for such loss.

Generally speaking, the employer has a duty to compensate the employee by giving him/her medical, nursing and hospital assistance, so he/she can recover physically and mentally and get back to work (article 23.rd subparagraph *a)*); compensate the employee by paying him/her a monetary compensation depending on the degree of the injury (articles 23.rd, subparagraph *b)* and article 48.th)[291].

Regarding the payments due date, compensation must be paid: in case of death, the day after the employee's death (article 56.th, n.er 2); in case of injuries that affect the employee's capacity to work, the day following the accident (article 126.th).

Regarding the place of payment, all the medical and hospital assistance must take place at the hospital or clinics where the treatments take place (article 27.th). Monetary compensation must be paid at the employee's or his/her family (in case of death) residence or at any other place as agreed (article 73.rd).

The entitlement to compensation arising from the right to reparation is inalienable, enforceable and cannot be waived (article 78.th).

Under the Portuguese legal system, the reparation of accidents at work must be guaranteed by insurance agencies, to prevent the insolvency of the employers and correspondingly to alleviate and guarantee the Social Security's financial sustainability.

As a consequence, the employer must endorse and transfer his/her responsibility to a certified insurance company by subscribing a work insurance policy. Subscription is mandatory and the form of insurance is approved by Government authorities (article 79.th).

[291] See PEDRO ROMANO MARTINEZ, *Direito do Trabalho*, cit., pp. 866 et seq.

12.4. Employer's fault-based liability

I. If the accident suffered by the employee is caused by a serious fault or negligence of the employer or its representatives or under a user-undertaking company, the liability of the employer is aggravated (article 18.th)[292].

If there is no fault of the employer, the only damages he/she must compensate are those that come from the death or the injuries suffered by the employee. The employer doesn't have to pay other patrimonial or non-patrimonial damages. This changes if the accident is caused by any fault or negligence of the employer. In the latter, the employer has to compensate all the patrimonial and moral damages suffered by the employee or his/her family, beyond the damages regarding death or body injuries.

If the fault or negligence is caused by the employer's representatives, the employer's liability is also aggravated under the "vicarious liability" doctrine.

The Vicarious Liability is based on a Latin term which means "Let the superior answer." It is an indirect liability.

In sum, vicarious liability applies in situations where one person is liable for the damages caused by the negligence of another. It is the legal principle under which employers are responsible for negligent acts of their employees. This includes employers being responsible for work accidents caused by fault or negligence of other employees. It is rooted in the theory of "enterprise liability".

In this case, the employer pays compensation to the employee but becomes entitled to a right of recourse against the employee who caused the accident.

12.5. Exclusion or reduction of liability

I. The legal regime on accidents at the workplace is imperative, i.e., it cannot be amended to provide for worst conditions by individual agreements[293].

Actually, article 12.th is clear on this issue stating that a convention that is contrary to the employee's rights or guarantees in case of accident at work

[292] See Luís Menezes Leitão, *Direito do Trabalho*, cit., pp. 361 et seq.

[293] See Pedro Romano Martinez, *Direito do Trabalho*, cit., pp. 876 et seq.

is null and void. On the other hand, the employee cannot waive his/her own rights regarding the reparation of accidents at work. Acts and contracts that seek to waive the rights conferred by law, are null and void.

Nevertheless, the Law admits some situations under which the employer is exempted to compensate the injured employee. Those are the cases of exclusion or reduction of liability expressed in article 14.th.

II. Under article 14.th, n.^{er} 1, the employer is not liable in the following events:

a) The accident was intentionally caused by the employee or because he/she breached a set of rules regarding health and safety;
b) The accident is caused by the injured or deceased employee´s serious negligence;
c) The accident is caused by a permanent or an accidental loss of psychological faculties of the employee, so long as this loss is caused by the execution of the work or if the employer or his representative, knowing of the existence of that loss of capacity, still allow the employee to continue practicing the activity he/she was doing.

The article also makes clear that there is a justification for the employee's breaching of safety conditions rules if the work accident results from violation of a legal rule or a rule established by the employer from which the employee,because of his/her degree of education or access to information, could not understand; or, having this level of education, was obviously difficult for him/her to understand (article 14.th, n.^{er} 2).

Under article 14.th, n.^{er} 3, serious negligence is understood as a reckless behavior in a high and relevant degree, which does not consist in an act or omission resulting from the normal danger associated with the work performed or professional practices.

13.
Breach of contract

13.1. General overview

I. The concept of obligation derives from the Latin etymon *obligare*, which means to bind.

It denotes a relationship between two persons which entitles one of them to claim, from the other, some act or omission recognized as capable of producing a legal effect.

The person that is entitled to the performance of an obligation, whatever its nature may be, is called the creditor, and the person who is under the obligation is called the debtor.

Obligatory rights are rights that only operate relatively, meaning against the person of the debtor.

An obligatory right consists, as such, in the fact that a particular person (debtor) is bound to do something in a specific way to benefit another person (creditor).

As a rule, an obligation cannot be created by any legal instrument other than a contract between the parties.

An agreement, constituted by concurrent declarations of at least two parties, is called a contract – an agreement between two or more parties which creates binding obligations as a result of an offer and an acceptance.

As a general rule, if the debtor doesn't comply with his/her obligation he/she incurs in a breach of contract and the breach can produce three different situations: default; delay (*mora*) or defective performance.

Default is a definitive breach of contract. Is a failure of the debtor to fulfill his/her contractual obligations. Delay (*mora*) occurs whenever the debtor doesn't fulfill his/her obligation when due, but performance is still possible. Defective performance occurs when there is a deficient or incomplete (partial) execution of the contract that does not fully satisfy its requirements and obligations. There is no default nor a delay, but the execution is insufficient.

II. The concepts of default, delay, and defective performance can be used within the employment relationship[294].

Both the employer and the employee can incur in a breach of contract and be liable for the violation of legal and contractual duties and obligations.

The Portuguese Labour Code follows the general rules comprised in the Portuguese Civil Code (e.g. article 798.º et seq.) but contains certain particularities.

The Portuguese Labour Code contains principles on the breach of the employment contract – articles 323.rd and 324.th – and contains specific solutions in case of delay, default or defective performance by both parties.

The most common situation is the employer's delay in paying the employee's monthly salary, but other events may surface as a breach of contract.

Whenever it happens, the law states a common solution, provided in article 323.rd of the Labour Code[295].

Article 323.rd provides the general effects of the breach of the employment contract, stating that the party that is guilty of failing to perform his/her duties is responsible for the damage caused to the counterparty. Particularly, the employer who is guilty of not complying with the salary payment shall pay the corresponding default interest at legal rate, or the higher rate established in an instrument of collective labour regulation. The lack of timely payment of remuneration entitles the employee to suspend or terminate the contract, in accordance with the provisions of this code. Moreover, in case of lack of punctual payment of the salary by the employer (article 324.th) the Labour Code states that the employer triggers the application of article 313.th – he/she cannot distribute profits or dividends, pay for supplies and respective interest or redempt quotas in any form; remunerate members of the social

[294] See PEDRO ROMANO MARTINEZ, *Direito do Trabalho*, cit., pp. 781 et seq.

[295] See PEDRO ROMANO MARTINEZ, *Código do Trabalho Anotado*, cit., notes on article 323.rf, pp. 750 et seq.

bodies by any means, in a percentage higher than the one paid to the respective workers; buy or sell shares or quotas to members of corporate bodies; make payments to creditors who do not hold a guarantee or privilege in preference to the claims of employees, unless such payments are intended to enable the business of the undertaking; make payments to employees that do not correspond to the apportionment of the amount available, in proportion to the respective remunerations; make donations, regardless of the title; waive rights with equity value; enter into loan agreements as lender; carry out cash withdrawals for purposes other than the business of the company. The act of disposal of the assets of the company during a situation of delay, or in the previous six months, is null and void.

13.2. Employer misconducts

I. In the case of employer's delay or default in accomplishing his/her duties, he/she incurs in liability under the general rules of the Civil Code and articles 323.rd et seq. of Labour Code.

As referred above, if there is a delay in paying the employee's monthly salary, i.e., if the employee doesn't receive the amount of the remuneration on the due date (278.th, n.er 5)the employer shall pay the corresponding default interest at the legal rate (4% – Regulatory ordinance, *Portaria n.er 291/2003*), or the higher rate established in a collective regulation instrument of work or agreement between the parties (323.rd).

If the delay in the payment of the employee's salary is longer then 15 days from its due date, the employee can suspend the contract by written notice to the employer and to the Ministry of Labor, with an advance notice of 8 days (325.th, n.er 1).

If there is a 60 days delay in the payment of the employee's salary from its due date, then the law considers it as default (more serious than a delay) and therefore the employee can terminate the contract with by delivering written notice to the employer within 30 days from delay (394.th and 395.th). In this case, the employee will be entitled to receive compensation (394.th n.ers 1, 2 and 5, and article 396.th)[296].

[296] See Joana Vasconcelos, *Código do Trabalho Anotado*, cit., notes on article 394.th – 396.th, pp. 899 et seq.

Moreover, the employee's salary benefits from the guarantees expressed in articles 333.º et seq., as follows: credit privileges (333.rd); solidarity liability within groups of corporations with reciprocal, domain or group participation (334.th); liability of partner, manager, board member or director (335.th); the payment of worker credits arising from employment contracts, or of their violation or termination, which cannot be paid by the employer by reason of insolvency or difficult economic situation, shall be ensured by the Salary Guarantee Fund, under the terms provided for in specific legislation (336.th); the credit of an employee arising from an employment contract, for its violation or termination shall prescribe one year after the termination of the contract (337.th) .

II. The employer may also incur in defective performance, whenever there is a deficient or incomplete (partial) execution of the contract that does not fully satisfy its requirements and obligations. a default nor a delay, but the contract is insufficiently executed.

There is, for example, a defective performance of the employer when there is a deficient or incomplete execution of the duty to train the employee (130 or of the duty to enact rules on health and safety (281.st).

In these situations, the employee may terminate the contract with just cause under the provisions of article 394 et seq., receiving compensation for it (396.th).

13.3. Employee misconducts

I. The employee must respect his/her contractual and legal duties, expressed in article 128.th. If he/she violates his/her duties, he/she will incur in a misconduct and can be held liable for that action. Besides, in that case the employer may exercise its disciplinary power in order to sanction the employee[297].

For instance, if the employee violates his/her duties of punctuality or assiduity (article 128.th, n.er 1, *b*)) he/she incurs in default or in delay and loses his/her salary corresponding to the period of absence (256.th). If it is

[297] See Pedro Romano Martinez, *Direito do Trabalho*, cit., pp. 808 et seq.

a mere delay, he/she can compensate his/her absence with extra work. The employer must allow this compensation.

If the employee presents an unjustified delay for longer than 60 minutes, the employer may not accept the provision of work for the entire day; if the delay exceeds 30 minutes, the employer may not accept the provision for half of the normal working period (256.th, n.er 4).

Usually default is partial. For example, if there is an unjustified absence of 2 days, the employee is entitled can claim the 20 business days he/she worked during that month.

II. The employee misconducts can lead to to exercise of the employer's disciplinary power by initiating a procedure for the application of a disciplinary penalty (318.th).

If the violation of the duties is very serious, the employer can dismiss the employee with just cause and without the need to pay any compensation (351.st). In this case, the employee is responsible for the damage caused to the employer (323.th).

III. The employee may also incur in defective performance, whenever there is a deficient or incomplete (partial) execution of the contract that does not fully satisfy its requirements and obligations. In these situations, there is neither a default nor a delay, but the contract is insufficiently executed.

There is, for example, a defective performance by the employee when he/she violates his/her duty of zeal and diligence (128.th, ner 1, *c*)) – he/she is working at his/her workplace and within the working schedule and as such there's no delay or default. Nevertheless, he/she is not working as he/she should.

In these cases, where there is a defective performance, the employer may apply a sanction against the employee (328.th). If it is a very serious violation, the employer may fire him/her with just cause by observing the legal requirements and procedures (351.st et seq.).

14.
Termination of the employment contract

14.1. General overview

I. Along with the mass of other private contracts, the employment contract, being a term contract or an open-ended contract, can be terminated[298].

The Portuguese Labour Code deals with the termination of the employment contract in the following terms [299].

As an overview, the employment contract may terminate by expiration, by mutual agreement (revocation), or by initiative of the employer or employee. On termination, employment law differs from the regime comprised in the Civil Code and applicable the majority of private contracts[300].

The reason is straightforward: considering the importance of the employment contract for the worker and his/her family, the law protects the employee against abusive and unfair dismissals. Hence, the law tries to protect the weaker party of the contract and the one that depends economically from the work: the employee[301].

The basic rule on this regard is the one which follows from the principle of job security enshrined in article 53.rd of the Portuguese Constitution – workers are guaranteed job security, and dismissal without fair cause or for

[298] See João Leal Amado, *Contrato de Trabalho*, cit., pp. 352 et seq.

[299] See Menezes Cordeiro, *Direito do Trabalho II*, cit., pp. 843 et seq.

[300] See Pedro Romano Martinez, *Direito do Trabalho*, cit., pp. 893 et seq.

[301] See Guilherme Dray, *O Princípio da Proteção do Trabalhador*, cit., pp. 769 et seq.

political or ideological reasons is prohibited. The same rule is expressed in article 338.th of the Labour Code, which forbids unfair dismissal or dismissal motivated for political or ideological reasons[302].

As a consequence, and as referred above, the Portuguese system does not apply the employment at will doctrine which exists in the common law countries[303], under which both the employee and the employer can terminate the contract with or without just cause.

Because of the importance of this subject, article 339.th determines that the legal regime regarding termination of contract is mandatory, which means it cannot be replaced by contract or by instrument of coletive labour regulation[304].

II. The forms of termination of the employment contract are expressed in article 340.th of the Labour Code.

Under this provision, the forms of termination are the following[305]:

a) Expiration;
b) Revocation;
c) Dismissal for a fact attributable to the employee;
d) Collective dismissal;
e) Dismissal for extinction of a job position;
f) Dismissal due to inadaptation;
g) Resolution by the employee;
h) Termination by the employee.

Let´s take a closer look at each of them.

[302] See Pedro romano Martinez, *Código do Trabalho Anotado*, cit., notes on article 338.th – 396.th, pp. 787 et seq.

[303] See Alvin L. Goldman and Roberto L. Corrada, *Labor Law in the USA*, cit., p. 98.

[304] See Maria do Rosário Ramalho, *Tratado de Direito do Trabalho – Parte II*, cit., pp. 32 et seq.

[305] See Pedro Romano Martinez, *Código do Trabalho Anotado*, cit., notes on article 340.th, pp. 792 et seq.

14.2. Expiration

I. Expiration occurs when contract terminates because it naturally comes to an end, because its function is accomplished (e.g. fixed term contract) or as it is rendered impossible due to the employee (employee's death or absolute inability) or to the employer (undertaking´s extinction)[306].

Under article 343, the employment contract expires in general terms, because:

a) It comes to term;
b) There is a supervening, absolute and definitive impossibility of the worker to provide his/her work or of the employer to receive it;
c) The worker retires, due to old age or disability.

II. The first cause for expiration is its natural end, whenever it is a fixed-term or an unfixed-term contract. Expiration takes place at the end of the term by declaration of one of the contractors[307].

Regarding expiration of the fixed-term contract, article 344 provides that this type of contract expires at the end of the stipulated period, or it's renewal, provided that the employer or the employee reports to the other party the will to do so, in writing, 8 to 15 days before the deadline expires[308].

Regarding expiration of an unfixed-term contract, article 345 states the unfixed-term employment contract expires when, provided the occurrence of the term, the employer notifies termination of the contract with a minimum previous notice of 7, 30 or 60 days, depending whether the contract lasted up to six months, two years or for a longer period.

If the expiration arises from a notification from the employer, the employee is entitled to a compensation corresponding to 18 days of basic salary and seniority payment for each full year of seniority, calculated in accordance with the formula expressed in article 366.th.

[306] See Maria do Rosário Ramalho, *Tratado de Direito do Trabalho – Parte II*, cit., pp. 761 et seq.

[307] See João Leal Amado, *Contrato de Trabalho*, cit., pp. 358 et seq.

[308] See Pedro Romano Martinez, *Código do Trabalho Anotado*, cit., notes on articles 344.th and 345, pp. 797 et seq.

II. The second cause occurs with the absolute and final supervenient impossibility of the worker to provide his/her work or of the employer in receiving it. For instance, if a truck driver has an accident and loses his legs and arms, he/she cannot work anymore as a driver. There's an absolute, definitive and supervenient event that makes the subsistence of the employment contract impossible. Therefore, the contract expires[309].

Secondly, the contract shall also expires, for example, in case of death of an individual employer. In this case, the contract terminates at the date of closure of the enterprise, unless the successor of the deceased continues the activity for which the employee is hired or if the company or establishment is transferred. (article 346). Also, the extinction of a corporate employer, when there's no transfer of the company or establishment, determines the expiry of the employment contract[310]. Finally, the total and definitive closure of the company determines the expiry of the employment contract, and triggers the procedure provided for in article 360.th et seq., with the necessary adaptations.

If the contract expires due to any reasons of the precedent paragraphs, the employee is entitled to a compensation calculated in accordance with article 366.th.

III. The third cause expressed in article 343 is retirement[311].

Article 348.th states that the employment contract of a worker that retires from old age converts into a fixed-term contract 30 days after both parties are aware of it. In this case, the contract will be subject to the regime defined in the Code for the fixed-term contracts, with the necessary adaptations and the following specificities:

a) The reduction of the contract, in writing, is waived;
b) The contract is valid for a period of six months, renewing for equal and successive periods, without being subject to maximum thresholds;

[309] See Maria do Rosário Ramalho, *Tratado de Direito do Trabalho – Parte II,* cit., pp. 767 et seq.
[310] See Pedro Romano Martinez, *Código do Trabalho Anotado,* cit., notes on articles 343.rd and 345.th, pp. 796 et seq.
[311] See Luís Menezes Leitão, *Direito do Trabalho,* cit., pp. 385 et seq.

c) Expiration of the contract is subject to prior notice of 15 to 60 days, depending on whether the initiative is of the employer or of the worker;
d) Expiration does not determine the payment of any compensation to the employee.

The same rules apply to a contract of employment of a worker that reaches the age of 70 years old, even if he/she doesn't retire.

14.3. Revocation

I. There is revocation when we have a mutual agreement between employer and employee to terminate the contract[312].

The employer and employee may agree to rescind and revoke the employment contract[313].

Under article 349.th, the agreement shall be set down in writing and signed by both parties. The document should expressly mention the date of conclusion of the agreement and the purported effects. If both parties establish a global pecuniary compensation for the employee, it is presumed that all employment credits of the employee, such as salary, holiday and christmas allowances, are already included and settled on the date of termination date[314].

II. In order to avoid situations in which the employee is compelled to accept revocation without a free and conscious will, the law states that the employee may revoke the agreement up until the 7.th day following the date of conclusion of the revocation agreement ("right to regret"). In order to make effective the referred "right to regret", the employee must give back any compensation he/she may have received from the employer due to the termination of the contract. The right to regret cannot be exercised if the

[312] See MARIA DO ROSÁRIO RAMALHO, *Tratado de Direito do Trabalho – Parte II*, cit., pp. 789 et seq.
[313] See JOÃO LEAL AMADO, *Contrato de Trabalho*, cit., pp. 365 et seq.
[314] See PEDRO ROMANO MARTINEZ, *Código do Trabalho Anotado*, cit., notes on article 349.th, pp. 809 et seq.

revocation agreement is duly dated and signatures are notarized in person as per the law (article 350).

14.4 Termination under the employer's initiative

14.4.1. General overview

I. Dismissal without just cause is prohibited in per article 53.rd of the Portuguese Constitution, but the employer can dismiss the employee for just cause[315].

The underlying reason is the following: although there is a general prohibition of dismissals without just cause, the employer can dismiss the employee if there is a motive that turns impossible the subsistence of the employment relationship, due to a fact attributable to the employee, or based on circumstances regarding economic or technological issues.

When this happens, there is a dismissal for just cause[316].

II. Dismissal for just cause takes place when the employer decides to terminate the contract based on a legal motive: for subjective or objective just cause.

The employer can dismiss the employee if the latter incurs in a very serious breach of contract. In this case we are dealing with subjective just cause (article 351.st et seq.).

The employer can also dismiss the employee for an objective just cause, based on reasons that cannot be imputable to the employee, if there is: (i) an economic crisis that justifies a collective dismissal (article 359.th et seq.); (ii) a cause extinction of a job post (article 367.th et seq.); or (iii) an employee is unsuitable to adapt to new changes to the workplace environment or to accomplish certain goals (article 373.rd et seq.).

We will now provide some insight into this.

[315] See Maria do Rosário Ramalho, *Tratado de Direito do Trabalho – Parte II*, cit., pp. 799 et seq.

[316] See Luís Menezes Leitão, *Direito do Trabalho*, cit., pp. 388 et seq.

14.4.2. Dismissal for subjective just cause

I. The employer may terminate the employment contract if there is serious misconduct by the employee that, by its consequences, makes immediately and practically impossible the subsistence of the employment relationship[317]. That's the normative concept of just cause stated in article 351.st, n.^{er} 1[318].

Since the concept of just cause is an undetermined concept, the Law tries to determine it by giving some examples of employee misconducts that can sustain his/her dismissal for just cause (n.^{er} 2).

In particular, there is just cause for fair dismissal if the employee incurs in one of the following events:

a) Illegitimate disobedience to orders given by hierarchically superior officials;
b) Violation of rights and guarantees of other employees of the company;
c) Repeatedly causing conflicts with workers of the company;
d) Showing lack of interest in the fulfillement, with due diligence, of obligations inherent to the exercise of the position to which he/she is assigned;
e) Serious damages to crucial interests of the company;
f) False statements regarding the justification of absences;
g) Unjustified absences from work that directly cause serious losses or risks to the company, or whose number reaches, in each calendar year, 5 consecutive or 10 interpolated absences, in the latter regardless of injury or risk;
h) Lack of compliance with safety and health rules at work;
i) Practice, within the company, of physical violence, injuries or other offenses punishable by law on employees of the company, elements of social bodies or on an individual employees not belonging to these bodies, their delegates or representatives;
j) Kidnapping or committing general crime against the freedom of the people mentioned in the previous paragraph;

[317] See João Leal Amado, *Contrato de Trabalho,* cit., pp. 371 et seq.

[318] See Pedro Romano Martinez, *Código do Trabalho Anotado,* cit., notes on article 351.st, pp. 814 et seq.

l) Non-compliance or opposition to comply with a judicial or administrative decision;
m) Abnormal productivity reductions.

The list stated in article 351.st, n.er 2, is an open list. One may find other actions that are not exemplified but may still be considered just cause.

Nevertheless, even if there is an action of the employee exemplified in article 351.st, n.er 2, we cannot say there is automatic just cause for dismissal. .st

II. We have to apply the so called "spiral of concretization" method: first, we have to find if there is a serious misconduct by the employee (n.er 1); secondly, we have to see if that misconduct is exemplified in the list of situations provided by law (n.er 2); thirdly, we have to find out whether this action is harmful to the employer and consider the degree of damage to the employer's interests, as well as type of the relationship between the parties or between the employee and his/her co-workers (n.er 3); finally, we shall get back to the concept stated in number 1 to conclude whether the misconduct at stake renders immediately and practically impossible the employment relationship. It will be the case, for example, of a misconduct that is so serious that breaks any confidence of the employer's over the employee's future in the corporation[319].

III. At times there is just cause for dismissal even if the action is not exemplified in article 351.st, n.er 1. That is the exceptional case of just cause for personal issues, regarding the employee's private life. As a rule, private events cannot be considered as a disciplinary infraction, as they belong to the employee's private sphere. This is the case, for example, of circumstances regarding the sexual or sentimental life of the employee, or facts related to his/her health or hobbies. Despite this general rule, certain events from the employee's private life can, exceptionally, be relevant for a dismissal for just cause. This was the case, for example, of a crew captain of a civil airplane who was seen on the eve of boarding drinking whisky in a Hotel and with several females at the same time, having been recognized by the passengers of that flight as commander of the airplane. This can also

[319] See Menezes Cordeiro, *Direito do Trabalho II*, cit., pp 934 et seq.

be the case of an employee of a Bank who is convicted in his or her private life of financial fraud, even though it occurred outside his or her job. Or it may be the case of two workers who work side-by-side who one day, during their rest time, seriously attacked each other in front of other colleagues, seriously degrading the good work environment in the company. In short and as a rule, facts of private life are irrelevant for just cause of dismissal. But exceptionally, if they harm the trust relationship between the parties or irreversibly affect the working environment, may constitute just cause for dismissal[320].

IV. The existence of a subjective just cause is a requirement (substantive requirement) for dismissal but is not enough to lawfully fire the employee.

The employer shall promote a special disciplinary procedure (formal requirement) to dismiss the employee, under articles 328.th et seq. and 352.nd et seq.[321]

The special procedure to dismiss contains four different phases: accusation (article 353.rd); defense (article 355.th); instruction (article 356.th) and decision (article 357.th)[322].

The accusation is based on a "fault-based notice for dismissal". In the event of any behavior likely to be grounds for just cause for dismissal, the employer shall inform the worker who has committed it the intention to dismiss him/her in writing, together with a detailed description of the facts imputed. On the same date, the employer shall send copies of the communication and the note of fault to the workers' committee and, if the worker is a trade union representative, to the respective trade union association (article 353.rd).The notification of the fault notice to the worker interrupts the count of the periods established in article 329.th [323].

The employee has the right to defend himself/herself under a due process, has 10 working days to consult the case and respond to the guilty

[320] See Menezes Cordeiro, *Direito do Trabalho II*, cit., pp. 963 et seq.

[321] See Maria do Rosário Ramalho, *Tratado de Direito do Trabalho – Parte II*, cit., pp. 822 et seq.

[322] See Pedro Romano Martinez, *Código do Trabalho Anotado*, cit., notes on articles 352.th – 357.th, pp. 818 et seq.

[323] See Menezes Cordeiro, *Direito do Trabalho II*, cit., pp. 984 et seq.

note, deducting in writing the elements that he/she considers relevant to clarify the facts and his/her participation in them; the worker is able to attach documents and request the evidentiary measures that are relevant to ascertain the truth (article 355.th).

After the defense, we have the instruction phase that comprises evidentiary mechanisms to determine the facts. The employer, by himself/herself or through an instructor appointed by him/her, shall carry out the evidentiary measures requested by the employee in his/her response to the note of guilt, unless the employer considers them delay mechanism, in this case he/she shall submit a reasoned plea in writing. The employer is not obliged to proceed to the hearing of more than three witnesses for each fact described in the fault-based notice for dismissal, nor more than 10 in total. The worker must ensure the presence of the witnesses he/she indicates. Upon completion of the probationary proceedings, the employer shall submit a copy of the file to the workers' committee and, if the worker is a union representative, to the respective trade union association, who may, within five working days, issue a reasoned opinion (article 356.th).

Finally, we reach the decision. After the accusation, the defense and the instruction, the employer may decide whether he/she wants to dismiss the employee, or to close the process for lack of evidence or if he/she concludes after all that there's no relevant misconduct. If the employer finds out that there is misconduct but concludes that is not so serious to justify a dismissal, then he/she can decide to apply a penalty, such as a reprehension or a monetary penalty, but not dismissal for just cause. The dismissal for just cause is the most serious sanction and therefore should be an *ultima ratio* – it is only applicable when misconduct is so serious that justifies termination of the contract.

The decision of dismissal shall be written and substantiated. After the decision is notified, it enters into force. If the decision is the dismissal for just cause, the employment contract terminates with its issuance (article 357.th).

V. In the event the employee is fired for subjective just cause, he/she lacks any right to specific compensation. He/she is only entitled to the general credits that become due as a result of termination (regular pay; holiday's pay; christmas pay; overtime pay if owed, etc). He/she may also be liable for damages caused to the employer under the liability regime in article 323.rd [324].

If the employee doesn´t agree with the dismissal, whether because he/she thinks there´s no just cause, or because he/she argues he/she had no chance to defend himself/herself, he/she can file a complaint against the employer to contest the dismissal by submitting an application to the competent court, within 60 days from receipt of the notice of dismissal (article 387.th).

14.4.3. Collective dismissal

I. There is an objective just cause to dismiss the employee when the employer may fire him/her due to a legal motive that is not based on the latter´s fault, on a misconduct or a breach of contract. In other words: the employee has done nothing wrong, but there is a legal motive (an objective motive) that gives the employer the chance to dismiss the employee whilst paying him/her a compensation[325].

The Law defines three types of objective just cause: collective dismissal (articles 359.th – 366.th); extinction of a job post (articles 367.th – 372.nd); and inadaptation or unsuitability of the employee to adapt (373.rd – 380.th)[326].

II. Collective dismissal is the dismissal of at least 2 (micro businesses or small undertakings) or 5 (medium or big corporations) employees made within a period of 3 months based on the closure of a business unit or the process of costs and personal reduction for market, structural or technological reasons (article 359.th).

It is commonly know that the collective dismissal is motivated by an economic crisis that impacts the employer. It is therefore a last option to save the company from insolvency[327].

[324] See Pedro Romano Martinez, *Código do Trabalho Anotado*, cit., notes on article 323.rd, pp. 749 et seq.

[325] See Maria do Rosário Ramalho, *Tratado de Direito do Trabalho – Parte II*, cit., pp. 822 et seq.

[326] See João Leal Amado, *Contrato de Trabalho*, cit., pp. 385 et seq.

[327] See Luís Menezes Leitão, *Direito do Trabalho*, cit., pp. 393 et seq.

The underlying idea is: facing an economic crisis, or needing to make a rearrangement in the corporation for market or technological reasons, the employer is face with the need to dismiss collectively more than 2 or 5 employees, depending on the size of the company (article 359.th). The law defines market reasons, structural motives and technological reasons.

Under the law (article 359.th, n.er 2), one may consider market reasons for a reduction of the company's activity caused by the foreseeable decrease in the demand of goods or services or caused by a supervenient impossibility to place those goods or services on the market; structural reasons entails an economic and financial imbalance, a change of activity, a restructure of the production organization or a replacement of products; technological reasons are changes in manufacturing techniques or processes, automation of production, control or transfer of cargoes, as well as the use of new technological information and communication tools.

III. Whenever an employer intends to promote a collective dismissal, he/she has to follow a specific procedure governed by law and split in three different phases: communication to the worker's representatives and the Ministry of Employment (360.th); negotiation with the worker's representatives and the Ministry of Employment (361.st and 362.nd); final decision (363.rd)[328].

The first phase is the communications phase, during which the employer shall inform his/her intention to dismiss collectively some workers (article 360.st). The communication shall include:

a) The grounds for collective dismissal;
b) The list of workers, broken down by organizational sectors of the company;
c) The criteria for selection of the workers to be dismissed;
d) The number of workers to be fired and the professional categories covered;
e) The period during which it is intended to carry out the dismissal;
f) The method for calculating the compensation to be generally granted to employees, where appropriate, without prejudice to the

[328] See Pedro Romano Martinez, *Código do Trabalho Anotado*, cit., notes on articles 360.th to 363.rd, pp. 831 et seq.

compensation established in article 366.th or in an instrument of collective labour regulation.

In the absence of the employee's representatives, the employer shall notify his/her intention to proceed with the dismissal, in writing, to each of the workers thar are planned to be dismissed, who may within five working days of receiving of the communication create an *ad hoc* commission, with a maximum of three or five members, depending whether the dismissal covers five or more workers.

The employer must also inform the Ministry of Employment of his/her intention to promote a collective dismissal, so that Ministry can be part of the negotiation that will take place from then on.

IV. The second phase is the negotiation process, during which parties will bargain in order to see if there is an alternative to collective dismissal. Within five days of the first communication, the employer has to promote a negotiation with the representatives of the worker with the intention to reach an agreement on the scale and effects of the measures to be applied, as well as other alternative measures such as the suspension of employment contracts; the reduction of normal periods of work; the conversion or professional reclassification; or the early retirement of the employees (article 361.st). The Ministry of Employment takes part in these negotiations in order to guarantee compliance with the law and provide technical assistance (article 362.nd). Finally, the employer has to decide. He/she can decide to implement one of the alternative measures that were bargained, or to go ahead and carry on with the collective dismissal[329].

V. The decision shall take place up to 15 days after the first communication (article 363.rd). If the employer decides to collectively dismiss the employees, he/she shall notify each worker concerned advancing the underlying reason for the dismissal; the date of termination; the amount, time and place of payment of the credits due to termination and the legal compensation.

This decision shall be in writing and the employer must inform the employees affected with the following previous notice:

[329] See Maria do Rosário Ramalho, *Tratado de Direito do Trabalho – Parte II*, cit., pp. 890 et seq.

a) 15 days, in the event of a worker with a seniority of less than 1 year;
b) 30 days, in the event of a worker with a seniority of 1 year or more and less than 5 years;
c) 60 days, in the event of a worker with a seniority equal to or greater than 5 years and less than 10 years;
d) 75 days in the event of a worker with a seniority of 10 years or more.

VI. As a consequence of an ongoing collective dismissal, the employee is entitled to a credit of hours to find a new job corresponding to two days a week whilst losing the right to a salary (364.th); to deliver notice of termination of the contract without just cause with only 3 days of previous notice (365.th); and to a specific compensation for the termination of the contract (366th)[330].

The compensation for collective dismissal corresponds to 12 days of basic salary and seniority subsidies ("seniorities" in Portuguese: "*diuturnidades*") for each full year of seniority. The compensation shall be determined as follows:

a) The amount of the basic monthly remuneration and seniority subsidies to be considered cannot exceed 20 times the minimum monthly guaranteed remuneration;
b) The total amount of the compensation may not exceed 12 times the basic monthly salary and daily allowances of the employee or, when the limit provided for in the previous paragraph is applicable, 240 times the minimum monthly guaranteed salary;
c) The daily value of basic and diurnal remuneration is the result of the division by 30 of the basic monthly remuneration and seniority payments;
d) In the case of a fraction of a year, the amount of the compensation shall be calculated proportionally.

The worker is presumed to accept the dismissal when he/she receives the compensation provided for in article 366.th. This assumption may be

[330] See Luís Menezes Leitão, *Direito do Trabalho*, cit., pp. 396 et seq.

rebutted provided that, simultaneously, the employee pays back or puts the compensation paid by the employer at the latter's disposition.

14.4.4. Dismissal for the extinction of a job post

I. The extinction of a job is the dismissal of an employee based on market, structural or technological reasons regarding the undertaking (article 367.th)[331].

The reasons are equivalent to those that support the collective dismissal (367.th, n.er 2).

The difference between the extinction of a job and collective dismissal is numerical – in first case we have the dismissal of 1 single employee; on the collective dismissal we have the dismissal of 2 to 5 workers, depending on the size of the undertaking.

Like the collective dismissal, the extinction of a job post depends on substantive and formal requirements to be lawful[332].

II. Substantive requirements are expressed at article 368.th, as follows[333]:

a) The reasons for the extinction are not attributable neither to the employer nor the employee;
b) The subsistence of the employment relationship seems practically and immediately impossible;
c) The extinguished job post is not performed by any fixed or unfixed term employee;
d) The collective dismissal process is not applicable (368.th).

If there is a plurality of identical work posts, in the determination of the work post to be terminated, the employer's decision shall, by reference to the respective holders, obey the following non-discriminatory criteria:

[331] See Maria do Rosário Ramalho, *Tratado de Direito do Trabalho – Parte II*, cit., pp. 899 et seq.

[332] See João Leal Amado, *Contrato de Trabalho*, cit., pp. 390 et seq.

[333] See Pedro Romano Martinez, *Código do Trabalho Anotado*, cit., notes on articles 367.th to 372.nd, pp. 846 et seq.

a) Worse performance evaluation, with previously known parameters by the worker;
b) Lower academic and professional qualifications;
c) Increased labour costs due to the maintenance of the employee as a worker;
d) Less experience in the function;
e) Lower seniority in the company.

The worker who, during the three months preceding the beginning of the dismissal procedure, has been transferred to a job that was extinguished, is entitled to be reassigned to the previous employment if it still exists, with the same basic remuneration[334].

III. Under the same terms of the collective dismissal, the extinction of a job post depends on a specific procedure with three different phases: communication to the worker's representatives and the Ministry of Employment (369.th); consultation with the worker's representatives and the Ministry of Employment (370.th); final decision (371.st).

Under article 369.th the employer shall inform, in writing, the employee´s representatives about:

a) The need to extinguish the job, indicating the reasons and the section or equivalent unit to which it relates;
b) The need to dismiss the worker who is assigned to the job and his/her professional category;
c) The criteria used for the selection of the workers to dismiss.

Within 10 days of the communication provided by the employer, the representative structure of the workers, the worker involved and, if the latter is a trade unionized worker, the respective trade union, shall communicate to the employer its reasoned opinion, in particular on the grounds referred to in article 368.th or the criteria of selection referred to in paragraph 2 of that article, as well as the alternative measures to mitigate the effects of dismissal.

[334] See Luís Menezes Leitão, *Direito do Trabalho*, cit., pp. 397 et seq.

Any worker involved or his representatives may, within three working days of the employer's notice, ask the Ministry of Employment to verify legal compliance of the dismissal with the requirements set out in article 368.th .The Ministry shall prepare and send to the applicant and the employer a report on the matter within seven days after receipt of the application (article 370.th).

After these phases, the employer has to decide whether he/she extinguishes the job or not.

IV. The decision shall take place within 5 days after the first communication. If the employer decides to dismiss he employee, he shall notify him/her of the decision of dismissal, expressing the reasons for the dismissal; compliance with the legal requirements; the criteria applied to choose the worker to dismiss; the amount, time and place of payment of the credits due to the termination and the legal compensation; finally, the date of the contract termination[335].

This decision shall be in writing and the employer must inform the employee affected with previous notice correspondent to:

a) 15 days, in the case of a worker with a seniority of less than 1 year;
b) 30 days, in the case of a worker with a seniority of 1 year or more but less than 5 years;
c) 60 days, in the event of a worker with a seniority equal to or greater than 5 years and less than 10 years;
d) 75 days in the event of a worker with a seniority of 10 years or more.

V. As a consequence of an ongoing extinction of a job post the employee is entitled to the same rights attributed in a collective dismissal event, above referred, namely (372.nd): credit of hours to find a new job (364.th); right to terminate the contract without just cause with only 3 days of previous notice (365.th); right to receive a specific compensation for the termination of the contract (366.th).

[335] See PEDRO ROMANO MARTINEZ, *Código do Trabalho Anotado*, cit., notes on article 361.st, pp. 853 et seq.

14.4.5. Dismissal for inadaptation or unsuitability

I. Dismissal for inadaptation or unsuitability to adapt occurs when termination of an employment contract is pursued by the employer, who based his/her decision on the employee's supervening lack of adaptability to the job (374.th, n.^{er} 1)[336].

In sum, it depends on the employee's supervenient unsuitability to adapt, which makes the subsistence of the relationship impossible due to one of the following situations[337]:

a) Continuous reduction of productivity or quality;
b) Repeated malfunctions in the tools and equipments used in the workplace;
c) Risks to the health and safety of workers or third parties.

The dismissal for unsuitability may also occur regarding managers or employees that perform complex tasks whenever written goals, previously agreed upon with the employer, are not met by the employee as a result of his/her unsuitability and if non-compliance renders the subsistence of the employment relationship virtually impossible (374.th, n.^{er} 2).

II. Dismissal for supervening unsuitability in the situation referred to in article 375.th, n.^{er} 1, can only take place provided the cumulative following cumulative requirements are fulfilled[338]:

a) Changes have been made in the workplace resulting from alterations in the manufacturing or marketing technologies or equipment used which occurred six months prior to the initiation of the procedure;
b) The employer provided for appropriate vocational training regarding said modifications at the workplace through a competent authority or certified training entity;

[336] See Maria do Rosário Ramalho, *Tratado de Direito do Trabalho – Parte II*, cit., pp. 919 et seq.

[337] See João Leal Amado, *Contrato de Trabalho*, cit., pp. 392 et seq.

[338] See Pedro Romano Martinez, *Código do Trabalho Anotado*, cit., notes on article 375.th, pp. 858 et seq.

c) The worker has been given, after training, a period of adaptation of at least 30 days;
d) There is no other available workplace compatible with the professional category of the worker.

Dismissal in the situations referred to in article 375.th, n.er 2, may take place:

a) Where new manufacturing processes or new technologies or equipment based on different or more complex technology has been introduced, which implies a modification of the functions related to the job;
b) If there has been no change in the workplace, the employee must be informed, with supporting documents, of the changes to his/her performance which sustain dismissal and allow the employee to respond to the presented elements in writing within a deadline of at least 5 business days.

III. Dismissal based on unsuitability to adapt depends on a specific procedure with three different phases: communication to the worker's representatives and the Ministry of Employment (376.th); consultation by the worker's representatives and the employee (377.th); final decision (378.th)[339].

Under article 376.th, the employer shall inform the worker and, if the latter is a trade union representative, the union, about:

a) The intention to proceed with the dismissal, indicating the reasons;
b) The changes made to the workplace, if that is the case;
c) The results of the vocational training, if that is the case.

Within 10 days after the notification provided for in article 376.th, the worker may request evidence of the facts advanced by the employer to ground the dismissal. If evidence has been requested, the employer shall inform the worker, the representative structure of the workers and, if it is

[339] See Luís Menezes Leitão, *Direito do Trabalho*, cit., pp. 402 et seq.

a union representative, the respective Trade Union, of the attained results (article 377.th).

After these communications, the employee and representative structure of workers may, within 10 working days, communicate his/her employer its reasoned opinion, and the grounds presented for dismissal.

Finally, after gathering those opinions, the employer has 30 days to carry out the dismissal, under penalty of expiry of the right, by written statement referring:

a) The reason for termination of the employment contract;
b) The confirmation of the requirements set forth in article 375th;
c) The amount, form, time and place of payment of compensation and overdue credits and those due as a result of the termination of the job;
d) The date of termination of the contract.

IV. As a consequence of an ongoing dismissal based on unsuitability to adapt, the employee is entitled to the same rights given in a collective dismissal event, namely the following (379.th): credit of hours to find a new job (364.th); the right to terminate the contract without just cause with only 3 days of advance notice (365.th); the right to receive specific compensation for the termination of the contract (366.th).

14.4.6. Unlawfulness of the dismissal

I. As stated above, the employment contract may terminate by dismissal of the employee pursued by the employer[340].

The dismissal of the employee shall be based on just cause (substantive requirement) and follow a specific procedure (formal requirement) endorsed by the employer.

Upon the initiative of the employer, we may have a dismissal based on a subjective just cause or an objective just cause. In both cases the lawfulness of the dismissal depends, as well, on the follow up of a specific procedure.

[340] See Luís Menezes Leitão, *Direito do Trabalho*, cit., pp. 403 et seq.

Under the prohibition of dismissals without just cause (articles 53.rd Constitution and 388.th Labour Code) the legality of the dismissal depends on the existence of just cause and cannot be based on ideological, political, ethnical or religious motives, otherwise it will be null.

On the other hand, if the employer does not comply with the formal procedure comprised in the Labour Code (articles 354.th et seq. for the subjective just cause; and articles 360.th, 369.th et seq., and 376.th et seq. for objective just cause), the dismissal will be considered illegal.

The law lists all those cases in which the dismissal is illegal[341].

II. Article 381.st states the general causes for unlawful dismissals, establishing that the dismissal taken by the employer is unlawful if it is based on the referred political, ideological, ethnic or religious reasons, even if a different motive is invoked; if the reason justifying the dismissal is declared void; or if the dismissal is not preceded by its legal procedure. Moreover, the dismissal is also unlawful if, in the event of dismissal of a pregnant or breastfeeding woman or during the enjoyment of initial parental leave, in any of its forms, the employer doesn't obtain the necessary consent from the governmental authority that stands for equal opportunities for men and women[342].

Beyond the existence of general causes, the Law also comprehends specific reasons for the unlawfulness of the dismissal, as follows:

a) Article 382.nd specifies other reasons for the illegality of the dismissal based on a subjective just cause (351.st);
b) Article 383.rd details other reasons for the illegality of the collective dismissal (359.th);
c) Article 384.th contains other reasons for the illegality of the job extinction (367.th);
d) Article 385.th details other reasons for the illegality of the dismissal based on unsuitability or inadaptability (373.rd).

[341] See João Leal Amado, *Contrato de Trabalho*, cit., pp. 396 et seq.

[342] See Pedro Romano Martinez, *Código do Trabalho Anotado*, cit., notes on articles 381.st – 382.th pp. 870 et seq.

III. Under article 382.nd, the dismissal based on a subjective just cause (351.st) is also null if the deadlines define in article 329.th are exceeded or if the disciplinary procedure is illegal. The disciplinary procedure is illegal whenever:

a) The employer misses the fault-based notice, or if the latter is not in writing or does not contain the circumstantial description of the facts attributable to the worker;
b) The employer fails to communicate his/her intention to dismiss along with the fault-based notice;
c) The right of the employee to consult or respond to the fault-based notice is breached or if the deadline for responding is not guaranteed;
d) The communication to the employee of the dismissal decision is not made in writing, or is not made under the requirements of articles 357.th, n.er 4, or 358.th, n.er 2.

Under article 383.rd, collective dismissal (359.th) is also null if the employer[343]:

a) Has not made the communication provided for in article 360.th, n.er 1 or 4, or the negotiation provided for in article 361.st, n.er 1;
b) Fails to observe the deadline for dismissal referred to in article 363.rd, n.er 1;
c) Has not made available to the dismissed employee, until the end of the period of notice, the compensation due and referred in article 366.th as well as other credits due become due – due or become due as a result of the termination of the contract.

Under article 384.th, the extinction of a job post (367.th) is also null if the employer[344]:

a) Does not comply with the requirements of article 368.th, n.er 1;

[343] See Pedro Romano Martinez, *Código do Trabalho Anotado*, cit., notes on article 383.rd, pp. 873 et seq.

[344] See Pedro Romano Martinez, *Código do Trabalho Anotado*, cit., notes on article 384.th, pp. 874 et seq.

b) Fails to comply with the provisions of article 368.th, n.er 2;
c) Has not made the communications provided for in article 369.th;
d) Has not made available to the dismissed worker, until the end of the period of notice, the compensation due as referred in article 366.th, by reference to article 372.nd, and other credits due or payable as a consequence of the termination of the employment contract.

Under article 385.th, dismissal for the employee's unsuitability (373.rd) is also null if the employer[345]:

a) Fails to comply with the provisions of article 374.th, n.er 3 and 4 or article 375.th, n.ers. 1 – 3;
b) Has not made the communications provided for in article 376.th;
c) Has not made available to the dismissed worker, up until the end of the period of notice, the compensation due to it and referred in article 366.th by reference to paragraph 1 of article 379.th and any credits due by virtue of the termination of the employment contract.

IV. The unlawfulness of the dismissal shall be declared by a Court of Law in response to an unfair dismissal claim filled by the employee against his/her former employer (article 387.th, n.er 1).

In case of dismissal based on a subjective just cause (351.st), the unfair dismissal claim shall be filled by the employee through a legal form request within the period of 60 days after the dismissal's decision is notified. During the legal dispute, the employer cannot present any more facts and grounds beyond those that were expressed in the final decision of the dismissal.

The unlawfulness of the collective dismissal shall be declared by a Court of Law in response to an unfair collective dismissal claim filled by the employee against his/her former employer (article 388.th, n.er 1). The unfair collective dismissal claim must be filled by the employee within the period of 6 months after the collective dismissal's decision is notified. During the legal dispute, the employer cannot present more facts and grounds beyond those that were expressed in the final decision of the collective dismissal.

[345] See Pedro Romano Martinez, *Código do Trabalho Anotado*, cit., notes on article 384.th, pp. 875 et seq.

V. The general effects of an illegal dismissal, are expressed in article 389.th [346].

Under this provision, whenever a dismissal is judicially declared unlawful, the employee is entitled to a severance compensation for all the moral and patrimonial damages he/she suffered as a result of the dismissal, as well as to resume work in the same undertaking with the same job description and seniority, unless an exception is applicable under articles 391.st and 392.nd.

The severance compensation is foreseen in article 389.th, which states the employee is entitled to receive a compensation for all the moral and patrimonial damages he/she suffered as a result of the dismissal.

Moreover, under article 390.th, the employee is also entitled to receive all the salaries he/she stopped receiving from the day he/she was illegally dismissed up to the day the unlawfulness was declared by the Court. These salaries are usually called interim wages. The amounts received by the employee (e.g. unemployment subsidies) accrued in the time between the dismissal and the Court decision, foreseen in article 390.th, n.er 2, shall be discounted in the value of the interim wages.

Under article 389.th, the illegally dismissed employee is also entitled to be reintegrated at work with the same job description and seniority, unless an exception is applicable under articles 391.st and 392.nd.

These are the main rights the unlawfully dismissed employee may claim. But the law provides him/her with some alternatives.

VI. Considering that an employee illegally dismissed may not want to resume work, as the relationship between him/her and the employer maybe irretrievably broken, article 391.st offers the employee the chance to opt for receiving a different compensation for the unlawful dismissal, instead of his/her reintegration at work.

In this case, the substitutive compensation varies between 15 and 45 days of monthly salary and seniority subsidies, according to Court criteria, depending on the degree of the employer's guilt and of the amount of the employee's wages, with a minimum of 3 monthly salaries.

The option between reinstatement at work or receiving a severance compensation is therefore a subjective right that can be exercised by the

[346] See Luís Menezes Leitão, *Direito do Trabalho*, cit., pp. 407 et seq.

employee. That means that, as a rule, this is an option that belongs to the employee and not to the employer. If the employee wants to resume work after the judicial declaration of illegality of dismissal, he/she may choose this option and the employer cannot oppose this. However, the law admits some exemptions to this rule.

VII. If the unlawful dismissal occurs at a micro undertaking or if the dismissed employee is a Member of the Board of Directors or a Director, the employer can ask the Court to not reinstate the employee, if he/she proves his/her return to work is seriously harmful to the company (article 392.nd). This request cannot proceed if the dismissal is based on a political, ideological, ethnical or religious motive, and ultimately is up to the Court to decide whether the employer's will in not reintegrating the employee is acceptable and justifiable or not. Hence, one may not say that the employer has a subjective right against the reinstatement. The employer can say he/she does not want to reinstate the employee, but the final decision belongs to the judge[347].

If the Court agrees with the employer's request not to reintegrate the employee, the latter will be entitled to receive a higher compensation than usual. This compensation will range from 30 to 60 days of salary and seniority subsidies, according to Court criteria, depending on the degree of the employer's guilt and of the amount of the employee's wages, with a minimum of 6 months salaries.

14.5. Termination by the employee

14.5.1. General overview

I. Along with other private contracts, the employment contract can also be terminated, whether it is a fixed-term or an open-ended contract, and the employee can terminate it at will by his/her own initiative. He/she can do it with just cause or without just cause. Having just cause he/she can terminate

[347] See PEDRO ROMANO MARTINEZ, *Código do Trabalho Anotado*, cit., notes on article 392.th, pp. 893 et seq.

the contract immediately. If there´s no just cause, he/she can deliver notice of termination of contract with previous notice.

There is termination of the employment contract by the employee if he/she terminates the contract based on an employer misconduct (default) that affects him/her seriously. In this case the employee can terminate the contract based on just cause without previous notice (article 394.th).

There is termination of the contract by the employee if he/she decides to terminate the contract without just cause through a "notice of termination"[348].

II. The underlying reason behind this regime is the idea that the employee is a citizen that benefits from a myriad of freedoms and fundamental rights. The termination of the contract by the initiative of the employee is based on the constitutional principle of freedom to work, enshrined in article 47.th of the Portuguese Constitution, in light of which everyone has the right to choose a job or type of work freely. The philosophy behind this rule is easy to grasp: no one can work against his/her own will and slavery is blatantly prohibited, as stated in article 4.th of the Universal Declaration of Human Rights – no one shall be held in slavery or servitude; slavery and slave trade shall be prohibited in all their possible forms.

Therefore, freedom of work also comprehends also the employee´s freedom to terminate the contract. Contrarily to the constitutional rule that forbids the employer´s dismissal without just cause (article 53.rd), the employee may terminate he employment contract without just cause.

14.5.2. Termination by just cause

I. In the event of just cause, the worker can immediately terminate the contract (article 394.th, n.er 1). The causes for termination of the contract with just cause can be divided into two types: just cause based on a serious

[348] See Maria do Rosário Ramalho, *Tratado de Direito do Trabalho – Parte II*, cit., pp. 937 et seq.

offense by the employer (article 394.th, n.er 2), or just cause based on objective causes (article 394.th, n.er 3)[349].

The employee can terminate the contract based on subjective just cause grounded on the employer's performance in the following situations (article 394.th, n.er 2)[350]:

a) Default of the employer in the payment of remuneration;
b) Violation of legal or conventional guarantees of the employee;
c) Application of abusive sanctions against the employee;
d) Lack of safety and health conditions at work;
e) Damage of the employee's pecuniary interests;
f) Offense to the physical or moral integrity, freedom, honor or dignity of the employee, punishable by law, including the practice of harassment by the employer or his/her representative.

Regarding subparagraph a), the law considers that a delay in timely payment of remuneration for a period of 60 days. There Is also a delay when the employer, at the request of the employee, declares in writing the forecast of non-payment of the missing remuneration until the expiration of that period of 60 days, is considered as default (article 394.th, n.er 5).

The employee can terminate the contract based on an objective just cause in the following situations (article 394.th, n.er 3):

a) The need to fulfill a legal obligation Is incompatible with the subsistence of the contract;
b) Substantial and lasting change of the working conditions lawfully attained by the employer and in the exercise of management powers;
c) Failures of punctual payment of the retribution not based on the employer's fault;
d) Transfer to the acquirer of the employer's position in the employment contract, as a result of the transfer of the undertaking, under to article 285.th, n.er 1 or 2, on the basis of article 286th, n.er 1.

[349] See Maria do Rosário Ramalho, *Tratado de Direito do Trabalho Parte II*, cit., pp. 941 et seq.

[350] See João Leal Amado, *Contrato de Trabalho*, cit., pp. 441 et seq.

II. The existence of just cause shall be analyzed under the same criteria employed in article 351.st, n.^{er} 3, regarding dismissal with just cause by the employer. In order to determine if there is just cause for the resolution of the contract by the employe one shall estimate the degree of the damages suffered by the employee; an existing good or bad relationship between the employer and the employee; and other relevant circumstances (article 394.th, n.4)[351].

The termination of the contract based on the facts foreseen in article 394.th, n.^{er} 2, i.e., grounded on subjective just cause, entitles the employee to receive a compensation between 15 and 45 days of basic remuneration and seniority subsidies for each full year of seniority, taking into account the value of the salaries and the degree of unlawfulness in the behavior of the employer, and in any event, shall not be less than 3 months of basic remuneration and seniority subsidies. Compensation can be higher whenever the patrimonial and moral damages suffered by the employee are higher than the value of the compensation depicted (396.th, n.^{er} 1 and 2).

If termination is based on objective just cause, foreseen in article 394.th, n.^{er} 3, the employee does not have the right to receive any compensation.

III. The notification of termination of the contract shall be delivered to the employer[352].

Under article 395.th the employee must communicate the termination to the employer, in writing, with a brief indication of the facts that justify it, within 30 days of the knowledge of said facts. In the case referred to in paragraph 5 of article 394.th, the deadline for termination is counted from the end of the period of 60 days or the declaration of the employer stating he/she will not pay the salary on the due date. If the basis of the termination is the need to fulfill a legal obligation incompatible with the subsistence of the contract (article 394th, n.^{er} 3, paragraph a)), the communication should be made as soon as possible.

The employer may require that the signature of the worker included in the declaration of termination is notarized in person. In this case, there must

[351] See Pedro Romano Martinez, *Código do Trabalho Anotado*, cit., notes on article 394.th, pp. 899 et seq.

[352] See Pedro Romano Martinez, *Código do Trabalho Anotado*, cit., notes on article 395.th, pp. 902 et seq.

be a period not exceeding 60 days between the date of recognition and the termination of the contract.

14.5.2. Notice of termination

I. The employee can terminate the employment at his/her will, based on the freedom to work principle (article 47.th of the Portuguese Constitution)[353]. In this case, termination is attained by the worker's offer of resignation or declaration that he/she is quitting the job[354].

Under article 400.th, the employee may deliver notice of termination of the contract regardless of just cause, by notifying the employer, in writing, at least 30 or 60 days in advance, depending on whether the contract is up to 2 years or more than 2 years old, respectively. Termination must be accomplished by written communication[355].

The instrument of collective labour regulation and the contract of employment may increase the period of notice up to six months if the employee occupies a position of administration or management or takes a representation or responsibility role.

In the event of a fixed-term contract, the delivery of notice of termination must be done with an advance notice of 15 or 30 days, in advance, depending on whether the contract had lasted for at least 6 months or less. In the event of an unfixed-term contract, for the purpose of the duration of the notice period, one must base that calculation on the duration of the contract already elapsed.

II. As stated above, the employee must previously inform the employer of the notice of termination of the contract. The employee, who does not comply, in whole or in part, with the notice period established in article 400.th must pay the employer a compensation equal to the basic remuneration and seniority subsidies corresponding to the fault period, without jeopardizing the right to compensation for damages caused by failure to comply with prior notice an obligation assumed in the pact of permanence

[353] See MARIA DO ROSÁRIO RAMALHO, *Tratado de Direito do Trabalho – Parte II*, cit., pp. 953 et seq.

[354] See ALVIN L. GOLDMAN and ROBERTO L. CORRADA, *Labor Law in the USA*, cit., p. 116.

[355] See JOÃO LEAL AMADO, *Contrato de Trabalho*, cit., pp. 430 et seq.

(article 401.st). In this case, the contract terminates, but the employee shall pay a compensation to the employer[356].

III. The law also provides a "right to regret", regarding the notice of termination of the contract. If the employee's signature does not have notarial recognition face-to-face, he/she can revoke the notice of termination up until the seventh day after the date on which it was received by the employer, by written communication.

IV. Finally, the Labour Code considers as an abandonment of work and therefore a tacit notice of termination, the occurrence of some facts regarding the employee's absence from work[357].

Under article 403.rd, the employee's absence from work sided with facts which likely indicate the intention not to resume it, is considered an abandonment of the job.

Moreover, the abandonment of the job is presumed in case of absence for at least 10 consecutive business days without the employer being informed of the reason for the absence.

The abandonment of the job must be treated as an employer delivery of notice to terminate the contract and can only be used by the employer after he/she informs the worker of the grounds for the abandonment or the presumption thereof, by registered letter with notice to the last known address of the worker. This presumption may be rebutted by the employee by presenting evidence of an event of force majeure impeding the communication to the employer of an absence justification.

In the event of abandonment of work, since the law considers it as a termination of contract without just cause and previous notice, the worker shall indemnify the employer in accordance with article 401.st.

[356] See Luís Menezes Leitão, *Direito do Trabalho*, cit., pp. 413 et seq.

[357] See Maria do Rosário Ramalho, *Tratado de Direito do Trabalho – Parte II*, cit., pp. 956 et seq.

15. Labour Law

15.1. General Overview

I. Labour Law deals with collective structures, collective bargaining and collective conflicts[358].

Labour Law is the discipline that deals with the relationship between employers and the collective structures that represent the employees, such as trade unions and workers committees. Labour Law also deals with collective bargaining, the instruments of collective labour regulations and labour conflicts, especially strikes.

It also establishes the procedure for concluding a collective agreement through collective bargaining, as well as its scope, content, dates of implementation and termination. Finally, it regulates collective conflicts such as the strike and creates procedures to overcome it, such as conciliation, mediation, and arbitration.

For all these reasons, Labour Law is very important and helps improving the lives of people, insofar as work is the most common source of income[359].

II. With regards to collective structures, Labour Law affirms the freedom of association principle and specifies the capacities and competences of certain collective bodies, such as trade unions and workers' committees as well as employers' organizations.

[358] See ALVIN L. GOLDMAN and ROBERTO L. CORRADA, *Labor Law in the USA*, cit., p. 217 et seq.

[359] See BRIAN LANGILLE, "Labour Laws's Theory of Justice", *The Idea of Labour Law*, cit., p. 112.

On another level, collective agreements are the most important source of labour law. They result from collective bargaining and guarantee the adaptation of the law to specific sector, as well as, social peace. They usually promote an improvement of working conditions and better entitlements for the employees[360]. For these reasons, as we´ll see further on, the Labour Code promotes colletive bargaining.

Finally, Labour Law also deals with conflicts between an employer or an association of employers and employees or trade unions regarding the entry into force or the performance of collective agreements or the claims for new working conditions. It contains several rules regarding labour conflicts and the instruments to overcome them, such as conciliation, mediation and arbitration

Let´s take a closer look at them.

15.2. Collective Structures

I. The existence of collective representatives, such as trade unions and employers' organizations, is usual[361].

Both the Portuguese Constitution and the Portuguese Labour Code refer to the existence of collective labour structures which represent the employees and the employers.

Both are grounded in the freedom of association principle, as a fundamental right enshrined in article 46.th of the Portuguese Constitution, under which citizens have the right to form associations freely and without the requirement for any authorization, on condition that such associations are not intended to promote violence and their purposes are not contrary to those of criminal law. Associations shall pursue their purposes freely and without interference from public authorities and may not be dissolved by the state or have their activities suspended other than in cases provided for by law and further on by a judicial decision. No one may be forced to belong to an association or be coerced to remain therein by any means.

[360] See SIMON DEAKIN, "The contribution of Labour Law to Economic and Human Development", *The Idea of Labour Law*, cit., pp. 156-175.

[361] See ALVIN L. GOLDMAN and ROBERTO L. CORRADA, *Labor Law in the USA*, cit., p. 282.

II. Article 440.th of the Labour Code affirms the referred freedom of association as well, stating that workers have the right to form trade unions aimed at the defense and promotion of their socio-professional interests. Employers have the right to establish employers' organizations at all levels to defend and promote their business interests[362].

Trade Unions organizations include trade unions, federations, unions and confederations.

Employers organizations include associations, federations, unions and confederations.

The statutes of federations, unions and confederations may admit direct representation of workers not represented by trade unions, or employers not represented by employers associations.

III. Article 443.rd provides the rights of associations, stating trade unions and employers associations have the right to[363]:

a) Conclude collective agreements;
b) Provide economic and social services to their members;
c) Participate in the drafting of employment legislation;
d) Initiate and intervene in legal and administrative proceedings to defend the interests of their members, in accordance with the law;
e) Establish relationships with or join other organizations of workers or employers at a national or international level.

Trade unions also have the right to participate in turnovers or corporations restructuring processes, regarding training policies or when there is a change in working conditions. Employers associations may not engage in the production of goods or services or in any way intervene in the market.

IV. Regarding the workers collective structures, article 404.th admits that for the collective defense and pursuit of their rights and interests, workers may create:

[362] See Luís Gonçalves da Silva, *Código do Trabalho Anotado*, cit., notes on article 440.th, pp. 974 et seq.
[363] See Luís Gonçalves da Silva, *Código do Trabalho Anotado*, cit., notes on article 440.th, pp. 978 et seq.

a) Trade Unions;
b) Workers Committees and subcommittees of workers;
c) Workers representatives for safety and health at work;
d) Other structures provided for by specific law, namely European Undertaking Committees.

Article 405.th contains a guarantee of autonomy and independence, stating that the structures of collective representation of workers are independent from the State, political parties, religious institutions or associations of any other nature. It is prohibited any interference from these bodies the organization of these structures namely in its financing.

Article 406.th prohibits any kind of discrimination, stating that null the agreement or other act aimed at making the employment of a worker conditional upon him or her becoming a member or affiliate or withdraw from a trade union in which he/she is registered. It Is also forbidden to dismiss, transfer or, in any way, harm a worker due to the exercise of rights relating to the participation or lack of participation in union membership. The violation of these rules constitutes a serious offense.

Articles 408.th to 411.th establish the rights of the members of the employees' collective structures. Firstly, they are entitled to a credit of hours (408.th) without losing salary, so that they can provide their activity as workers representatives against the employer; secondly, they have the right to be absent (409.th) whenever they use the credit of hours and they still need additional time to fulfill their duties as representatives, although in the latter it being reflected on their salary; thirdly, they benefit from special protection against dismissal and disciplinary procedure (410.th), since the law presumes that dismissal of a representative is without just cause and, as a consequence, is null; finally, they have a special protection against workplace transfer (411.st) – the law states that in case of an individual transfer the agreement of the employee is always mandatory. In this case, the employer cannot unilaterally transfer, the employee on the basis of article 194.th [364].

IV. The Worker's Committee is a permanent association based on the right of association aimed at defending and promoting the interests of

[364] See Luís Gonçalves da Silva, *Código do Trabalho Anotado*, cit., notes on articles 405.th to 411.st, pp. 938-951.

employees within the Undertaking. Worker's Committees are legitimized under article 54.th of the Portuguese Constitution, which expresses their rights and competences.

Basically, article 54.th of the Portuguese Constitution puts forth the entitlements of worker committees, sustaining that employees are entitled to create workers committees to advocate for their interests and to promote their democratic intervention within the undertaking. The members of the employees committee shall enjoy the legal protection provided to trade union delegates.

The following are the rights of the workers committee:

a) Receive all the information necessary for the exercise of its activity;
b) Exercise management control in the undertakings;
c) Participate in the restructuring process of the company, especially regarding training sessions or when there is a change in working conditions;
d) Participate in the drafting of employment legislation and the economic and social plans that comprise the respective sector;
e) Manage or participate in the management of the company's social works;
f) Promote the election of employees representatives to the corporate bodies of the companies belonging to the State or to other public entities.

Article 415.th contains the general principles relating to committees, subcommittees and coordinating committees. In light of said provision, workers shall be entitled to set up, in each undertaking, a worker committee to defend their interests and exercise their rights. This is provided both in the Constitution and in the law. Subcommittees of workers may be established in the undertaking geographically dispersed. Every employee of the company, regardless of age or function, has the right to participate in the constitution of the representation structures and in the adoption of the respective statutes, and also has the right to elect and be elected.

Under article 417.th, the number of workers commission members may not exceed the following[365]:

[365] See Luís Gonçalves da Silva, *Código do Trabalho Anotado*, cit., notes on article 417.th, pp. 956 et seq.

a) In an undertaking with fewer than 50 employees, 2 members;
b) In an undertaking with 50 or more employees and less than 200, 3 members;
c) In an undertaking with 201 to 500 workers, 3 to 5 members;
d) In an undertaking with 501 to 1000 workers, 5 to 7 members;
e) In a undertaking with more than 1000 employees, 7 to 11 members.

The number of members of the subcommittee of workers shall not exceed the following:

a) In an establishment with 50 to 200 employees, 3 members;
b) In an establishment with more than 200 employees, 5 members.

In an establishment with less than 50 employees, the function of the subcommittee shall be held by a single member.

The number of members of the coordinating committee may not exceed the number of committees of workers coordinated by it, nor the threshold of 11 members.

The workers commission is entitled, in particular to, (article 423.rd):

a) Receive the information necessary for the exercise of its activity;
b) Exercise control over the management of the undertaking;
c) Participate, among others, in the process of turnover or restructuring of the company, in the preparation of vocational training plans and reports and in procedures intended to change working conditions;
d) Participate in the drafting of labour legislation, directly or through its coordinating committees;
e) Manage or participate in the management of the company's social works;
f) Promote the election of workers' representatives to the bodies of public business entities;
g) Meet, at least once a month, with the management body of the company for the discussion of matters related to the exercise of their rights[366].

[366] See Luís Gonçalves da Silva, *Código do Trabalho Anotado*, cit., notes on article 423.rd, pp. 961 et seq.

V. A Trade Union is a permanent association, based on the right of association, and aims at advocating for the socio-professional interests of its members.

Trade Unions may promote the interests of the employees within and outside the Undertaking, namely by entering Into collective bargaining and by summoning strikes. As such, they have more competences than the workers committees[367]. They often perform, in addition, other functions ranging from operating trade skills, training programs, recreational activities, and sponsoring retirement homes[368].

The union associations cover trade unions, federations, unions and confederations.

Under article 442.nd, a Trade Union is a permanent association of employees for the defense and promotion of their socio-economic interests; a Federation is an association of unions of employees of the same profession or sector of activity; an Union of trade unions is an association of trade unions in regional basis; a Confederation is the national association of trade unions, federations and unions[369].

Although they can defend the employees outside the corporate universe, workers and trade unions have the right to engage in trade union activity within the company, through trade union delegates, trade union commissions and inter-union commissions.

Under article 463.rd the maximum number of trade union delegates benefiting from the entitlements provided in this Code is defined as follows[370]:

a) In an undertaking with less than 50 unionized workers, 1 member;
b) In an undertaking with 50 to 99 unionized workers, 2 members;
c) In an undertaking with 100 to 199 unionized workers, 3 members;
d) In an undertaking with 200 to 499 unionized workers, 6 members;

[367] See Guilherme Dray, *The Influence of the United States of America on Reaffirming the Principle of Equality in Employment in Portuguese Speaking Language Countries*, cit., pp. 24 et seq.

[368] See Alvin L. Goldman and Roberto L. Corrada, *Labor Law in the USA*, cit., p. 282.

[369] See Luís Gonçalves da Silva, *Código do Trabalho Anotado*, cit., notes on article 442.th, pp. 976 et seq.

[370] See Luís Gonçalves da Silva, *Código do Trabalho Anotado*, cit., notes on article 463.rd, pp. 1000 et seq.

e) In an undertaking with 500 or more unionized workers, the number will result from the following formula: 6 + [(n-500): 200].

The right to union activity through union delegates includes the right to: hold meetings (461.st); to facilities (464.th); to advertise (465.th); to information (466.th); credit of hours (467.th)

With regards to the right to meet in the workplace, article 461.st stipulates that workers may meet in the workplace, upon summons by one third or 50 workers of their establishment, or by the trade union or inter-union commission. The meetings may take place outside the working hours of the majority of workers, without prejudice to the normal operation of shifts or additional work; or during working hours of the majority of workers up to a maximum of 15 hours per year, which counts as the length of effective service, provided that the operation is urgent and that essential services are guaranteed.

With regards to the right to facilities, article 464.th states the employer shall make available to trade union delegates an appropriate place for the performance of their duties, within the company, made available on a permanent basis in a company or establishment with 150 or more employees.

Article 465.th provides the right to advertise and to deliver information. Trade union delegates shall have the right to display, in an appropriate place provided by the employer, conventions, communications, information or other documents relating to trade union performance and interests of the workers, as well as to deliver them without prejudice to the normal operation of the Company.

Trade union delegates also have the right to information and to consult the following matters, in addition to others referred to by law or collective agreement (article 466.th)[371]:

a) Recent evolution and probable future evolution of the company's activity and economic situation;
b) The situation, structure and likely evolution of employment in the undertaking or establishment and possible preventive measures, particularly when reduction of the number of workers is at stake;

[371] See Luís Gonçalves da Silva, *Código do Trabalho Anotado*, cit., notes on article 466.th, pp. 1003 et seq.

c) A decision likely to trigger substantial change in the organization of the work contracts.

With regards to the credit of hours, article 467.th states that trade union delegates shall be entitled, for the performance of their duties, to a credit of 5 hours per month, or 8 hours per month if he/she is part of an inter union committee.

VI. Along with the existence of workers collective structures, the law also admits employers organizations to promote the corporations interests.

Employers organizations may, under the Law, take part in collective bargaining, conclude collective agreements and provide economic and social services to their members. They may also represent their associates within the context of legislative and administrative agencies and advocate economic and social policies on behalf of the industries they represent[372].

These organizations can be divided into the following types:

The Association of Employers is the permanent association of persons, individuals or groups of private law, holders of a company, which usually employs workers; a Federation is the association of employers associations of the same sector of activity; an Union is the association of associations of regional-based employers; a Confederation is the National Association of Employers Associations, federations and unions.

The Labour Code guarantees the employers freedom to register in an association of employers to represent him/her in his/her area of activity – article 444.th, n.er 3.

The law provides the independence of employers organizations with regards to the State, political parties, religious institutions and any equivalent institutions, and prohibits its interference in their organization and direction – article 405.th, n.er 1.

Article 443.rd establishes the powers of employers organizations. Under the law, trade union associations and employers organizations have the right to[373]:

[372] See Alvin L. Goldman and Roberto L. Corrada, *Labor Law in the USA*, cit., p. 316.

[373] See Luís Gonçalves da Silva, *Código do Trabalho Anotado*, cit., notes on article 443.rd, pp. 978 et seq.

a) Conclude collective agreements;
b) Provide economic and social services to its members;
c) Participate in the drafting of labour legislation;
d) Initiate and intervene in legal proceedings and administrative proceedings regarding the interests of its members, in accordance with the law;
e) Establish relationships or join, at national or international level, organizations, respectively, of workers or of employers.

Employers organizations may not engage in the production or marketing of goods or services or otherwise intervene in the market.

The Labour Code establishes the mandatory content of the statutes of employers associations (article 450.th, n.^{er} 1). The employer's organizations are subject to the subsidiary application of the general regime of the right of association – article 441.st.

The termination of employer's organizations may be judicial, if its extinction is judicially determined, or voluntary, if it results from the deliberation of their members.

15.3. Collective bargaining

I. Collective agreements are the most important specific source of labour law. They are a result of the collective bargaining between employers and trade unions and are regulated by law. They often promote changes in the conditions or terms of employment, fostering better working conditions[374].

As stated, they usually promote better working conditions and foster the employees' entitlements, creating more beneficial regimes than those provided in the Labour Code. They are also a powerful instrument of adaptation of the law to specific sectors or undertakings, and also to promote social peace within the corporations and the whole economy of a country[375].

Collective bargaining is a safeguard to ensure that everyone's interests are considered. Workers speak together as a body using their strength in numbers, and employers or employers organizations may also bargain as a

[374] See Alvin L. Goldman and Roberto L. Corrada, *Labor Law in the USA*, cit., p. 217.
[375] See João Leal Amado, *Contrato de Trabalho*, cit., pp. 28 et seq.

unity knowing that reaching a deal may achieve social peace within their companies, which is crucial for their competitiveness.

For all these reasons, collective bargaining is very important and should be protected as such.

II. Collective bargaining is at the heart of labour relationships, which should pertain to be peaceful and economically productive. Therefore, Labour Law has always played and still plays an important role in the development of labour relationships: "*Labor relation laws have contributed to industrial peace and largely freed our economy from clipping strikes and labor turmoil*"[376].

The important role played by trade unions, particularly in the industrial sector, was strengthened in the U.S. after the 1930 Great Depression and cannot be decoupled from the Labour Law currently established in our societies[377]. The greatest labour achievements obtained mainly through collective industrial agreements, were not always peaceful. Labour fights occurring during the 19 century, especially in the United States railway sector, became well know: these disputes were known by largely conflictive times and, in some cases, by violence, being led either by the first U.S. nation-wide trade unions – the National Labour Union (NLU) and later its successor, the Knights of Labour –, or by employers[378]. The situation became unsustainable: the collective labour struggles, or "mass picketing", characterized by the concentration of workers protesting against their working conditions[379], was converted into unruled actions of extreme violence, sometimes lasting for weeks – sometimes, these labour disputes resembled a military operation more than a strike. The aggression and violence were raging on both sides and the situation needed to be tackled.

At an initial stage, in the absence of legal provisions to protect trade union activities, U.S. courts acted against workers, criminalizing their actions– it was

[376] See David E. Strecker, *Labor Law. A Basic Guide to the National Labor Relations Act*, p. 2.

[377] See Guilherme Dray, *The Influence of the United States of America on Reaffirming the Principle of Equality in Employment in Portuguese Speaking Language Countries*, cit., pp. 24 33. We'll follow this book within the next paragraphs.

[378] See Robert A. Gorman/Matthew W. Finkin, *Basic Text on Labor Law*, cit., p. 2.

[379] See Amhed A. White, "Workers Disarmed: The Campaign Against Mass Picketing and the Dilemma of Liberal Labor Rights", *Harvard Civil Rights – Civil Liberties Review*, Harvard Law School, Vol. 49, no. 1, Winter 2014, pp. 59 et seq.

the era of the criminal conspiracy doctrine, in light of which collective and concerted actions of workers, in order to demand better working conditions, in particular through strikes, were qualified as illegal. The 1806 decision of the Philadelphia Court in *Cordwainer's* case is a clear depiction of this period. In a collective and concerted way, the workers of a shoe factory demanded a salary increase from their employers. The employers, who were in a difficult economic situation, did not accept this claim and, instead of negotiating with the workers, decided to refer the case to the courts in order to incriminate them. The Court decided to condemn the workers for criminal conspiracy, and as such the criminal conspiracy doctrine was created[380]. Under this doctrine, a worker could demand a salary increase from his/her employer individually; but the collective and concerted action of workers for this same purpose was considered illegal. Also, in this period, criminal syndicalism laws arose, criminalizing trade unionism which advocated or performed acts of disorder that could affect or change the industries' ownership or control – in this regard, the 1919 California's Criminal Syndicalism Act is particularly emblematic. This law criminalized trade union acts that could disrupt the correct functioning of the production units. In this respect, the case *Whitney v. California* (1927) became well-known: based on that 1919 legislative act, the U.S. Supreme Court condemned the activist and daughter of a good family, Charlotte Anita Whitney, for allegedly being a member of the Communist Labour Party and for having embraced and promoted a dangerous and subversive ideology, "*tending to incite crime, disturb the public peace, or endanger the foundations of organized government and threaten its overthrow*"[381]. On a second stage, the employers themselves began restricting the hiring of workers, also setting as a condition for employment the previous signing of agreements waiving unionization. Thus, job applicants or employees would waive their trade-union membership as a precondition for their hiring or the maintenance of their employment. The commonly called "yellow dog contracts" then appeared – through the employment agreement, the employee would agree with the employer to renounce to unionization. Otherwise, the employer would have the right to terminate the contract on specific grounds with just cause. The U.S. Supreme Court

[380] See Walter Nelles, "The First American Labor Case", *Yale Law Journal, Vol. XLI, December 1931*, n^{er}. 2, p. 165 et seq.

[381] See at Whitney v. California, 274 U-S- 357 (1927).

admitted the legality of these agreements in light of the "liberty of contract" principle. In the case *Adair v. United States* (1908)[382], the U.S. Supreme Court even declared invalid a 1898 legislative act of the Congress (*Erdman Act*) that prohibited employers of the railway sector from discriminating workers on the basis of being members of a "labour organization". The Supreme Court considered that the 1898 *Erdman Act* violated contractual freedom and the Fourteenth Amendment, and therefore was unconstitutional. "Yellow dog contracts" were acceptable, as they were part of the structure of contractual freedom. Considering this theory, employers and workers could freely negotiate and dispose of content of the employment agreement. The same happened in 1915, in case *Coppage v. Kansas* (1915). In this case, the Supreme Court followed Adair's case law and declared the illegality of a Kansas State legislative Act that considered the yellow dog contracts as illegal, considering they violated principles of contractual freedom and the due process clause of the Fourteenth Amendment.

On a third stage, in the late 19th century and the first quarter of the 20th century, employers began to bring labour injunctions against workers, i.e. court orders intended to paralyze strike actions, the disrespect of which would be considered as civil disobedience – "*Concerted activities in support of unionization – strikes, picketing and boycotts (of the employer or its products) – were treated as conspiracies which restrained trade and which inflicted irreparable damage upon the affected employer*"[383]. In a first moment, labour injunctions were also accepted by the U.S. Supreme Court. Even when some States started legislating against labour injunctions, the Supreme Court declared some of those legislative acts as invalid, namely in the case *Truax v. Corrigan* (1921) ([384]), regarding an Arizona State's legislative Act. This case can be summarized as follows: workers of The English Kitchen in Bisbee's restaurant began a strike and organized themselves in pickets in front of the restaurant. As a result, the business and restaurant's turnover fell abruptly. The restaurant owners brought a labour injunction against the workers, who in turn invoked the Arizona's Statute, which authorized peaceful picketing

[382] See Adair vs. United States, 208, U.S. (1915).

[383] See Robert A. Gorman/Matthew W. Finkin, *Basic Text on Labor Law*, Second Edition, cit., p. 2.

[384] See *Truax v. Corrigan*, 257, U.S., 312 (1921).

and prohibited labour injunctions. Before the case, the U.S. Supreme Court considered that the Arizona's Statute was invalid.

Something had to be done. The State could not continue observing in a passive way these collective labour fights, both aggressive and violent, and of no help to the country's social, and economic development.

Finally, in 1932, the Congress approved the *Norris-La Guardia Act,* in light of which courts were prevented from issuing injunctions in the context of labour disputes, save for exceptional circumstances.

Henceforth, the State began to legislate on labour issues.

III. Following the 1929 stock market crash and the 1930 Great Depression, the U.S. was thrown into a black hole with more than a quarter of unemployed active population, with failing banks and companies and a paralyzed economy. In 1933 the then elected President, Franklin Delano Roosevelt, launched a political program called "New Deal", with the purpose of restoring the U.S. economy and helping those who had suffered most with the Great Depression[385].

The New Deal brought about a significant number of legal reforms, especially in the period between 1933 and 1935, intended to boost the economy, either through laws approved by the Congress or Executive Orders issued by the President. Around this time, in 1933, the following legal documents were approved: the *National Industrial Recovery Act,* to promote the industry's recovery; the *Emergency Banking Act,* to ensure the financial restructuring of the banking sector; the *Agricultural Adjustment Act,* to regulate agriculture production; and the *Home Owner's Refinancing Act,* to prevent the loss of homeowners' mortgages. Given the social and political situation, President F. Roosevelt and the Congress also understood they could no longer deny trade unions a leading part in U.S. economy. Maintaining the status quo and denying any legitimacy to trade unions would only result in permanent (violent) conflicts in the productive sector, harmful to economic growth.

A step further should be taken. Collective negotiation would boost national economy.

[385] See GUILHERME DRAY, *The Influence of the United States of America on Reaffirming the Principle of Equality in Employment in Portuguese Speaking Language Countries*, cit., p. 30.

In 1935, the *Wagner Act* was approved, representing a new legislative framework with the aim of creating "a bold new era in labour relations"[386].

The *Wagner Act* recognized in its preamble the existence of an unequal treatment between employers and employees, underlining the purely formal nature of the workers freedom of contract. For the first time, this legislative act gave workers the legitimacy to act collectively and concertedly, defending them from employers' external interference and compelling the latter to negotiate with trade unions in good faith. Also for the first time, in the case *National Labour Relations Board* v. *Jones & Laughlin Steel Corp* (1937), the U.S. Supreme Court, analyzing the constitutionality of *Wagner Act*, acknowledged the workers' right to self-organization as a fundamental right, assuming that trade unions were essential "*to give laborers an opportunity to deal on an equality basis with their employer*"[387]. Later, in 1938, the *Fair Labour Standards Act* was approved, and for the first time a national minimum wage (twenty-five cents an hour) and a maximum limit of normal working hours (forty-four hours a week) were established. In 1947, the *Wagner Act* was reformed by *Taft-Hartley Act*, which strengthened the collective action rights and established the right to work. In turn, this right determined the nullity of contractual clauses that made the access to or the maintenance of employment dependent on non-unionization. In other words, the nullity of the aforementioned "yellow dog contracts".

Henceforth, collective bargaining began to have a prevailing role, guaranteeing "*fairness in employment (...) without the need for direct government intervention*"[388].

IV. The Portuguese legal framework also acknowledges the power of collective bargaining.

The Portuguese Constitution expresses this idea, stating that "*Trade unions have the competence to exercise the right to enter into collective agreements, a right which shall be guaranteed as laid down in the law*" (article 56.th).

386 See LAWRENCE M. FRIEDMAN, *American Law in the 20th Century*, Yale University Press, cit. p. 167.

387 See *National Labor Relations Board v. Jones & Laughlin Steel Corp*, 301 U.S. 1 (1937).

388 See ROBERT A. GORMAN/MATTHEW W FINKIN, Basic Text on Labor Law, Second Edition, cit., p. 8.

The Labour Code also qualifies the collective conventions as a specific source of Labour Law (article 1.st) and admits three different types (article 2.nd). Under article 2.nd, collective agreements can be specified as follows: collective employment contract, which is an agreement concluded between a trade union and an employers association; a collective employment agreement, as an agreement signed between a trade union and several employers for several undertakings or plants; and the single-undertaking agreement, which is an agreement concluded between a trade union and an employer of a specific plant or undertaking.

On the other hand, article 485.th of the Labour Code bearing in mind the importance of collective bargaining, establishes the duty of the State to promote collective negotiations between employers and employees. The State should promote collective bargaining, so that collective agreements are applicable to the largest number of workers and employers[389].

V. The conclusion of a collective agreement follows a negotiation process, governed by law – article 486.th to 490th [390].

The negotiation process begins with the presentation of a draft proposal by one of the parties to the other to enter into a new or to review an existent collective agreement (article 486.th.). The proposal must be written form and justified (article 486.th).

The recipient of the proposal should reply in writing and in a grounded manner within 30 days from its reception unless there has been another agreed deadline or a longer deadline indicated by the proponent (article 487.th, n.er 1). The reply is mandatory.

The reply should contain the respondent's position on each of the clauses of the proposal, by accepting or repudating them or by suggesting an alternative (counter proposal) (article 487.th, n.er 2).

The Labour Code affirms that the parties should give priority to some matters and respect the principle of good faith during negotiations – articles 488.th and 489.th. Whenever possible, the parties should prioritize such matters as salary, duration and organization of work, considering a needed

[389] See Luís Gonçalves da Silva, *Código do Trabalho Anotado*, cit., notes on article 485.th, pp. 1032 et seq.

[390] See Luís Gonçalves da Silva, *Código do Trabalho Anotado*, cit., notes on articles 486.th to 490.th, pp. 1033 et seq.

adjustment to the overall expenses increase resulting thereof, as well as health, safety and hygiene at work. The non-viability of the initial agreement concerning above the indicated matters does not justify the departure of negotiations.

The collective bargaining must respect the *bona fide* principle.

Under article 489.th, the parties shall respect, throughout the collective bargaining, the principle of good faith, namely by responding, as soon as possible, to proposals and counterproposals, observing the negotiation protocol, if it exists, and making meetings and contacts aimed at preventing and solving conflicts. Representatives of trade unions and employers associations shall, whenever necessary, consult workers and employers, but cannot invoke such a need to obtain suspension or interruption of any acts. Each party must provide the other party with the necessary information requested, in so far as it is not. It may not be refused, in the course of the negotiations of a collective employment agreement or a single-undertaking agreement, the supply of reports and accounts of companies already published as well as the number of workers, by professional category, within the scope of the agreement to be concluded[391].

The union association, the employers' association or the employer that is not represented at a meeting summoned in accordance with the negotiation protocol concluded by them, commit a serious misconduct.

For the drafting of the negotiating proposal and its response, as well as during negotiations, the government agencies of the Ministry of Employment and of the Ministry of the area of activity at stake shall provide the parties with all the availeble information. The parties must send the proposals and answers, with its respective reasons, to the Ministry of Employment area within 15 days after their presentation (article 490.th).

VI. Collective agreements obey a mandatory content safeguard.

Under article 492.nd, n.[er] 1, of the Labour Code, the collective agreement must indicate the following:

a) Designation of the entities involved;
b) Name and quality of the representatives of the entities involved;

[391] See Luís Gonçalves da Silva, *Código do Trabalho Anotado*, cit., notes on article 489.th, pp. 1037 et seq.

c) Scope of the sector of activity, professional and geographical application, except in the case of a revision that does not change the scope of the revised convention;
d) Date of conclusion;
e) Revised convention and its date of publication, if applicable;
f) Expressed values of basic remuneration for all professions and professional categories, if they have been agreed;
g) An estimate of the numbers of employers and workers covered by the Convention;
h) Collective labour regulation instrument and its date of publication.

Under article 492.nd, n.er 2, of the Labour Code, collective agreements shall regulate the following:

a) Relationships between the parties to the agreement, the compliance with the Convention, means of conflict resolution and their application or review;
b) Vocational training actions, tailored to the needs of the worker and employer;
c) Working conditions relating to safety and health;
d) Measures aimed at the effective application of the principle of equality and non-discrimination;
e) Other rights and duties of workers and employers, namely basic remuneration for all professions and professional categories;
f) The procedures for settling disputes arising from contracts of employment, including through conciliation, mediation or arbitration;
g) The definition of services necessary for the safety and maintenance of equipment and facilities and minimum services indispensable to satisfy unmet social needs, if the activity of the employers meets social needs, as well as the means necessary to secure them in a strike situation;
h) The effects of the Convention in the event of its expiration, regarding the workers covered by it until another instrument of collective bargaining is endorsed.

VII. The collective agreement has four different scopes: personal (496.th to 498th); material (492.nd); geographical (492.nd, 1, c)); and regarding its duration (500.th).

Regarding personal scope, article 496.th comprises the principle of filiation, under which the collective agreement binds the employers who sign It and those registered in the signatory employer associations as well as the signing unions and the employees that are members of the signing union associations. When, within the framework of an undertaking, one or more collective agreements or arbitration decisions are applicable, an employee that is not a member of any trade union association can choose which of those instruments shall apply (article 497.th)[392].

The material scope of the collective employment convention corresponds to the sector of activity and its professional application. Under article 492.nd, n.^{er} 1, subparagraph c), the collective agreement shall indicate its sector of activity and professional application.

The geographical scope corresponds to the territorial area where the collective employment conventions will be applicable. Conventions may be national or regional. Under the referred article 492.nd n.^{er} 1, c), the collective agreement shall also indicate its geographical application. It can have a national or local reach.

A collective agreement will remain in force for the period established therein and is renewed according to its terms (article 499.th). If the Convention does not provide for a term of validity, its duration corresponds to a period of one year and is successively renewed for an equal period.

VIII. Once concluded, the collective agreement shall be delivered, to deposit, to the Ministry of Employment.

Deposit of said instruments depends on the following requirements:

a) Was concluded by those with the needed capacity;
b) Be accompanied by evidence of representation of the entities;
c) Comply with the provisions of paragraph 1 of article 492.nd;
d) Be accompanied by a consolidated text, if applicable;
e) Comply with the provisions of paragraph 3, as well as the consolidated text.

[392] See Luís Gonçalves da Silva, *Código do Trabalho Anotado*, cit., notes on article 496.th, pp. 1045 et seq.

The application for deposit must be decided within 15 days of receipt of the agreement by the competent department. Refusal of the deposit shall be notified to the parties, with the return of the collective agreement, the consolidated text and evidence of representation. If the deposit application is not decided within the legal deadline it is considered to have been deposited.

VIII. The expiration of the collective agreement is not automatic.

In case of termination the agreement remains applicable during the period of negotiation, conciliation, mediation or voluntary arbitration for, at least, 12 months (article 501.st). Whenever an interruption of the negotiation, conciliation, mediation or voluntary arbitration occurs, for a period exceeding 30 days, the agreement ceases to apply but this suspension cannot exceed the period of 18 months[393].

After the referred period the agreement shall remain in force for 45 days after which either party notifies the Ministry of Employment as well as the other party, that the negotiation process has ceased.

In the absence of prior agreement on the effects which occur in event of lapse, the Minister of Employment notifies the parties within the deadline depicted above, so that they can agree on the definition of such effects.

After the expiration and up until the entry into force of another arbitration agreement or decision, the effects agreed by the parties or, failing this, those already produced by employment contract as regards to: remuneration of the employee, category, length of working time, social protection schemes whose benefits are substitutive of those guaranteed by the general social security scheme or with protocol of substitution of the National Health Service, parental rights and rules regarding health and safety.

In addition to the effects mentioned in the preceding paragraph, the employee will benefit from other rights and guarantees arising from labour legislation.

Article 502.nd of the Labour Code establishes that a collective agreement may be terminated by revocation or expiration.

In addition, the collective agreement or part thereof may be temporarily suspended in its application: (i) in the event of a business crisis; (ii) and

[393] See Luís Gonçalves da Silva, *Código do Trabalho Anotado*, cit., notes on article 501.th, pp. 1053 et seq.

for market, structural or technological reasons, catastrophes or other occurrences that have seriously affected the normal activity of the company. The suspension is only allowed if it is indispensable to ensure the viability of the company and the maintenance of the jobs. The agreement between the employers' associations and the trade union' associations must be written form.

VIII. There are also rules regarding succession of collective agreements – article 503.rd.

In this rule, the lawmaker intends to have the parties maintain the working conditions of the previous collective agreement in event of replacement..

With regards to the succession of collective agreements, the law states that a subsequent agreement fully revokes a preceding agreement, except for those matters where the parties expressly granted an exception. But it also establishes that the mere succession of collective agreements cannot be used to reduce the general protection level of employees. Under the law, the rights arising from the collective agreements can only be reduced by a new agreement whose text expressly states an overall more favorable regime (503.rd, n.^{er} 3).

This is a tenet of the principle of the employees′ protection[394].

15.4. Collective disputes

I. Collective conflicts are common in a labour relation[395]. The reason is easy to strike: the interests of the employer and the employees are contrary. On one hand, employees want the best independent job for the highest salary they can attain, if possible with time for leisure and to conciliate private and professional life; on the other hand, employers pertain to maximize their production and profit making capacity by decreasing expenses, namely by paying lower salaries and more hours of work[396].

Bearing that in mind, the existence of labour disputes is normal and at the heart of the creation and development of Labour Law. They were important

[394] See GUILHERME DRAY, *O Princípio da Proteção do Trabalhador*, cit., pp. 5238 et seq.
[395] See ALVIN L. GOLDMAN and ROBERTO L. CORRADA, *Labor Law in the USA*, cit., p. 21 et seq..
[396] See SIMON DEAKIN/GILLIAN MORRIS, *Labour* Law, cit., pp. 20 et seq.

for the construction the current model of society and to the human and economic development[397].

A collective labour dispute is a conflict between employers and employees regarding the entry into force or the performance of collective agreements or the claims for new working conditions. It is the core idea of Labour Law[398].

Collective labour disputes may include conflicts regarding negotiation, review, interpretation or application of a collective agreement, or grounded on new claims from the employees regarding working conditions – salaries, working schedules, promotions, rights and duties, etc.

Within the topic of collective disputes, the right to strike is considered the most important and emblematic collective labour conflict.

II. A strike is an interruption of work by the initiative of trade unions or an *ad hoc* assembly of employees in order to achieve better working conditions. It is a claim over an employer or an association of employers regarding labour issues aimed at improving working conditions. It is a constitutional right (article 57.th).

Lock-out is an interruption of work upon the initiative of an employer or an association of employers in order to achieve concessions from employees. Contrarily to the strike, the lock out is constitutionally forbidden (article 57.th).

Besides the strike, we have different types of collective conflicts organized by the employees, such as boycotts, demonstrations or picketing. Only the strike is legally prescribed, as we'll see further on.

Labour disputes can bring problems: problems for the companies, for the employees and for the economy as a whole. So, in order to solve them, the law contains a pack of instruments to deal with labour disputes.

III. The means to solve a collective dispute are negotiation, conciliation, mediation and arbitration.

Negotiation consists on the attempt to solve the collective labour dispute through direct dialogue between the parties, which, if successful, may lead

[397] See Simon Deakin, "The contribution of Labour Law to Economic and Human Development", *The Idea of Labour Law*, cit., pp. 156-175.

[398] See Adrián Goldin, "Global Conceptualizations and Local Constructions", *The Idea of Labour Law*, cit., pp. 69-87.

to the conclusion of an instrument of collective labour regulation (if the dispute is about a collective agreement), or to an answer to the employees demands and therefore to the cancelation or termination of a strike.

Conciliation is a mechanism to solve a collective labour dispute, particularly one resulting from the conclusion or revision of a collective agreement (article 523.rd, n.^{er} 1), and is a special form of negotiation. It is conducted by a third party: the Conciliator. Conciliators are impartial experts from the Ministry of Employment. They implement new approaches to bring the two parties together and come to an agreement, but they do not come up with proposals[399].

Mediation is a form of collective labour dispute resolution that is halfway between conciliation and arbitration. It is not limited to stimulating the approximation of the parties, since the mediator may present proposals for the resolution of the conflict, but without deciding it by himself/herself. Mediation is regulated in articles 526.th et seq. of the Labour Code[400].

Arbitration is the attempt to solve a collective conflict by third parties, the arbitrators, who intend to reach a solution for the dispute. If the conflict is about the conclusion or review of a collective agreement, the parties may submit it to voluntary arbitration (506.th). Statutory arbitration is prescribed in article 508.th. After the expiration of a collective agreement, arbitration will be necessary (510.th). If the conflict concerns other issues such as the interpretation or application of a collective agreement, voluntary arbitration may be used to solve it (articles 506.th and 529.th). The arbitral decision may be considered as an instrument of collective labour regulation (article 2.nd)[401].

Besides these mechanisms, we may also have the intervention of the Government or the courts.

The Government can intervene in the resolution of collective disputes through the extension administrative act (article 514.th) or the administrative employment conditions act (article 517.th), applying to employers and

[399] See Luís Gonçalves da Silva, *Código do Trabalho Anotado*, cit., notes on article 523.rd, pp. 1124 et seq.

[400] See Luís Gonçalves da Silva, *Código do Trabalho Anotado*, cit., notes on article 523.rd, pp. 1129 et seq.

[401] See Luís Gonçalves da Silva, *Código do Trabalho Anotado*, cit., notes on article 529.th, pp. 1134 et seq.

employees that were not bound by any instrument of collective labour regulation a collective agreement already in force applicable to other employers or employees of the same sector of (article 514.th), or by creating a new legal instrument (article 517.th). By doing it, the Government can help the employee's in best achieving their claims and goals and thus in solving the conflict.

Whenever the dispute involves the interpretation or enforcement of a preexistent instrument of collective labour regulation, the conflict may be overcome by the courts. In these cases, the court may rule on the interpretation or application of a collective labour regulation instrument, or on issues related to the strike whenever there is a legal claim.

15.5. Right to strike

I. The strike is the most important collective dispute instrument[402].

A strike is a collective and concerted abstention of work upon the initiative of trade unions in order to achieve concessions and benefits from an employer or an association of employers on labour issues. Since the definition is not stringent, it includes situations such as any concerted stoppage of work or interruption of operations by employees[403].

The right to decree and join a strike is a fundamental right (57.th Constitution)[404] also enshrined in article 530.th of the Labour Code[405].

Despite the general right to strike, the law governs its enforcement and organization, to minimize damages for the employers and the community as a whole, especially whenever the strike occurs with key sectors, such as healthcare, transports, public health, education, energy, water supply, security, etc. For that reason and because the constitutional right to strike can affect other constitutional rights (such as the right to free circulation,

[402] See Tonia Novitz, *International and European Protection of the Right to Strike. A Comparative Study of Standards Set by the International Labour Organization, the Council of Europe and the European Union*, Oxford, 2003.

[403] See Alvin L. Goldman and Roberto L. Corrada, *Labor Law in the USA*, cit., p. 401.

[404] See Jorge Miranda/Rui Medeiros, *Constituição Portuguesa Anotada*, cit., notes on article 57.th.

[405] See Pedro Romano Martinez, *Código do Trabalho Anotado*, cit., notes on article 530.th, pp. 1135 et seq.

or the right to access healthcare services), the law imposes rules regarding the legitimacy to declare it, the notice of strike that must be fulfilled, the minimum services that must be provided and the effects of the strike on the employment contract.

In a nutshell, the law imposes certain procedural requirements before a work stoppage can lawfully be initiated[406].

II. Primarily, the legitimacy to declare the strike belongs to trade unions (531st, n.er 1). Exceptionally, when the majority of employees aren't unionized, it is possible to have a decision taken by an *ad hoc* assembly of employees – the strike committee (531st, n.er 2).

The strike declaration requires prior statutory notice (534.th) of 5 or 10 business days, depending on the corporation's sector of activity.

The notice must be delivered to the employer and the Ministry of Employment in writing or through the media (534.th, n.er 2) and must indicate the date of the commencement of the strike and its duration, as well as a proposal of services to guarantee the safety and maintenance of equipment and minimum services if it is a corporation that provides social services that cannot be discontinued.

The idea behind the previous notice is to give the employer and society the chance to minimize the negative effects of the strike[407].

Article 536.th et seq. announces the effects of the strike.

Basically, the strike suspends the employment contract of the adherent worker, including the right to retribution and the duties of subordination and attendance. That means that the employee is authorized to be absent from work but loses his/her retribution.

Nevertheless, during the strike, in addition to the rights, duties and guarantees of the parties that do not presuppose the effective provision of work (such as duties of loyalty, confidentiality and courtesy), the rights provided by social security legislation and benefits due to a work accident or occupational disease remain in force. The period of suspension shall be considered for the purposes of seniority and shall not be detrimental to the effects arising from it. Additionally, because the strikers remain employees,

[406] See Alvin L. Goldman and Roberto L. Corrada, *Labor Law in the USA*, cit., p. 411.

[407] See Pedro Romano Martinez, *Código do Trabalho Anotado*, cit., notes on article 534.th, pp. 1138 et seq.

a striker who returns to work must be treated as a returning worker –one that has been laid off or benefited from a leave of absence – and not as a new employee[408].

Moreover, during the strike, there is a prohibition of replacement of strikers and therefore the employer may not, during the strike, replace strikers with persons who, at the date of the prior notice, did not work in the corresponding establishment or service and may not, from that date, admit employees for that purpose (article 535.th)[409].

The law also allows, during the strike, strike picketing – the trade union association or strike committee may organize pickets to carry out activities to persuade, by peaceful means, the employees to join the strike whilst respecting the freedom of work of those who want to do so (article 533.rd).

III. The obligation to provide minimum services during the strike is very important and reveals the idea of fair balance upon which it is based. The employees have the constitutional right to strike, but it cannot cause damages to the community as a whole when it occurs in vital sectors of activity.

For that reason, one of the obligations of the employees during the strike is to carry out the minimum services necessary to ensure the satisfaction of social needs that cannot be disrupted. These services are anchored on other constitutionally protected rights and interests. The law tries to achieve a balance between these rights and interests and the right to strike.

The obligation to provide minimum services depends on two assumptions (article 537.th n.er 1): the strike occurs in a company or establishment intended to provide to social needs that cannot be disrupted; the provision of certain services by striking workers should prove indispensable to the satisfaction of the protected needs.

In a company or establishment intended to meet unforeseeable social needs, the trade union association that declares the strike, or the strike committee and the adhering employees shall ensure, during the same, the provision of the minimum services indispensable to their satisfaction. Under the law, it is considered a company or establishment that is intended to

[408] See Alvin L. Goldman and Roberto L. Corrada, *Labor Law in the USA*, cit., p. 409.
[409] See Pedro Romano Martinez, *Código do Trabalho Anotado*, cit., notes on article 535.th, pp. 1141 et seq.

meet unforeseeable social needs those which belong to one of the following sectors (article 537.th, n.er 2):

a) Post and telecommunications;
b) Medical services and hospital care;
c) Public health, including the performance of funerals;
d) Energy and mining services, including fuel supplies;
e) Water supply;
f) Firefighters;
g) Public-service services that ensure the satisfaction of essential needs whose performance is the State's responsibility;
h) Transports, including ports, airports, railways and trucking stations, relating to passengers and the transportation of animals, foodstuffs and goods essential to the national economy, including loading and unloading;
i) Transport and security of monetary values.

The trade union association that declares the strike, or the strike committee in the case referred to in article 531.st, n.er 2, and the adherent employees must also provide, during the strike, the necessary services for the safety and maintenance of equipment and installations (article 537.th, n.er 3).

The employees assigned to the provision of the services shall remain, to the strict minimum necessary for such service, under the authority and direction of the employer, and are entitled to remuneration[410].

IV. The definition of the minimum services that must be provided in each specific strike is very important, so the parties and the community may know in advance what services will be provided. The method to define the minimum services is expressed in article 538.th Basically, they can be defined by an instrument of collective labour regulation, by agreement; by an administrative act issued by the Minister of Employment; or by arbitration.

As per the law, the minimum services to be provided shall be defined by a collective labour regulation instrument or by agreement between the

[410] See PEDRO ROMANO MARTINEZ, *Código do Trabalho Anotado*, cit., notes on article 537.th, pp. 1145 et seq.

employees representatives and the employers or the association of employers covered by the prior notice of strike.

In the absence of this provision in a collective labour regulation or agreement, the competent department of the Ministry of Employment shall call upon the entities to negotiate an agreement on minimum services and the means necessary to ensure them. In the negotiation of minimum services for a strike the Department proposes minimum services substantially identical to those two previous strikes. In the absence of agreement within three days after the strike notice, the minimum services and the means necessary to ensure them are defined:

a) By a duly substantiated administrative order issued by the Minister of Employment and the Minister responsible for the sector of activity covered by the strike;
b) By an arbitral court in the event the strike targets a public sector company, established under the terms of the specific law on compulsory arbitration.

The definition of minimum services must respect the principles of necessity, adequacy and proportionality. The order and decision of the arbitral court shall take effect immediately after its notification to the entities covered by the strike (employers and trade unions) and shall be posted at the premises of the company, establishment or service, and information points for the employees. The representatives of striking employees shall designate the employees who are assigned to the provision of the minimum services and inform the employer thereof within twenty-four hours before the start of the strike period. If they do not do so, the employer is free to make such designation[411].

In case of breach of the obligation to provide minimum services, the Government may determine the requisition or mobilization, under the terms provided in specific legislation (article 541.st, n.er 3) – Decree-Law n.er 637/74, of November 20.th.

[411] See Pedro Romano Martinez, *Código do Trabalho Anotado*, cit., notes on article 538.th, pp. 1148 et seq.

V. The strike terminates by agreement, by unilateral decision issued by the trade unions or the strike committee that triggered it, or at the end of the period for which it was declared (article 539.th).

Usually, strikes are decreed for short periods, so the most common form of termination is the term of the period in which the strike was decreed.

In the case of strikes summoned for an indefinite period, these usually terminate with the total or partial acceptance of the employees' claims and under a termination agreement.

The law also stipulates that the act that implies coercion, prejudice or discrimination of a worker by reason of adhesion or no adhesion to a strike is null and void (article 540.th)[412].

VI. The strike is unlawful if it is declared by those who don't have the competence to decree it; if the previous notice was not respected; or if its reasons and motives are unlawful, namely for being against the Constitutional order or whenever they violate the principle of proportionality.

Whenever the strike is unlawful, the absence of the employee who joined is unjustified and may trigger a disciplinary procedure and the potential liability of the employee who committed the disciplinary infraction The absence of a worker by reason of adhesion to the strike declared or executed in a way contrary to the law is considered an unjustified absence (article 541.st)[413].

[412] See Pedro Romano Martinez, *Código do Trabalho Anotado*, cit., notes on article 540.th, pp. 1152 et seq.

[413] See Pedro Romano Martinez, *Código do Trabalho Anotado*, cit., notes on article 541.st, pp. 1153 et seq.

BIBLIOGRAPHY

ABRANTES, José João, *Direito do Trabalho II – Direito da Greve*, Almedina, Coimbra, 2013.

—. "Álcool e drogas no meio laboral.", *Estudos em Memória do professor Doutor José Dias Marques*, Almedina, Coimbra, pp. 355-361, 2007.

—. *Contrato de Trabalho e Direitos Fundamentais*, Almedina, Coimbra, 2005.

—. "A Autonomia do Direito do Trabalho, a Constituição Laboral e o Artigo 4º do Código do Trabalho.", in *Estudos sobre o Código do Trabalho*, Coimbra Editora, 2004.

—. *Estudos sobre o Código do Trabalho*, Almedina, Coimbra, 2004.

—. "O novo Código do Trabalho e os direitos de personalidade do trabalhador", *A Reforma do Código do Trabalho*, Centro de Estudos Judiciários/Inspecção Geral do Trabalho (org.), Coimbra Editora, 2004, pp. 161-171.

—. "Contrato de trabalho e Meios de Vigilância da Actividade do Trabalhador (Breves Considerações)", *Estudos em Homenagem ao Prof. Doutor Raul Ventura, Vol. II*, Coimbra Editora, 2003, pp. 809 e ss.

—. "Contrato de trabalho a termo., *Estudos do Instituto de Direito do Trabalho, Vol. III*, Almedina, Coimbra, 2002, pp. 157-177.

—. *Contrat de travail et droits fondamentaux: contribution a une dogmatique commune europeenne, avec reference speciale au droit allemand et au droit portugais*. Frankfurt:

PETER LANG, 2000.

—. "Do tratado de Roma ao Tratado de Amsterdão – a caminho de um Direito do Trabalho europeu?", *Questões Laborais*, nº 16 de Ano 7-2000.

—. "Contrato de trabalho e direitos fundamentais., *II Congresso Nacional de Direito do Trabalho*, de António José Moreira (coord.), pp. 105 e ss. Coimbra: Almedina, 1999.

—. "Breve apontamento sobre o regime jurídico do contrato de trabalho a prazo", *Direito do Trabalho- Ensaios*, Cosmos, Lisboa, 1995, pp. 93-101.

—. "Formação e Evolução Histórica do Direito do Trabalho.", *Direito do Trabalho-Ensaios*, Cosmos, Lisboa, 1995, pp. 20 e ss.

—. *Do contrato de trabalho a prazo*, Almedina, Coimbra, 1992.

ACIDIANO, Peter/AUCEJO, Esteban/HUSSEY, Andrew/SPENNER, Kenneth, "Racial Segregation Patterns in Selective Universities", *The Journal of Law & Economics*, The University of Chicago Press, Vol. 56, number 4, November 2013: 1039 et seq.

ACKERMAN, Bruce, *We The People, II, Transformations*, United States of America: Harvard University Press, 2000.

—. *We The People, III, The Civil Rights Revolution*, Cambridge, Massachusetts: Harvard University Press, 2014. Ackerman, Bruce ALMEIDA, Tatiana Guerra, "Período experimental. Breves notas para o estudo comparativo dos regimes jurídicos português e espanhol.", *Estudos de Direito do Trabalho em Homenagem ao Professor Manuel Alonso Olea*, Almedina, Coimbra, 2004, pp. 589-613.

ALVAREZ, Anselmo Prieto/FILHO, Wladimir Novaes, *Constituição dos EUA, Anotada*, 2nd edition. São Paulo: LtR, 2008.

ALVIN, L. Goldman/CORRADA, Roberto L., *Labor Law in the USA*, Third Revised Edition, Law and Business. The Netherlands: Wolters Kluwer, 2011.

AMADO, João Leal. –. *Contrato de trabalho*, 3ª edição,Coimbra Editora, 2011.

—. *Contrato de trabalho – à luz do novo Código do Trabalho*, Coimbra Editora, 2009.

—. "Contrato de trabalho e condição resolutiva (breves considerações a propósito do Código do Trabalho).", *Estudos de Direito do Trabalho em Homenagem ao Professor Manuel Afonso Olea*, Almedina, Coimbra, 2004, pp. 343-356;

—. "A Proteção do Salário." *Suplemento do Boletim da Faculdade de Direito da Universidade de Coimbra*, Vol. XXXIX, 1995: pp. 1 e ss.

AMADO, João Leal/VICENTE, Joana Nunes, "Contrato de trabalho intermitente.", *IX-X Congressos Nacionais de Direito do Trabalho. Memórias, de António José Moreira* (org.), Almedina, Coimbra, 2007, pp. 117 e ss.

ARNESON, Richard. "Equality of Opportunity", *The Stanford Encyclopedia of Philosophy*, Edward N. Zalta (ed.), Fall Edition 2008.

ARTHURS, Harry, "Labour Law after Labour", in *The Idea of Labour Law*, by Guy Davidov & Brian Langille, 190-208, United Kingdom: Oxford University Press, 2013.

BANCROFT, George, *History of the Formation of the Constitution of the United States of America*, Vol. 2, United States of America: D. Appleton and Co., 1889.

Bastos, Celso Ribeiro, *Curso de Direito Constitucional*, 22nd ed., São Paulo: Editora Saraiva, 2010.

Blackstone's Employment Law Practice 2019, Edited by Gavin Mansfield QC, Lydia Banerjee, Damian Brown QC, Simon Forshaw, Anthony Korn, Eleena Misra, David Reade QC, and Catherine Taylor.

Bonavides, Paulo, "Constitucionalismo Luso-Brasileiro: influxos recíprocos", in *Perspectivas Constitucionais: nos 20 anos da Constituição de 1976*, Jorge Miranda (org.), 51 et seq. Coimbra: Coimbra Editora, 1996.

—. *Curso de Direito Constitucional*, 30th ed. São Paulo: Editora Saraiva, 2015.

—. *Curso de Direito Constitucional: A Importância do Princípio da Igualdade*, São Paulo: Malheiros Editores, 2001.

Breyer, Stephen, *Making Our Democracy Work. A Judge's View*, New York: Alfred A. Knopf, 2010.

Brito, Pedro Madeira De. –. anotação aos artigos 97º a 99º, 115º a 125º, 126º a 129º, 135º, 139º a 149º, 157º a 160º e 193º a 196º, *Código do Trabalho Anotado*, 9ª edição, Pedro Romano Martinez, Luís Miguel Monteiro, Joana Vasconcelos, Pedro Madeira de Brito, Guilherme Dray e Luís Gonçalves da Silva. Coimbra: Almedina, 2013.

—. *Contrato de trabalho da administração pública e sistema de fontes*, *Repositório da Universidade de Lisboa*, Faculdade de Direito, FD – Teses de Doutoramento, 2010.

Brito, Rodrigo Toscano de. –. "Estado de Perigo e Lesão: entre a previsão de nulidade e a necessidade de equilíbrio das relações contratuais." in *Novo Código Civil, Questões controvertidas no direito das obrigações e dos contratos*, Série Grandes Temas de Direito Privado, Vol. 4. São Paulo: Editora Método, 2005.

Brunner, Christiane/Bühler, Jean-Michel/Waeber, Jean-Bernard. –. *Commentaire du contrat de travail*, 3ª ed., Lausanne: Réalités Sociales, 2011.

Bruton, Henry/Farirris, David. –. "Travail et développement." *Revue International do Travail*, vol. 138 (1999), nº 1, 1999: pp. 5 e ss.

Brockhoff, J. R. "A Lesson on Tolerance", in *Rethoric, Religion and the Civil Rights Movement*, David W. Houck & David E. Dixon editors., 2006: 172 et seq.

Cabeza, Jaime/Diéguez, Gonçalo, *Derecho del Trabajo*, Segunda Edición. Madrid/Barcelona: Marcial Pons, 2003.

Cabo, Sérgio Gonçalves do. –. "O novo regime do contrato de trabalho a prazo." *Revista Jurídica da Associação Académica da Faculdade de Direito de Lisboa*, nº 15, 1992: pp. 85-123.

Cabral, Rita Amaral. –. "O direito à reserva sobre a intimidade da vida privada." *Boletim da Faculdade de Direito da Universidade de Coimbra*, XLIX, 1993: pp. 479-585.

—. "O Direito à Intimidade da Vida Privada (Breve reflexão acerca do artigo 80º do Código Civil)." in *Separata dos Estudos em Memória do Professor Doutor Paulo Cunha*, pp. 26 e ss. Lisboa, 1988.

Calder, Alan/Colley, John/Stettinius, Wallace/Doyle, Jacqueline/Logan, George. *What is Corporate Governance*, New York: The Mcgraw-Hill, 2004.

Camanho, Paula Ponces. –. "O Contrato de trabalho a termo." in *A Reforma do Código do Trabalho*, de Centro de Estudos Judiciários/Inspeção Geral do Trabalho, pp. 300-304. Coimbra: Coimbra Editora, 2004.

—. "Limites da Contratação a Termo." In *Código do Trabalho – Alguns Aspectos Cruciais*, pp. 85-86. Cascais: Principia, 2003.

—. "Contrato de Trabalho a Tempo Parcial." in *Estudos do Instituto de Direito do Trabalho*, Vol. IV, pp. 205 e ss. Almedina, 2003.

—. "Algumas reflexões sobre o regime jurídico do contrato de trabalho a termo." *Juris et de Jure*, 1998: pp. 969-986.

Campos, Carlos Alexandre de Azevedo. "A Evolução do Ativismo Judicial na Suprema Corte Norte-Americana (II).", *Revista Brasileira de Direito Constitucional, Year 2* (2013), pp. 6515-6571.

Carrion, Valentim. –. *Comentários à Consolidação das Leis do Trabalho*, 26ª edição. São Paulo: Editora Saraiva, 2001.

—. *Comentários à Consolidação das Leis do Trabalho*, 24ª edição. São Paulo: Editora Saraiva, 1999.

Carter, Ian. –. "Positive and Negative Liberty." *The Stanford Encyclopedia of Philosophy*, Edward N. Zalta (ed.), (Spring) de 2012.

Carvalho, António Nunes De. –. "Código do Trabalho, a Revisão de 2009." in *Mobilidade Funcional (do Código de Trabalho de 2003 à revisão de 2009)*, de Paulo Morgado de Carvalho (coord.), Coimbra: Coimbra Editora, 2011.

—. "Duração e Organização do Tempo de Trabalho no Código do Trabalho", *VI Congresso Nacional de Direito do Trabalho. Memórias*, pp. 95 e ss. Coimbra, 2004.

—. "Reflexões sobre a carreira profissional (a propósito do Código do Trabalho)." in *Estudos de Direito do Trabalho em Homenagem ao Professor Manuel Alonso Olea*. Coimbra: pp. 123-161, 2004.

—. "O pluralismo do Direito do Trabalho." in *III Congresso Nacional de Direito do Trabalho. Memórias*, de António Moreira (coord.), pp. 269-294. Coimbra: Almedina, 2001.

—. *Das Carreiras Profissionais no Direito do Trabalho.*, Lisboa, 1990.

CARVALHO, Catarina. –. "A Regulamentação Nacional do Tempo de Trabalho e o Direito Comunitário: Omissões e Incompatibilidades." *Questões Laborais,* nº 27 (2006), 2006: pp. 33 e ss.

—. "A mobilidade geográfica dos trabalhadores no Código do Trabalho." in *VII Congresso Nacional de Direito do Trabalho,* de António Moreira (coord.), pp. 43 e ss. Coimbra: Almedina, 2004.

CAUPERS, João. –. *Os Direitos Fundamentais dos Trabalhadores e a Constituição. Coimbra*: Almedina, 1985.

CENTENO, Mário. –. *O Trabalho, Uma visão de mercado. Lisboa*: Fundação Francisco Manuel dos Santos, 2013.

CORDEIRO, Menezes. –. *Direito do Trabalho, I, Direito Europeu Dogmática Geral Direito Coletivo,* Almedina, Coimbra, 2019;

—. *Direito do Trabalho, II, Direito Individual,* Almedina, Coimbra, 2019;

—. *Tratado de Direito Civil Português, I, Introdução, Fontes do Direito, Interpretação da Lei, Aplicação das Leis no Tempo, Doutrina Geral,* 4ª edição, Reformulada e Atualizada. Coimbra: Almedina, 2012.

—. *Da Modernização do Direito Civil, I – Aspectos Gerais.* Coimbra: Almedina, 2004.

—. "Da Natureza Civil do Direito do Consumo." *O Direito,* Ano 136, 2004: pp. 605--640.

—. *Tratado de Direito Civil Português, I, Parte Geral.* Coimbra: Almedina, 2002.

—. "Justas Causas de Despedimento." in *Estudos do Instituto de Direito do Trabalho, Vol. II, Justa Causa de Despedimento,* de Pedro Romano Martinez (coord.), pp. 15 e ss. Coimbra: Almedina, 2001.

—. "A liberdade de expressão do trabalhador." in *II Congresso Nacional de Direito do Trabalho.* Memórias de António José Moreira (coord.), pp. 16-37. Coimbra: Almedina, 1999.

—. "O respeito pela esfera privada do trabalhador." in *I Congresso Nacional de Direito do Trabalho,* de António José Moreira (coord.), pp. 20 e ss. Coimbra: Almedina, 1998.

—. *Da Boa fé no Direito Civil.* Coimbra: Almedina, 1997.

—. "Dos Conflitos Temporais de Instrumentos de Regulamentação Colectiva de Trabalho." in *Estudos em Memória do Professor Doutor João de Castro Mendes,* pp. 460 e ss. Lisboa: Lex, 1995.

—. *Manual de Direito do trabalho.* Coimbra: Almedina, 1991.

—. "Da Constitucionalidade das Comissões de Serviços Laborais." *Revista de Direito e de Estudos Sociais XXXIII, nºs. 1/2,* 1991: pp. 129 e ss.

—. "O Princípio do Tratamento Mais Favorável no Direito do Trabalho." *Direito e Justiça, volume de Homenagem ao Prof. Doutor Cavaleiro Ferreira*, volume III, 1987/1988: pp. 111 e ss.

CHATTERJI, Aaron K./RICHMAN, Barak D.,"Understanding the Corporate in Corporate Social Responsibility", *Harvard Law & Policy Review, Progressive Visions of The Corporation*, Volume 2, Number 1, n.d.

CIHON, Patrick J./CASTAGNERA, James Ottavio, *Employment & Labor Law*, Sixt Edition. Mason, South-Western Cenage Learning, 2008.

COOLEY, Thomas M., *Princípios Gerais de Direito Constitucional nos Estados Unidos da América*, Campinas, Ed. Russel, 2002.

CORDEIRO, A. Barreto Menezes, *Do Trust no Direito Civil*, Coimbra, Almedina, 2014. CORDEIRO, Menezes, *Tratado de Direito Civil, I, Introdução, Fontes do Direito, Interpretação da Lei, Aplicação das Leis no Tempo, Doutrina Geral*, 4ª edição, Revista, Coimbra, Almedina, 2012.

DAVIDOV, Guy. "Re-Matching Labour Laws with Their Purpose.", in *The Idea of Labour Law*, by Guy Davidov & Brian Langille, 179-189, United Kingdom, Oxford University Press, 2013.

—. *A Purpositive Approach to Labour Law*, Oxford, 2018.

DAVIDOV, Guy/LANGILLE, Brian. –. "Understanding Labour Law: A Timeless Idea, a Timed-Out Idea, or an Idea Whose Time has Now Come", *The Idea of Labour Law, Edited by Guy Davidov & Brian Langille*, Oxford University Press, United Kingdom, 2013, pp. 1-10.

DEAKIN, Simon/GILLIAN Morris. –. *Labour Law*, 3ª edição. Londres: Butterworths, 2001.

DEAKIN, Simon. –."The Contribution of Labour Law to Economic and Human Development", *The Idea of Labour Law*, Edited by Guy Davidov & Brian Langille, Oxford University Press, United Kingdom, 2013, pp. 156-175.

DELGADO, Maurício Godinho. –. *Curso de Direito do Trabalho*, 9ª ed. São Paulo: LTR Editora, 2010.

—. *Princípios de Direito Individual e Coletivo do Trabalho*. São Paulo: LTR Editora, 2001.

DRAY, Guilherme.

—. *Equality, Welfare State and Democracy*, Almedina/The Luso-American Development Foundation, Coimbra, 2018.

—. *The Influence of the United States of America on Reaffirming the Principle of Equality in Employment in Portuguese Speaking Language Countries*, Almedina/The Luso-American Development Foundation, Coimbra, 2017.

—. Anotação aos artigos 13º a 96º, 126º a 129º, 165º a 162º e 288º a 293º, *Código do Trabalho Anotado, 11ª edição*, Pedro Romano Martinez, Luís Miguel Monteiro, Joana Vasconcelos, Pedro Madeira de Brito, Guilherme Dray e Luís Gonçalves da Silva, Almedina, Coimbra, 2017.

—. *A influência dos Estados Unidos da América na Afirmação do Princípio da Igualdade no Emprego nos Países da Lusofonia*, Almedina, Coimbra, 2016.

—. *O Princípio da Proteção do Trabalhador*, Almedina, Coimbra, 2015.

—. *O Princípio da Proteção do Trabalhador*, Ltr, São Paulo, 2015.

—. "A Jurisprudência da Crise", *Revista de Direito e de Estudos Sociais*, janeiro-setembro 2015, Ano LVI (XXIX da 2.ª Série), n.º 1-3, pp. 155 e ss..

—. "Comunicações Eletrónicas e privacidade no contexto laboral", *Prontuário de Direito do Trabalho, II*, 2016, Centro de Estudos Judiciários, Almedina, Coimbra, 2016, pp. 103-131.

—. "Direitos fundamentais e retrocesso social – o sentido do Direito do Trabalho, a experiência portuguesa & o caso brasileiro", *Revista do Tribunal Superior do Trabalho*, Volume 83, n.º 3, julho/setembro 2017, Tribunal Superior do Trabalho, Brasil.

—. "O Livro Verde Sobre As Relações Laborais & o mercado de trabalho português da última década", *Revista de Direito e de Estudos Sociais*, janeiro-dezembro 2017 Ano LVIII (XXXI da 2.ª Série), n.º 1-4, pp. 155 e ss.

—. "O direito à reserva da intimidade da vida privada. O artigo 80.º do Código Civil de 1966", *Revista de Direito Civil*, Centro de Investigação de Direito Privado, Faculdade de Direito da Universidade de Lisboa, Ano II (2017), Número 3, António Menezes Cordeiro (Dir.), pp. 673-699.

—. "Liberdade e dever de não concorrência", *Estudos de Direito do Trabalho, em Homenagem ao Professor António Monteiro Fernandes*, Parte I, Bernardo da Gama Lobo Xavier, Maria do Rosário Palma Ramalho, José João Abrantes, João Leal Amado, David Falcão, Sérgio Tenreiro Tomás (Coordenação), Nova Causa – Edições Jurídicas, Lisboa, 2017, pp. 434-449.

—. "Constituição Laboral: actualidade ou revisão?", *II Congresso Europeu de Direito do Trabalho, os Desafios Atuais do Direito do Trabalho*, José João Abrantes (Coordenação Científica), Almedina, Coimbra, 2018, pp. 25-57.

—. "As convenções fundamentais da OIT: receção normativa e dificuldades de aplicação", IV Encuentro Ibérico de Derecho del Trabajo. Los Convenios de la OIT: su incidência en los ordenamentos de Portugal Y España, Documentación Laboral, Revista de la Associación Española de Derecho del Trabajo y de la

Seguridad Social, n-º 116, Año 2019, Vol. I, Ediciones Cinca, Mayo 2019, pp. 23-35.

—. "A Globalização e as Novas Tendências do Mercado de Trabalho. Teletrabalho e Deslocalização do Trabalho. O caso Português», in *II Congresso Internacional de Direito (Brasil – Europa), Análise Contemporânea do Direito em Face da Globalização e da Crise Económica*, org. Instituto de Direito do Trabalho da Faculdade de Direito de Lisboa, Programa de Pós-Graduação em Direito da PUC/SP e Comunidade de Juristas de Língua Portuguesas, pp. 81-92. Coimbra: Almedina, 2010.

—. "Igualdade e Não Discriminação." in *Separata de Código do Trabalho, a Revisão de 2009*, pp.123-138. Coimbra: Coimbra Editora, 2009.

—. *Direitos de Personalidade – Anotações ao Código Civil e ao Código do Trabalho*. Coimbra: Almedina, 2006.

—. "Período anual de férias: articulação entre o regime do Código do Trabalho e o do Acordo Colectivo de Trabalho Vertical do Sector Bancário." in *Separata da Revista "O Direito"*, pp. 657-685. Coimbra: Almedina, 2005.

—. "O Sentido Jurídico do Princípio da Igualdade: Perspectiva Luso-Brasileira." *Revista Brasileira de Direito Constitucional*, nº 2, Jul./Dez. de 2003: pp.113-137.

—. "Trabalho Temporário." in *Estudos do Direito do Trabalho*, IV, pp. 101-143. Coimbra: Almedina, 2003.

—. "Teletrabalho, Sociedade de Informação e Direito", *Estudos do Instituto de Direito do Trabalho*, Volume III, Almedina, Coimbra, 2002, pp. 261-287.

—. "Autonomia privada e igualdade na formação e execução de contratos individuais de trabalho." in *Estudos do Instituto de Direito do Trabalho*, I, pp. 83-95. Coimbra: Almedina, 2001.

—. "Justa causa e esfera privada." in *Estudos do Instituto de Direito do Trabalho*, II, de Pedro Romano Martinez (coord.), pp. 35-91. Coimbra: Almedina, 2001.

—. *O Princípio da Igualdade no Direito do Trabalho – sua aplicabilidade no domínio específico da formação de contratos individuais de trabalho*. Coimbra: Almedina, 1999.

Duarte, David. –. "An Experimental Essay on the Antecedent and Its Formulation." in *Estudos de Homenagem ao Prof. Doutor Jorge Miranda, Volume VI*, Edição da Faculdade de Direito da Universidade de Lisboa, pp. 119-139. Coimbra: Coimbra Editora, 2012.

—. *A norma de legalidade procedimental administrativa. A teoria da norma e a criação de normas de decisão na discricionariedade instrutória*. Coimbra: Almedina, Colecção Teses, 2006.

Dubois, Louis/Blumann, Claude. –. *Droit matériel de l'Union Européenne*, 4ª ed. Paris: Montchrestien, 2006.

DUGUIT, Leon. –. *Traité de droit constitutionnel*, t. 3, 2ª edição. Paris: Fontemoing, 1923.

DUQUESNE, François. –. *Le Droit du Travail, Éditions actualisée avec les reformes votées et les chantiers sociaux 2008/2009*. Paris: Gualino éditeur, 2009.

ENGELS, Friedrich. –. *A situação da classe trabalhadora em Inglaterra*, tradução portuguesa. Porto: Edições Afrontamento, 1975.

FELICIANO, Guilherme Guimarães. –. *Do Pré-Contrato de Trabalho, O Contrato Preliminar de Trabalho no Iter da Contratação Laboral: Abordagem Comparativa e Jusfundamental*. São Paulo: Editora LTR, 2010.

FERNANDES, António Monteiro. –. *Direito do Trabalho*, 12ª edição. Coimbra: Almedina, 2004.

FINNIS, John. –. *Natural Law and Natural Rights*, Second Edition, New York, Oxford University Press, 2011.

—. "Natural Law Theories", *The Stanford Encyclopedia of Philosophy*, First published Mon Feb 5, 2007; substantive revision Mon Jul 25, 2011, disponível em HYPERLINK "http://plato.stanford.edu/entries/natural-law-theories/" http://plato.stanford.edu/entries/natural-law-theories/ .

FOGLIA, Laura. –. "Il Welfare in Europa: realtà e prospettive per un nuovo modelo sociale." *In Sviluppo e ocupazione nel mercato globale*, de Giuseppe Ferraro (coord.), pp. 379-393. Milano, Giuffré Editore, 2004.

NICOLA. –. "The Legal Characterization of Personal Work Relations and The Idea of Labour Law", *The Idea of Labour Law*, Edited by Guy Davidov & Brian Langille, Oxford University Press, United Kingdom, 2013, pp. 190-208.

FULLINWIDER, Robert. –. "Affirmative Action." *The Stanford Encyclopedia of Philosophy*, Edward N. Zalta (ed.), (Fall Edition) de 2013.

GALANTINO, Luisa. –. *Diritto del Lavoro, Unidecisa Edizione*. Torino: G. Giappichelli Editore, 2001.

GARCIA, Maria da Glória Ferreira. –. *Estudos sobre o Princípio da Igualdade*. Coimbra: Almedina, 2005.

—. "Princípio da Igualdade, Fórmula Vazia ou Fórmula "Carregada"de sentido?" *Boletim do Ministério da Justiça* (358), 1987.

GARILLI, Alessandro. –. "Tutela della persona e tutela della sfera privata nel rapporto di lavoro." *Rivista Critica del Diritto Privato*, Ano X – 3, 1992.

GARRONE, Pierre. –."La discrimination indirecte en droit communautaire: vers une théorie générale." *Revue trimestrielle de droit européen*, nº 3, 1994: pp. 425 e ss.

GODOY, Arnaldo Sampaio de Moraes. –. *Direito do Trabalho e Globalização*. Teresina: Disponível em http://jus.com.br/ revista/texto/6042/direito-do-trabalho-e-globalizacao, 2004.

GOLDIN, ADRIÁN. –. "Global Conceptualizaions and Local Constructions", *The Idea of Labour Law*, Edited by Guy Davidov & Brian Langille, Oxford University Press, United Kingdom, 2013, pp. 69-87.

GOMES, Irene. –. "A comissão de serviço." in *A Reforma do Código do Trabalho*, de Centro de Estudos Judiciários/Inspeção Geral do Trabalho, pp. 370 e ss. Coimbra: Coimbra Editora, 2004.

—. "Considerações sobre o regime jurídico do contrato a termo certo no Código do Trabalho." *Questões Laborais, nº 24*, s.d.: pp. 137-169.

GOMES, Januário da Costa. –. "O Problema da Salvaguarda da Privacidade Antes e Depois do Computador." *Boletim do Ministério da Justiça*, 319, 1982: pp. 28 e ss.

GOMES, Júlio Vieira. –. "Da interpretação e integração das convenções colectivas.", *Novos Estudos de Direito do Trabalho*, pp. 121 e ss. Coimbra: Wolters Kluwer Portugal e Coimbra Editora, 2010.

—. *Direito do Trabalho, Volume I, Relações Individuais de Trabalho*. Coimbra: Coimbra Editora, 2007.

—. "O contrato de trabalho a termo certo ou a tapeçaria de Pénelope." In *in Estudos do Instituto de Direito do Trabalho, Volume IV*, pp. 35-101. Coimbra: Almedina, 2003.

—. "Do uso e abuso do período experimental." *Revista de Direito e de Estudos Sociais, Ano XXXI*, nº 1-2, 2000: pp. 57 e ss.

GOSEPATH, Stefan. –. "Equality." *The Stanford Encyclopedia of Philosophy*, Edward N. Zalta (ed.), (Spring Edition) de 2011.

GOUVEIA, Jorge Bacelar. –. *Manual de Direito Constitucional*, 4ª edição, Revista e Actualizada. Coimbra: Almedina, 2011.

—. "Os direitos de participação dos representantes dos trabalhadores na elaboração da legislação laboral." *In Estudos do Instituto de Direito do Trabalho*, de Pedro Romano Martinez (coord.), pp. 109152. Coimbra: Almedina, 2001.

GUERRA, Amadeu. –. *A privacidade no local de trabalho. As novas tecnologias e o controlo dos trabalhadores através de sistemas automatizados. Uma abordagem ao Código do Trabalho*. Coimbra: Almedina, 2004.

Häberle, Peter. –. "A dignidade humana como fundamento da comunidade estatal." in *Dimensões da dignidade: ensaios de filosofia do direito e direito constitucional*, pp. 89-152. Porto Alegre: Livraria do Advogado, 2005.

HANSEN, Johan/PLATENGA, Janneke. –. "Analyse comparative de l´égalité des chances dans l'Union européenne." *Revue Internationale du Travail*, vol. 138 (1999), nº 4, Número Spécial: Femmes, Genre et Travail (deuxième partie), 1999.

HART, H.L.A.– *The Concept of Law, Third Edition,Clarendon Law Series*, Oxford University Press, New York, 2012.

HEERS, Jacques. –. *Le travail au Moyen Âge, 2nd edition.* Paris: Presses universitaires de France, 1968.

HENRIQUES, Miguel Gorjão. –. *Direito Comunitário,* 4ª edição. *Coimbra*: Almedina, 2006.

HESPANHA, António Manuel. –. *Cultura Jurídica Europeia, Síntese de um MIlénio. Mem Martins*: Publicações Europa-América, 2003.

HOFFMAN, Reid/BEN Casnocha/CHRIS Yeh. –. "Tours of Duty – The New Employer-Employee Compact." *Harvard Business Revue,* June de 2013: pp. 49 e ss.

HÖRSTER, Heinrich Ewald. –. *A Parte Geral do Código Civil Português, Teoria Geral do Direito Civil.* Coimbra: Almedina, 1992.

ICHINO, Pietro. –. *Il contrato di lavoro, Vol. I.* Milano: Giuffre, 2003.

IVANOVA, Maria N. –. "The Great Recession and the State of American Capitalism." *Science & Society, Vol. 77, nº 3,* The Guilford Press, New York/London, July de 2013: 294 e ss.

JÚNIOR, Cesarino. –. "Direito Processual do Trabalho." in *Tratado de Direito Judiciário do Trabalho,* de Wilson de Souza Campos Batalha, pp. 533 e ss. São Paulo: Editora LTR, 1977.

KAHN-FREUNDK, Otto. –. *Trabajo y Derecho.* Madrid: Centro de Publicaciones Ministerio de Trabajo y Seguridad Social, 1987.

KILLMISTER, Suzy. –. "Autonomy and the Problem of Socialization." *Social Theory and Practice,* Volume 39, nº 1, Department of Philosophy The Florida State University, January de 2013: pp. 95 e ss.

KIRK, John A. –. "Racial Inequality in the Post-Civil Rights Era South." *Social Policy, Organizing for Social & Economic Justice,* Volume 42, nº 2, New Orleans, Summer de 2012: pp. 14 e ss.

LANGILLE, Brian. –. *The Idea of Labour Law,* Edited by Guy Davidov & Brian Langille, Oxford University Press, United Kingdom, 2013, pp. 101-119.

LANQUETIN, Marie Thérèse. –. "L'égalité de traitment entre les femmes et les hommes en matiére d'emploi et de travail: a propos de la directive 2006/54/ CE du 5 juillet 2006 (directive "refonte")." *Droit Social, nº 7/8, 2007*: pp. 861- 878.

–. "L'égalité entre les femmes et les hommes: sur la directive 2002/73/CE du 23 septembre 2002." *Droit Social,* 2003, 3, 2003: pp. 312-322. –. "Discriminations à raison du sexe." *Droit Social,* nº 7/8, 1998: pp. 688 e ss.

LEITÃO, Luís Menezes., *Direito do Trabalho,* 3ª edição. Coimbra: Almedina, 2012.

—. "Dispositivos tecnológicos de protecção e direito de acesso do público." *Revista da Ordem dos Advogados,* Jul.-Set. de 2011: 735-749.

—. *Direito do Trabalho.* Coimbra: Almedina, 2008.

—. "A protecção de dados pessoais no contrato de trabalho." in *A Reforma do Código do Trabalho*, de Centro de Estudos Judiciários/Inspeção Geral do Trabalho, pp. 123-138. Coimbra: Coimbra Editora, 2004.

—. *Código do Trabalho Anotado*. Coimbra: Almedina, 2004.

—. "O Direito do Consumo: Autorização e Configuração Dogmática." In *Estudos do Instituto de Direito do Consumo*, Volume I, Instituto de Direito do Consumo, Faculdade de Direito da Universidade de Lisboa, de Luís Menezes Leitão (coord.), pp. 11 e ss. Coimbra: Almedina, 2002.

—. *Direito das Obrigações, Vol. I., Introdução; Da Constituição das Obrigações*. Coimbra: Almedina, 2000.

LEITE, Carlos Henrique. –. *Curso de Direito Processual do Trabalho*, 2ª ed. São Paulo: Editora LTr., 2004.

LEITE, Jorge/Almeida, F. Jorge Coutinho de. –. *Legislação do Trabalho*. Coimbra: Editora Coimbra, 1999.

LEITE, Jorge. –. "Contrato de trabalho a prazo: Direito português e Direito comunitário." *Questões Laborais*, nº 27, 2006: pp. 1 e ss.

—. "A comissão de serviço." *Questões Laborais*, nº 16, ano VII, 2000, 2000: pp. 157 e ss.

—. "Contrato a termo para lançamento de nova actividade." *Questões Laborais*, nº 5, s.d.: pp. 76-87.

LEVY, Leonard. –. *Constitutional History, 1776-1789*, vol. 1. Nova Iorque: Encyclopedia of the American Constitution, 1986.

LOMBARDI, Giorgio. –. *Potere privato i diritti fondamentali*. Torino: G. Giappichelli Editore, 1970.

LOPES, Ribeiro. –. *Direito do Trabalho – Sumários Desenvolvidos das Aulas – policopiado*. Lisboa, 1977-1978.

LÓPEZ, Manuel Carlos/Manuel Álvarez de la Rosa. –. *Derecho del Trabajo, Décimoctava edición*. Madrid: Editorial Universitaria Ramón Areces, 2010.

LOPEZ, Maria Fernández. –. "El princípio de igualdad en el Derecho Social Europeo." in *I Jornadas sobre la Comunidad Europea*. Sevilha, 1994.

LOURENÇO, Paula Meira. –. "Os deveres de informação no contrato de trabalho." *Revista de Direito e de Estudos Sociais*, nºs 1-2, 2003: pp. 29 e ss.

LYON-CAEN, Antoine/ISABELLE, Vacarie. –. *Droits fondamentaux et Droit du Travail, Mélanges Verdier*. Paris: Dalloz, 2001.

MACHADO, Susana Sousa. –. *Contrato de trabalho a termo*. Coimbra: Coimbra Editora, 2009.

MACKINNON, Catharine. –. *Sexual Harassement of Working Women: A Case of Sex Discrimination*. Yale: Yale University Press, 1979.

MAGANO, Octavio Bueno. –. "Princípios do Direito do Trabalho e os avanços da tecnologia." in *Os Novos Paradigmas do Direito do Trabalho* (homenagem a Valentin Carrion), de Rita Maria Silvestre/Amauri Mascaro Nascimento (coord., pp. 81 e ss. São Paulo: Editora Saraiva, 2001.

MARTINEZ, Pedro Romano. –. *Direito do Trabalho,* Instituto de Direito do Trabalho da Faculdade de Direito de Lisboa, 7ª edição. Coimbra: Almedina, 2015.

—. Anotação aos artigos 4º a 12º, 112º a 110º, 126º a 129º, 130º a 134º, 281º a 284º, 323º a 332º e 337º a 393º, *Código do Trabalho Anotado,* 11ª edição, Pedro Romano Martinez, Luís Miguel Monteiro, Joana Vasconcelos, Pedro Madeira de Brito, Guilherme Dray e Luís Gonçalves da Silva. Coimbra: Almedina, 2013.

—. *Direito do Trabalho,* Instituto de Direito do Trabalho da Faculdade de Direito de Lisboa, 5ª edição. Coimbra: Almedina, 2010.

—. *Da Cessação do Contrato,* 2ª edição. Coimbra: Almedina, 2006.

—. "A justa causa de despedimento." in *Estudos do Instituto de Direito do Trabalho,* Vol. II, *Justa Causa de Despedimento.,* pp. 93 e ss. Coimbra: Almedina, 2001.

—. "Os Novos Horizontes do Direito do Trabalho." in *III Congresso Nacional de Direito do Trabalho* – Memórias, de António José Moreira (coord.), pp. 326 e ss. Coimbra: Almedina, 2001.

—. "Os princípios e o Direito do Trabalho em Portugal." in *Os Novos Paradigmas do Direito do Trabalho* (homenagem a Valentin Carrion), de Rita Maria Silvestre/ Amauri Mascaro Nascimento (coord.), pp. 27 e ss. São Paulo: Editora Saraiva, 2001.

MARTINEZ, Rey. –. "El derecho fundamental a no ser discriminado por razón de sexo." In *La discriminación por razón de sexo tras 25 años de la Constituición española,* pp. 25 e ss. Madrid: Consejo General del Poder Judicial, 2004.

MARTINZ, Ana Maria Guerra. –. *Curso de Direito Constitucional da União Europeia.* Coimbra: Almedina, 2004.

—. *As origens da constituição norte-americana, uma lição para a Europa.* Lisboa: Lex – Edições Jurídicas, 1994.

MARTINS, Pedro Furtado. –. "Questões sobre Trabalho Temporário." *Revista de Direito e de Estudos Sociais,* nº 1, (1999): pp. 65 e ss.

MARTINS, Sérgio Pinto. –. *Direito do Trabalho,* 25ª edição. São Paulo: Editora Atlas, 2009.

MAZZONI, Giuliano. –. *Manuale di Diritto del Lavoro,* 6ª ed., Volume Primo. Milano: Giuffrè Editore, 1988.

MAZZOTTA, Oronzo. –. *Trattato di Diritto Privato, Diritto del Lavoro,* 3ª ed. Milano: Giuffrè Editore, 2008.

MCDONALD, Laughlin/JOHN A. Powell.-. *The Rights of Racial Minorities*, Second Edition. Illinois: Southern Illinois University Press, 1993.

MELGAR, Alfredo Montoya. -. *Derecho del Trabajo*, 30ª ed. Madrid: Tecnos, 2009.

—. "Tendencias actuales del derecho del trabajo en España." in *Tendencias Actuales del Derecho del Trabajo. Perspectiva Iberoamericana*, de M. Pasco/M. Ackermán/A. Montoya/J. M. Galiana/A. V. Sempere A. Plá/W. D. Giglio, pp. 117 e ss. Murcia: Universidad de Murcia, 1990.

MELGAR, Montoya/GALIANA Moreno/NAVARRO Sempere. -. *Derecho Social Europeu*. Madrid: Tecnos, 1994.

—. "Direitos, liberdades e garantias - alguns aspectos gerais." in *Estudos sobre a Constituição, obra colectiva*, I, de Jorge Miranda (coord.), pp. 93 e ss. Lisboa, Petrony, 1977.

MESQUITA, Andrade. -. *Direito do Trabalho*, 2ª edição. Lisboa: Associação Académica da Faculdade de Direito de Lisboa, 2004.

MEYER, Francis. -. "La discrimination en fonction de l'âge en droit communautaire: aperçu de la jurisprudence recente de la Cour de Justice de l'Union européenne." *Droit Ouvrier*, nº 755, 2011: pp. 350 e ss.

MIRANDA, Jorge/RUI Medeiros. *Constituição Portuguesa Anotada*, Tomo *I, Introdução Geral*,. Coimbra: Coimbra Editora, 2007.

—. *Constituição Portuguesa Anotada, Tomo III, Organização do Poder Politico/Garantia e revisão da Constituição/Disposições finais e transitórias*,. Coimbra: Coimbra Editora, 2007.

MIRANDA, Jorge. -. *Manual de Direito Constitucional, Direitos Fundamentais*, Tomo IV, 5ª edição. Coimbra: Coimbra Editora, 2012.

—. *Manual de Direito Constitucional*, Tomo II - Constituição, 6ª edição. Coimbra: Coimbra Editora, 2007.

—. *Manual de Direito Constitucional, Direitos Fundamentais*, Tomo IV. Coimbra: Coimbra Editora, 1988.

—. *Manual de Direito Constitucional, Preliminares. A Experiência Constitucional*, Tomo I. Coimbra: Coimbra Editora, 1988.

—. "Princípio da Igualdade." in *Polis/Enciclopédia Verbo da Sociedade e do Estado*, vol. 3, pp. 401 e ss. Lisboa, São Paulo: Verbo, 1985.

MONTEIRO, Luís Miguel. -. anotação aos artigos 100º a 101º, 111º a 114º, 135º, 139º a 149º, 150º a 156º, 161º a 164º e 197º a 257º, *Código do Trabalho Anotado*, 9ª edição, Pedro Romano Martinez, Luís Miguel Monteiro, Joana Vasconcelos, Pedro Madeira de Brito, Guilherme Dray e Luís Gonçalves da Silva. Coimbra: Almedina, 2013.

Moreira, Teresa Coelho. –. "A discriminação em razão da idade no contexto de uma população envelhecida na UE." in *Igualdade e Não Discriminação, Estudos de Direito do Trabalho,* pp. 9-78. Coimbra: Almedina, 2013.

—. "Discriminação com base na orientação sexual dos trabalhadores." in *Igualdade e Não Discriminação, Estudos de Direito do Trabalho,* pp. 129-163. Coimbra: Almedina, 2013.

—. "O ónus da prova em casos de discriminação." in Igualdade e Não *Discriminação, Estudos de Direito do Trabalho,* pp. 79-127. Coimbra: Almedina, 2013.

—. "As novas tecnologias de informação e comunicação: um Admirável Mundo Novo do trabalho?" in *Estudos de Homenagem ao Prof. Doutor Jorge Miranda,* Volume VI, Edição da Faculdade de Direito da Universidade de Lisboa, pp. 953-973. Coimbra: Coimbra Editora, 2012.

—. "A conduta e a orientação sexuais do trabalhador." in *Estudos de Direito do Trabalho em Homenagem ao Professor Manuel Alonso Olea,* de António Monteiro Fernandes (org.), pp. 613-645. Coimbra: Almedina, 2004.

Moura, Barros. –. *A Convenção coletiva entre as Fontes de Direito do Trabalho.* Coimbra: Almedina, 1984.

Nascimento, Amauri Mascaro. –. *Curso de Direito do Trabalho,* 14ª edição, revista. São Paulo: Editora Saraiva, 1997.

Neto, José Francisco Siqueira. –. "Princípios de Direito do Trabalho e economia de mercado." in *Os Novos Paradigmas do Direito do Trabalho* (homenagem a Valentin Carrion), de Amauri Mascaro/Rita Maria Silvestre (coord.) Nascimento, pp. 129 e ss. São Paulo: Editora Saraiva, 2001.

Nickel, James. –. "Human Rights." *The Stanford Encyclopedia of Philosophy,* Edward N. Zalta (ed.), (Summer Edition) de 2013.

Nino, Carlos Santiago. –. *Ética y derechos humanos.* Buenos Aires: Editorial Paidós, 1984.

Novais, Jorge Reis. –. *Teoria jurídica dos direitos sociais enquanto direitos fundamentais.* Coimbra: Coimbra Editora, 2010.

—. *As restrições aos direitos fundamentais não expressamente autorizados pela Constituição.* Coimbra: Coimbra Editora, 2003.

—. "Renúncia a direitos fundamentais." in *Perspectivas Constitucionais – Nos 20 anos da Constituição de 1976,* volume I, de Jorge Miranda (org.), pp. 263-335. Coimbra: Coimbra Editora, 1997. Olea, Alonso/Baamonde, M. Emilia Casas. –.Derecho del Trabajo, 23ª edição. Madrid: Civitas, 2005.

Novitz, Tonia, *International and European Protection of the Right to Strike. A Comparative Study of Standards Set by the International Labour Organization, the Council of Europe and the European Union*, Oxford, 2003.

Olea, Alonso. *De la Servidumbre al Contrato de Trabajo*. Madrid: Tecnos, 1979.

Paladin, Livio. –. *Eguaglianza, Enciclopedia del Diritto*, vol. XIV. Milano: Giuffrè, 1965.

Palmer, R.R. –. *The Age of Democratic Revolution – A Political History of Europe and America*, 1760-1780. Princeton: Princeton University Press, 1959.

Parreira, Isabel. –. "O Assédio Moral no Trabalho." in *V Congresso Nacional de Direito do Trabalho*, Memórias, de António José Moreira (coord.), pp. 209- -247. Coimbra: Almedina, 2003.

—. "Assédio Sexual no Trabalho." in *IV Congresso Nacional de Direito do Trabalho*, Memórias, de António José Moreira (coord.). Coimbra: Almedina, 2002.

Pedrazzoli, Marcello. –. "Prestazione d'opera e parasubordinazione." *Rivista di diritto del lavoro*, 1984: pp. 506-556.

Pelissier, Jean/Supiot, Alain/Jeammaud, Antoine. –. *Droit du Travail*, 24e edition. Paris: Dalloz, 2008.

—. *Droit du Travail*. Paris: Dalloz, 2006.

Pera, Giuseppe/Marco Papaleoni. –. *Diritto del Lavoro*, 7ª ed. Padova: Cedam, 2003.

Pera, Giuseppe. –. *Compendio di Diritto del Lavoro*. Milan: Giuffrè, 2003.

—. *Compendio di Diritto del Lavoro*, 5ª ed. Milano: Giuffré Editore, 2000. –. Diritto del Lavoro, 6ª ed. Padova: Cedam, 2000.

Perelman, Chaim. –. *Liberty, Equality and Public Interest, Equality and Freedom, Past, Present and Future*. Wiesbaden: Steiner, 1977.

Pérez, Jesus Gonzalez. –. *La Dignidad de la Persona*, Civitas. Madrid: Civitas, 1986.

Perone, Giancarlo. –. "Direitos do trabalhador como indivíduo. Os direitos sociais." In *Os Novos Paradigmas do Direito do Trabalho* (homenagem a Valentin Carrion), de Rita Maria Silvestre/Amauri Mascaro Nascimento (coord.), pp. 60 e ss. São Paulo: Editora Saraiva, 2001.

Pinto, Mário/Martins, Furtado/Carvalho, Nunes. –. *Comentário às Leis do Trabalho. Lisboa:* Lex, 1994.

Pinto, Mário. –. *Direito do Trabalho*. Lisboa: Universidade Católica, 1996.

Pinto, Paulo Mota. –. "O direito à reserva da intimidade da vida privada." *Boletim da Faculdade de Direito da Universidade de Coimbra*, LXIX (1993), 1993: pp. 479- -485.

Rachleff, Peter. –. "Labor History for the Future, Vol. 42, nº 3." *Social Policy, Organizing for Social & Economic Justice*, New Orleans, LA, Fall de 2012: pp- 34 e ss.

Ramalho, Maria Do Rosário. –. *Tratado de Direito do Trabalho, Parte I – Dogmática Geral*, 6ª edição. Coimbra: Almedina, 2016.

—. *Tratado de Direito do Trabalho, Parte II – Situações Laborais Individuais,* 4ª ed. Coimbra: Almedina, 2012.

—. Tratado de Direito do Trabalho, Parte III, Situações Laborais Colectivas, 6ª ed. Coimbra: Almedina, 2016.

—. *Direito Social na União Europeia.* Coimbra: Almedina, 2009.

—. "Igualdade e não discriminação em razão do género no domínio laboral – situação portuguesa e relação com o direito comunitário." in *Estudos de Direito do Trabalho,* I, pp. 227-246. Coimbra: Almedina, 2003.

—. "O Direito do Trabalho numa sociedade em mutação acelerada e o problema da igualdade de tratamento entre trabalhadores e trabalhadoras." in *Estudos de Direito do Trabalho,* I, pp. 215-225. Coimbra: Almedina, 2003.

—. "O novo Código do Trabalho. Reflexões sobre a proposta de lei relativa ao novo Código do Trabalho." in *Estudos de Direito do Trabalho,* I. Coimbra: Almedina, 2003.

—. "Contrato de trabalho e direitos fundamentais." in *Estudos em Homenagem à Professora Doutora Isabel Magalhães Collaço*, Vol. II, pp. 393-417. Coimbra: Almedina, 2002.

—. *Da Autonomia Dogmática do Direito do trabalho.* Coimbra: Almedina, 2001.

—. *Do Fundamento do Poder Disciplinar Laboral.* Coimbra: Almedina, 1993.

Rawls, John. –. *Justice as Fairness: A Restatement, ed. by Erin Kelly.* Cambridge: Harvard University Press, 2001.

—. *Theory of Justice. Massachusetts*: Harvard University Press, 1971 (republicado em 1999).

—. *Political Liberalism,* 1993, tradução portuguesa, Liberalismo politico. Lisboa: Editorial Presença, 1996. –. Political Liberalism. Columbia University Press, 1993.

Redinha, Maria Regina. –. "Os direitos de personalidade no Código do Trabalho: actualidade e oportunidade da sua inclusão." in *A Reforma do Código do Trabalho,* de Centro de Estudos Judiciários/Inspecção Geral do Trabalho (org.), pp. 161-171. Coimbra: Coimbra Editora, 2004.

—. "Assédio Moral ou Mobbing no Trabalho." in *Estudos em Homenagem ao Prof. Doutor Raúl Ventura,* Volume II, pp. 833- -847. Coimbra: Coimbra Editora, 2003.

—. "Utilização de Novas Tecnologias no Local de Trabalho (algumas questões)." in *IV Congresso Nacional de Direito do Trabalho,* de António Moreira (org.), pp. 115-125. Coimbra: Almedina, 2002.

—. "O Teletrabalho." in *II Congresso Nacional de Direito do Trabalho,* pp. 95 e ss., de António José Moreira (coord.), pp. 95 e ss. Coimbra. Almedina, 1999.

—. *Relação Laboral Fragmentada. Estudo sobre o Trabalho Temporário*. Coimbra: Coimbra Editora, 1995.

RICHARDI, Reinhard. –."Arbeitsrecht und Zivilrecht." *Zeitschrift für Arbeitsrecht*, 1, 1974: pp. 3-27.

RIVERO, Jean. –. "La protection des droits de l'homme dans les rapports entre personnes privées." In *René Cassin – Amicorum Discipulorumque Liber*. Paris: A. Pardone, 1971.

ROCCELLA, Massimo. –. *Manual di Diritto del Lavoro*, 4ª edição. Torino: G. Giappichelli Editore, 2010.

ROCCELLA, Massimo /TIZIANO Treu. –. *Diritto del Lavoro della Comunità Europea*, 3ª ed. Padova: CEDAM, 2002.

RODRIGUES, Américo Plá. –. "Los princípios y el derecho del trabajo en Uruguay." In *Os Novos Paradigmas do Direito do Trabalho* (homenagem a Valentin Carrion), de Rita Maria Silvestre/Amauri Mascaro Nascimento (coord.), pp. 53 e ss. São Paulo: Editora Saraiva, 2001.

—. *Princípios de Direito do Trabalho*. São Paulo: Editora LTR, 1997.

—. *Curso de derecho laboral*. Montevideo: Acali, 1978.

ROTMAN, David. –. "How Technology is Destroying Jobs." *MIT Technology Review*, Volume 116, nº 4, Massachusetts Institute of Technology, Boston, July/August de 2013: pp. 28 e ss.

SABINO, João Filipe Moreira. –. "Os Direitos Fundamentais nas Relações de Trabalho." In *Direitos Humanos e Direito do Trabalho*, de Flávia/Luciana Paula Vaz de Carvalho (coord.) Piovesan, pp. 64 e ss. São Paulo: Editora Atlas, 2010.

SANTORO-Passarelli, Francesco. –. *Nozioni di Diritto del Lavoro*. Napoli: Giuffré Editore, 1995.

—. *Nozioni di Diritto del Lavoro*, 35ª edição. Napoli: Casa Editrice Dott. Eugenio Jovene, 1995.

SANTOS, Sabina Pereira dos. –. *Direito do Trabalho e Política Social na União Europeia*. Cascais: Principia, 2000.

SARLET, Ingo Wolfgang. –. *A eficácia dos direitos fundamentais*, 6ª ed. Porto Alegre: Livraria do Advogado, 2006.

SEN, Amartya. –. *A ideia de justiça*. Coimbra: Almedina, 2012.

SILVA, Filipe Fraústo da. –. "30 Anos de Contrato de Trabalho a Termo." In *A Reforma do Código do Trabalho*, de Centro de Estudos Judiciários/Inspecção Geral do Trabalho (coord.), pp. 271-274. Coimbra: Coimbra Editora, 2004.

SILVA, Luís Gonçalves Da. –. anotação aos artigos 1º a 3º e 404º a 529º, *Código do Trabalho Anotado*, 9ª edição, Pedro Romano Martinez, Luís Miguel Monteiro,

Joana Vasconcelos, Pedro Madeira de Brito, Guilherme Dray e Luís Gonçalves da Silva. Coimbra: Almedina, 2013.

—. "O Código do Trabalho face à Constituição." in *Estudos de Direito do Trabalho (Código do Trabalho)*, volume I, 2ª ed., pp. 18 e ss. Coimbra: Almedina, 2008.

—. "Princípios Gerais da Contratação Coletiva no Código do Trabalho." in *Estudos de Direito do Trabalho (Código do Trabalho)*, volume I, 2ª ed., pp. 179 e ss. Coimbra: Almedina, 2008.

—. *Da Eficácia Normativa das Convenção coletiva*, Colecção Cadernos Laborais, nº 1, Instituto de Direito do Trabalho. Coimbra: Almedina, 2002.

Sousa, Miguel Teixeira de. –. *Introdução ao Direito*. Coimbra: Almedina, 2013.

—. "Positivismo e Valores." in *Estudos de Homenagem ao Prof. Doutor Jorge Miranda*, Volume VI, Edição da Faculdade de Direito da Universidade de Lisboa, pp. 403-415. Combra: Coimbra Editora, 2012.

Sousa, Rabindranath Capelo de. –. *O direito geral de personalidade*. Coimbra: Coimbra Editora, 1995.

Sreenivasan, Gopal. –. "Justice, Inequality, and Health." *The Stanford Encyclopedia*, (Spring Edition) de 2009.

Supiot, Alain. –. *Transformações do trabalho e o futuro do Direito do trabalho na Europa*. Coimbra: Coimbra Editora, 2003.

—. "Transformations du travail et devenir du droit du travail: une prospective européene." *Revue Internationale du Travail*, vol. 138 (1999), nº 1, 1999: pp. 33 e ss.

–. *Le travail en perspectives*. Paris: Librairie LGDJ, 1998.

Supiot, Alain/Casas, María Emilia/Munck, Jean de/Hanau, Peter/Johansson, Andres/Meadows, Pamela/Mingione, Enzo/Salais, Robert/Heijden, Paul Va Der. –. *Transformações do Trabalho e futuro do Direito do Trabalho na Europa*. Coimbra: Coimbra Editora, 2003.

Supiot, Alain/Gerard Lyon-Caen/Jean Pelissier. –. *Droit du Travail*, Paris: Dalloz-Sirey, 2000.

Svolos, Alex. –. *Le Travail dans les Constitutions Contemporaines*. Paris: Librairie du Recuel Sirey, 1939.

Swan, Kyle. –. "Republican Equality." *Social Theory and Practice*, Volume 38, nº 3, Department of Philosophy, The Florida State University, July de 2012: pp. 432 e ss.

Teyssié, Bernard. –. *Droit européen du travail*, 4ª ed. Paris: Litec, 2010.

–. *Droit du Travail, 1. Relations individuelles de travail*, 12ª edição. Paris: Litec, 1992.

Thomsen, Frej Klem. –. "But some Groups Are More Equal Than Others: a critical revew of the Group-Criterion in the concept of discrimination." *Social Theory and Practice*, Volume 39, nº 1, Department of Philosophy The Florida State University, January de 2013: pp. 120 e ss.

THÜSING, Gregor. –. "Following the U.S. Example: european Employment Discrimination Law and the Impact of Council Directives 2000/43/EC and 2000/78/ EC." *The International Journal of Comparative Labour Law and Industrial Relations*, vol. 19, nº 2, Summer de 2003.

VALENTE, Joana Nunes. –. *A fuga à relação de trabalho (típica)*. Coimbra: Coimbra Editora, 2008.

VASCONCELOS, Joana. –. anotação aos artigos 136º a 138º, 258º a 280º, 285º a 287º, 294º a 322º, 333º a 336º e 394º a 403º, Código do Trabalho Anotado, 11ª edição, Pedro Romano Martinez, Luís Miguel Monteiro, Joana Vasconcelos, Pedro Madeira de Brito, Guilherme Dray e Luís Gonçalves da Silva. Coimbra: Almedina, 2017.

—. *A Revogação do Contrato de Trabalho*, Almedina, Coleção Teses de Doutoramento, Coimbra, 2011.

—. "O conceito de justa causa de despedimento. Evolução legislativa e situação actual." in *Estudos do Instituto de Direito do Trabalho, Vol. II, Justa Causa de Despedimento*, Instituto de Direito do Trabalho da Faculdade de Direito da Universidade de Lisboa, de Pedro Romano Martinez (coord.), pp. 15 e ss. Coimbra: Almedina, 2001.

VEIGA, Motta. –. *Direito do Trabalho Internacional e Europeu*. Lisboa: Universidade Lusíada, 1994.

VENTURA, Raúl. –. *Teoria da Relação Jurídica de Trabalho, Estudos de Direito Privado*. Porto: Imprensa Portuguesa, 1944.

—. *Droit du Travail*, 11ª ed. Paris: Dalloz, 1999.

VERDIER, Jean-Maurice. –. *Libertés et travail. Problématique des droits de l'homme et rôle du juge*. Paris: Recueil Dalloz Sirey, 1988.

VILLALON, Jesus Cruz/CARACUEL, Manuel Ramón Alarcon. –. *La igualdad de trato en el Derecho Comunitario Laboral*, Madrid: Aranzadi Editorial, 1997.

WALLON, Ch. Lenoir e B. –. "Informatique, travail et libertés." *Droit Social*, nº 3, Março de 1988: pp. 2-241.

WAQUET, Philippe. –. "La vie personelle du salarié." *Droit Social*, Dalloz, Paris, 2004: pp. 23 e ss.

WEDDERBURN, Lord. –. *Los Derechos Laborales en Gran Bretaña y en Europa*. Madrid: Centro de Publicaciones – Ministerio de Trabajo y Seguridad Social, 1994.

WEISS, Manfred. –. "Re-Inventing Labour Law?", *The Idea of Labour Law*, Edited by Guy Davidov & Brian Langille, Oxford University Press, United Kingdom, 2013, pp. 43-57.

XAVIER, Bernardo Lobo. –. *Contratação coletiva – cláusulas de paz, vigência e sobrevigência, Código do Trabalho – alguns aspectos cruciais*. Cascais: Principia, 2003.

—. "Contrato de trabalho a prazo." *Revista de Direito e de Estudos Sociais*, nº 4, 1998: pp. 424-436.

—. *Regime Jurídico do Contrato de Trabalho Anotado*, 2ª edição. Lisboa, 1972.

XAVIER, Bernardo Lobo, com a colaboração de P. Furtado Martins, A. Nunes de Carvalho, Joana Vasconcelos e Tatiana Guerra De Almeida. –. *Manual de Direito do Trabalho*. Lisboa: Verbo, 2011.